Historicising the Women's Liberation Movement in the W

The Women's Liberation Movement (WLM) of the late 1960s, 1970s and 1980s emerged out of a particular set of economic and social circumstances in which women were unequally treated in the home, in the workplace and in culture and wider society. As part of the WLM, women collected together in disparate groups and contexts to express their dissatisfaction with their role and position in society, making their concerns apparent through consciousness-raising and activism.

This important time in women's history is revisited in this collection, which looks afresh at the diversity of the movement and the ways in which feminism of the time might be reconsidered and historicised. The contributions here cover a range of important issues, including feminist art, local activism, class distinction, racial politics, perceptions of motherhood, girls' education, feminist print cultures, the recovery of feminist histories and feminist heritage, and they span personal and political concerns in Britain, Canada and the United States. Each contributor considers the impact of the WLM in a different context, reflecting the variety of issues faced by women and helping us to understand the problems of the second wave. This book broadens our understanding of the impact and the implication of the WLM, explores the dynamism of women's activism and radicalism, and acknowledges the significance of this movement to ongoing contemporary feminisms.

The chapters in this book were originally published as a special issue of *Women's History Review*.

Laurel Forster is a Senior Lecturer at the University of Portsmouth, UK, where she researches women's cultural history and media representations of gender. She has published on gender politics and activism, war zones and the domestic sphere, and literary modernism. Her recent book, *Magazine Movements: Women's Culture, Feminisms and Media Form* (2015), reflects her specialism in periodicals. Her current projects include a study of political magazine cultures and a history of British Women's Print Media.

Sue Bruley is a Reader in Modern History at the University of Portsmouth, UK. She specialises in women and gender relations in twentieth-century Britain, particularly in regard to oral testimony. Her last book was *The Women and Men of 1926, The General Strike and Miners' Lockout in South Wales* (2011). She is currently leading a project recovering oral feminist histories in the city of Portsmouth.

Historicising the Women's Liberation Movement in the Western World

1960–1999

Edited by
Laurel Forster and Sue Bruley

Routledge
Taylor & Francis Group

LONDON AND NEW YORK

First published 2018 by Routledge

2 Park Square, Milton Park, Abingdon, Oxon OX14 4RN
605 Third Avenue, New York, NY 10017

Routledge is an imprint of the Taylor & Francis Group, an informa business

First issued in paperback 2021

Copyright © 2018 Taylor & Francis

All rights reserved. No part of this book may be reprinted or reproduced or utilised in any form or by any electronic, mechanical, or other means, now known or hereafter invented, including photocopying and recording, or in any information storage or retrieval system, without permission in writing from the publishers.

Notice:
Product or corporate names may be trademarks or registered trademarks, and are used only for identification and explanation without intent to infringe.

Publisher's Note

The publisher has gone to great lengths to ensure the quality of this reprint but points out that some imperfections in the original copies may be apparent.

British Library Cataloguing in Publication Data
A catalogue record for this book is available from the British Library

ISBN13: 978-0-8153-4821-4 (hbk)
ISBN13: 978-0-367-53060-0 (pbk)

Typeset in Minion Pro
by codeMantra

Publisher's Note
The publisher accepts responsibility for any inconsistencies that may have arisen during the conversion of this book from journal articles to book chapters, namely the possible inclusion of journal terminology.

Disclaimer
Every effort has been made to contact copyright holders for their permission to reprint material in this book. The publishers would be grateful to hear from any copyright holder who is not here acknowledged and will undertake to rectify any errors or omissions in future editions of this book.

Contents

Citation Information — vii
Notes on Contributors — ix

Introduction: Historicising the Women's Liberation Movement — 1
Sue Bruley and Laurel Forster

1 Etchings from the Attic: looking back at feminist print-making from the 1980s — 5
   Lisa Taylor

2 Women's Liberation at the Grass Roots: a view from some English towns, c.1968–1990 — 27
   Sue Bruley

3 The Women's Movement and 'Class Struggle': gender, class formation and political identity in women's strikes, 1968–78 — 45
   George Stevenson

4 White Women, Anti-Imperialist Feminism and the Story of Race within the US Women's Liberation Movement — 60
   Say Burgin

5 'A Job That Should Be Respected': contested visions of motherhood and English Canada's second wave women's movements, 1970–1990 — 74
   Lynne Marks, Margaret Little, Megan Gaucher and T.R. Noddings

6 The 1944 Education Act and Second Wave Feminism — 94
   Phillida Bunkle

7 Spreading the Word: feminist print cultures and the Women's Liberation Movement — 114
   Laurel Forster

CONTENTS

8   Fighting for Recovery: foremothers and feminism in the 1970s   134
Janet Floyd

9   Theorising the Women's Liberation Movement *as* Cultural Heritage   149
D-M Withers

Index   165

Citation Information

The chapters in this book were originally published in *Women's History Review*, volume 25, issue 5 (October 2016). When citing this material, please use the original page numbering for each article, as follows:

Introduction
Historicising the Women's Liberation Movement
Sue Bruley and Laurel Forster
Women's History Review, volume 25, issue 5 (October 2016) pp. 697–700

Chapter 1
Etchings from the Attic: looking back at feminist print-making from the 1980s
Lisa Taylor
Women's History Review, volume 25, issue 5 (October 2016) pp. 701–722

Chapter 2
Women's Liberation at the Grass Roots: a view from some English towns, c.1968–1990
Sue Bruley
Women's History Review, volume 25, issue 5 (October 2016) pp. 723–740

Chapter 3
The Women's Movement and 'Class Struggle': gender, class formation and political identity in women's strikes, 1968–78
George Stevenson
Women's History Review, volume 25, issue 5 (October 2016) pp. 741–755

Chapter 4
White Women, Anti-Imperialist Feminism and the Story of Race within the US Women's Liberation Movement
Say Burgin
Women's History Review, volume 25, issue 5 (October 2016) pp. 756–770

Chapter 5
'A Job That Should Be Respected': contested visions of motherhood and English Canada's second wave women's movements, 1970–1990
Lynne Marks, Margaret Little, Megan Gaucher and T.R. Noddings
Women's History Review, volume 25, issue 5 (October 2016) pp. 771–790

CITATION INFORMATION

Chapter 6
The 1944 Education Act and Second Wave Feminism
Phillida Bunkle
Women's History Review, volume 25, issue 5 (October 2016) pp. 791–811

Chapter 7
Spreading the Word: feminist print cultures and the Women's Liberation Movement
Laurel Forster
Women's History Review, volume 25, issue 5 (October 2016) pp. 812–831

Chapter 8
Fighting for Recovery: foremothers and feminism in the 1970s
Janet Floyd
Women's History Review, volume 25, issue 5 (October 2016) pp. 832–846

Chapter 9
Theorising the Women's Liberation Movement as Cultural Heritage
D-M Withers
Women's History Review, volume 25, issue 5 (October 2016) pp. 847–862

For any permission-related enquiries please visit:
http://www.tandfonline.com/page/help/permissions

Notes on Contributors

Sue Bruley is a Reader in Modern History at the University of Portsmouth, UK. She specialises in women and gender relations in twentieth-century Britain, particularly in regard to oral testimony. Her last book was *The Women and Men of 1926, The General Strike and Miners' Lockout in South Wales* (2011). She is currently leading a project recovering oral feminist histories in the city of Portsmouth.

Phillida Bunkle studied at Smith College, Northampton, USA; Oxford University, UK; and as a Kennedy Fellow at Harvard University, Cambridge, USA. She is a Founder of the Academic Women's Association and Women's Health Action, and introduced Women's Studies as a degree subject in New Zealand. She later became an MP and Minister in the Government of New Zealand, including among her numerous portfolios the role of Associate Minister of Women's Affairs. She is now retired in the UK.

Say Burgin is Assistant Professor in Twentieth-Century US History at Dickinson College, USA, and a Research Associate with the Research Centre Visual Identities in Art and Design, University of Johannesburg, South Africa. She researches, writes and teaches on race, gender and twentieth-century social movements in the US.

Janet Floyd is Professor of American Literature and Culture at King's College London, UK. She has published on the nineteenth-century American West (first on the figure of the pioneer woman, and then on the cultural significance of the gold and silver mining rushes) and on domestic space and culture. She is currently working on a study of practices of friendship in late nineteenth-century America. She is the author of *Claims and Speculations: Mining and Writing in the Gilded Age* (2012).

Laurel Forster is Senior Lecturer in Media Studies at the University of Portsmouth, UK. Her research interests are in women's writing and women's cultures. She has published on representations of femininity and feminism on television and film; on domesticity; on modernism, especially the writings of May Sinclair; and on women's magazines and their cultural significance. She is author of *Magazine Movements* (2015) and is editing a history of women's periodical cultures in Britain.

Megan Gaucher is Assistant Professor in the Department of Law and Legal Studies at Carleton University, Ottawa, Canada. Her research interests focus on the intersections between citizenship, family, gender, sexuality and race in Canadian immigration and refugee law and policy. She is the author of *Keeping it in the Family: The (Re-) Production of Conjugal Citizens Through Canadian Immigration Policy and Practice* (forthcoming).

NOTES ON CONTRIBUTORS

Margaret Little is Professor and the Sir Edward Peacock Chair in Gender and Politics at Queen's University, Kingston, Canada. She is currently working on three projects: marginalized mothers' activism, 1960s–1980s; white feminist racism; and the (in)effectiveness of food insecurity programs. She is the author of *If I Had a Hammer: Women's Retraining That Really Works* (2006), and *No Car, No Radio, No Liquor Permit: The Moral Regulation of Single Mothers in Ontario, 1920–1996* (1998).

Lynne Marks is Professor of History at the University of Victoria, British Columbia, Canada. She teaches on Canadian history, women's and gender history, and the social history of religion. She is the author of *Infidels and the Damn Churches: Irreligion and Religion in Settler British Columbia* (2017). She is currently working on a project that explores the relationship between Canadian second wave feminism and motherhood and family.

T.R. Noddings is currently completing a PhD in the Department of History at Northwestern University, Illinois, USA. He studies the history of mass media Protestantism in the United States in the Gilded Age and Progressive era, with a particular focus on print evangelism and revivals. He is especially interested in the interconnections between media, urbanity, gender and the family in the creation of nineteenth- and twentieth-century evangelical Christian identities.

George Stevenson is a Research Fellow at Southampton University, UK, exploring understanding of the volunteer writers for the Mass Observation Archive. He completed his PhD at the University of Durham, UK, on the importance of class in the British women's movement, c. 1968–1979. Linked to his primary research, he is also interested in researching the way that public historical narratives are constructed and to what extent it is possible for those outside the formal historical apparatus to develop and disseminate 'popular' narratives.

Lisa Taylor is Head of Media at Leeds Beckett University, UK. She has published on media studies, popular film, music and art. In 2008 *A Taste for Gardening: classed and gendered practices* was published, an ethnography about the relationship between lifestyle television and gardeners. She is currently working on an ethnography of responses to demolition in an ex-industrial textile village.

D-M Withers is a Research Fellow at the University of Sussex, UK, working on the Leverhulme-funded project The Business of Women's Words. D-M co-authored *The Feminist Revolution: the Struggle for Women's Liberation* (2018) and is the author of *Feminism, Digital Culture and the Politics of Transmission: Theory, Practice and Cultural Heritage*, which won the 2016 Feminist and Women's Studies Association Book prize.

INTRODUCTION

Historicising the Women's Liberation Movement

Sue Bruley and Laurel Forster

ABSTRACT
The Women's Liberation Movement of the late 1960s, 1970s and 1980s emerged out of a set of economic and social circumstances where women collected together in disparate groups and contexts to express their dissatisfaction with their role and position in society. Through consciousness-raising and activism women raised their voices, profiles and visibility. This important moment of women's history is revisited in this collection of essays, which look afresh at the diversity of the movement and ways in which we might historicise the feminism of the time.

Women's liberation, also now known as 'second wave feminism', is commonly taken to be the upsurge in feminist activism and other feminist practices, agency and organisation in Europe, North America and many other developed countries between the mid 1960s and the mid 1980s. The economic and social context for the women's liberation movement (WLM) was post war affluence, rising living standards and increased educational opportunities. The WLM arose from, and was very much part of, what is termed 'new social movements' of the 1960s, particularly an end to the threat of nuclear war, anti-apartheid, opposition to the Vietnam war and civil rights. Women were frustrated and angry by their continued second class status in the post war world. The WLM produced widespread structural and attitudinal change which had a profound impact on the western world in the late twentieth century. By developing an 'imagined community' of feminism, women created a new sense of female selfhood.[1]

As Stephanie Gilmore has written, 'if we are to have a feminist future we need a feminist past upon which to stand and build'.[2] This should not be a 'celebratory' history, but a 'usable past'. It follows then that the notion of recovery is also problematic if it is to be more than celebration. As Janet Floyd suggests in her article, the notion of recovery and appropriation is a sensitive and contentious issue, even regarding the most revered of American feminist foremothers. The history of the WLM has been distorted by media portrayals of 'bra burning' feminists protesting about beauty contests in metropolitan centres such as London and the East coast of the USA, and by an unquestioning acceptance of criticisms of the movement as urban, racist and classist. This ignored the feminist activism of other regions and focussed on white middle-class women. Sue

Bruley's article on 'Women's Liberation at the Grass Roots', draws attention to the regionality of the WLM by concentrating on the diverse organisation and local activism and engagement of women's liberation in five urban communities across England. Feminist history is a dynamic and contested terrain, and is currently undergoing a reassessment to include a wider range of female agency and a broader range of political starting points for women's work and women's organisations intending to improve the position of women in society. This special edition of *Women's History Review* contributes to that reassessment of the second wave of feminism. For instance, we understand now that by highlighting the 'black machismo' of the Black Panthers in the US in the 1960s we ignored the fact that two thirds of the membership of the Panthers were women who learned leadership and organising skills which stood them in good stead in the WLM.[3] As Becky Thomson has argued, the traditional or 'hegemonic' approach to the history of the WLM 'does not recognise the centrality of the feminism of women of color in Second Wave history'.[4] Entering into this debate in this volume, Say Burgin problematises the relationship of white US feminists to the issue of race. By focusing on white anti-imperialist Boston feminists and their conjoining of issues of racism and sexism, Burgin argues against simplistic narratives about race in the WLM. The impact of postcolonial discourse has led to a refocused history of the WLM which underlines the importance of 'intersectionality', i.e., the interconnectedness of class, race and gender.[5] The category 'woman' is not simply a product of gender discourse. To uncover the history of Afro-American, Latina, Asian, West Indian and other minority women in second wave feminism we need a more inclusive definition of feminist activism which would encompass mixed gender organisations where women flourished and brought about real change in these years.[6]

The idea of 'waves' in feminist history has itself been challenged by Nancy Hewitt which has led to a more nuanced, less white dominated and less suffrage based history of the 'first wave' from the 1840s to the 1920s.[7] Beyond the first wave there was a continuing stream of feminist thought and activism. There is no denying, however, that there was a great burst of feminist energy—mass activism, theoretical texts and literature—between the 1960s and 1980s which distinguishes it from the periods both before and after. In the US in 1970 thirteen texts were produced relating in some way to the WLM.[8] By the mid 1980s in many states the onslaught of neo-liberal right-wing policies put feminism back on the defensive. This period needs to be studied as a distinct phenomenon in its own right. The WLM was hugely diverse, impacting differently according to different local circumstances, national and community needs. In Quebec, for instance, feminists saw their feminism as integral to their French Canadian identity.[9] Many women opted to work within local, autonomous, self-governing WLM groups, often with a 'consciousness raising' element.[10] There were, though, less radical feminist groups in the US such as the National Organisation of Women (NOW) which adopted formal bureaucratic structures. There was a constant tension between institutionalisation and local, autonomous grass roots campaigning; pragmatic realism versus revolutionary idealism. In Canada feminists were ready to accept state funding, whilst many others saw this as being 'co-opted' into the system. For most feminists, paid employment was the route to economic independence, but the longstanding maternalist, 'mothering' stream within feminism continued to assert women's right to choose to stay at home and raise their children, on state benefits if necessary. Marks and Little focus on a marginalised group of Canadian mothers who campaigned for welfare support to enable women to choose to be working mothers or stay at home mothers. This was at odds with those feminists who wanted women to assert their equality through their presence in the workplace, and Marks and Little highlight the differences, and different relationships to the WLM, on this issue between liberal, socialist and conservative groups of mothers.

The desire by the media to designate leaders was strongly resisted across the board, 'second wavers' were insistent that there were no 'stars' in the WLM. Transnational influences were very significant. Cheaper foreign travel meant that many American women brought feminist ideas and literature to Europe in the late 1960s, adding impetus to the nascent European WLM. The idea to 'take back the night' first happened in the US when a woman was murdered on her way back from work. It spread to Europe and in the late 1970s and early 1980s torch-lit, nocturnal 'reclaim the night' marches were held in red light districts all over the UK, often resulting in clashes with 'porn' shop owners and police.[11] Despite huge diversity in organisational forms, campaigns and chronology, in essence the core aims of the WLM were very similar: economic equality and access to education, affordable child care; freely determined sexuality, an end to sexual violence and the right to control fertility; political and legal equal equality. Of course, these issues are complex and meant different things to different women, often depending on class and ethnicity. Phillida Bunkle explores the impact of grammar school and university education on girls who benefitted from the 1944 Education Act, who used their education to shape the women's movement through the written word or to develop consciousness through their own reading. On the issue of working class women and the WLM, George Stevenson has sought to foreground working women through a history of four women-centred industrial strikes and disputes in Britain. These reveal complex links to the trade union and women's liberation movements, demonstrating intersections between class, race and gender based issues. Women also expressed their feminism creatively through visual media, performance arts and other cultural outlets. This is not simply a peripheral element but an essential aspect of the dynamism of the WLM. Lisa Taylor, a feminist artist, discusses, in her illustrated article, the creative and political environment surrounding her activist printmaking, and offers a contemporary reflection upon, and re-evaluation of, her practice from a vantage point of theoretically-informed feminism. Women's culture can be discerned and detected through the artefacts and creativity of the WLM, and D-M Withers envisages aspects of the WLM as cultural heritage. She argues that, through publicly oriented projects, exhibitions and feminist archives, women's histories of the WLM reveal women's communities, feminist cultural traditions and a multiplicity of voices. Laurel Forster, in her essay, also points to the diversity of feminist voices and perspectives, discernible through the varied ways that women engaged with print cultures. A wide range of feminisms, all of which found a home in the WLM, may be traced through feminist involvement with, and commitment to, publishing, print and feminist magazines.

It is vital that we continue to develop the history of the WLM. Towards this end a conference was held at the University of Portsmouth in July 2014, 'Situating Women's Liberation, Historicizing a Movement'. This collection of papers has been developed from that conference. The aim of the conference was to bring new discussions of the WLM to the fore, sometimes introducing new perspectives, and sometimes recasting existing debates in a new light. The WLM represents an important moment of consciousness-raising and self-expression for a wide range of women across the world, and therefore is a crucial movement in the history of the feminist journey towards gender equality. Feminist writers of the WLM have themselves chosen to consider further contexts for, and offer new perspectives on, their earlier writings.[12] The original essays in this collection also help us to broaden our understanding of the impact and implication of the WLM and therefore make a valuable addition to WLM historiography.

Notes

1. Stephanie Gilmore (2013) *Groundswell: grassroots feminist activism in post war America* (London: Routledge), p. 129; Celia Hughes (2012) Realigning Political and Personal Selfhood: narratives of activist women in the late 1960s and 1970s, *Women's History Magazine*, 68, pp. 22–27.
2. Gilmore, *Groundswell*, p. 19.
3. Carol Giardina (2010) *Freedom for Women, Forging the Women's Liberation Movement 1953–70* (USA: University of Florida), pp. 5, 12, 116, 214. For the UK see Natalie Tomlinson (2012) The Colour of Feminism: white feminists and race in the women's liberation movement, *History*, 97, pp. 453–475.
4. Becky Thompson (2002) Multiracial Feminism: recasting the chronology of second wave feminism, *Feminist Studies*, 28(2), pp. 337–359.
5. See Lela Fernandez (2010) Unsettled 'Third Wave Feminism': feminist waves, intersectionality and identity politics in retrospect, in Nancy A. Hewitt (Ed.) *No Permanent Waves: recasting histories of US feminism* (New Jersey, USA: Rutgers University Press), pp. 98–112.
6. Thompson, 'Multiracial Feminism', p. 338.
7. Nancy A. Hewitt (Ed) (2010) Introduction, in Nancy A. Hewitt (Ed) *No permanent waves: recasting histories of US feminism* (New Jersey, USA: Rutgers University Press), pp. 1–7.
8. Giardina, *Freedom for Women*, p. 231.
9. Constance Backhouse & David H. Flaherty (Eds) (1992) *Challenging Times: the women's movement in Canada and the US* (Montreal: McGill), Introduction, p. 5.
10. For Consciousness Raising in the UK, see Sue Bruley (2013) Consciousness Raising in Clapham: women's liberation as 'lived experience' in south London in the 1970s, *Women's History Review*, 22(5), pp. 717–738.
11. Beatrix Campbell & Anne Coote (1982) *Sweet Freedom: the struggle for women's liberation* (London: Pan), pp. 204–205. See also *Women's Voice*, May 1979, p. 5, for details of sixteen women who came to trial in April 1979 following arrests at a Reclaim the Night demonstration the previous November.
12. Sheila Rowbotham, Lynne Segal & Hilary Wainwright (2013 [1979]) *Beyond the Fragments: feminism and the making of socialism*, 3rd edn (Pontypool: The Merlin Press).

Etchings from the Attic: looking back at feminist print-making from the 1980s

Lisa Taylor

ABSTRACT
Drawing on autobiographical memories of the influence of the Women's Liberation Movement, this article discusses feminist etchings made for my final undergraduate show. Etching, historically related to satire, was deliberately chosen to mock the disparaging treatment of the female artist. The article offers both an experiential and a contextual discussion of the atmosphere of social activism, political activity and consciousness-raising of the WLM as well as the journalism and feminist art history scholarship which informed my practice. Further, the article evaluates the potential naivety of my feminist strategy of 'body art', as it risked being misunderstood as conventional sexually explicit imagery of female sexuality.

Introduction

Back in the 1980s, I wore Doc Martens, listened to post-punk and made irreverent art that urged its audience to ask questions about legitimated versions of art history which denied the existence of female artists.[1] Here I showcase some of the art pieces I made through an act of remembering; using hindsight I re-visit the relationship between art practice and what the Women's Liberation Movement meant to me as a young feminist student in the mid-1980s. It looks back to the politics of the atmosphere and the feminist scholarship, journalism and artistic activity that was formative and deeply influential in terms of the visual imagery of the etchings I made in 1986. The form of this article is deliberately experimental: it weaves autobiographical remembering of the experience of becoming alert to feminism as a student through a discussion of my print-making, while setting the work produced against the historical context of the feminist fervour for social activism which began in the late 1960s.[2] It considers both the efficacy and the problems of the textual strategies I used to make art which created illustrative meanings about how women were positioned in art history. Finally, by visualising what kind of art I might make today would contain, it draws a comparison with the present concerns of feminism.

A few words about how this piece came into being. One of my PhD students, a feminist performance artist, persuaded me to present a discussion of the etchings I present here at a conference entitled 'Playful Acts: Gender, Performance and Visibility'.[3] It was part of a number of 'happenings' organised for International Women's Day at Leeds Metropolitan University in March 2014. Later that week, I joined a march through the city centre heralded up front by a gargantuan papier mâché brassiere, made in the colours of women's suffrage which had been built by art and design undergraduates (see Figure 1). Passers-by were mildly interested and bemused. The march concluded with a ritualised burning ceremony in a small piece of wasteland in the cultural quarter of Leeds. Encircling the bra, we were encouraged, as it blazed, to shout out one-by-one key words which defined what feminism meant. Women, men and small children shouted things like 'choice' and 'freedom'. I realised that I was taking part in feminist social activism: a practice which, these days, is much less visible in contemporary culture. Taking part in these events triggered a need to take stock using a sense of periodicity.[4]

I write now, twenty-nine years later, as a result of working as a television, film and media scholar with a particular interest in gender and class, from a differently informed feminist location. My work has been concerned with the meaning of (mostly classed) femininity in visual forms such as popular cinema,[5] lifestyle[6] and reality television.[7] My work on the relationship between British gardening television and aesthetic garden practices in the domestic garden involved working as an ethnographer, combining the culturalist strand of the cultural studies tradition with a feminist approach to understanding lived culture by listening to voices 'from below'.[8] Intellectually there are affinities between cultural studies and feminism: both are concerned with the role of lived experience and both valorise the aim to represent the voices, lives and experiences of the silenced and the

Figure 1. Celebrating International Women's Day: the gigantic brassiere. Leeds, March 2014. Source: Author's photograph.

subaltern.[9] My work also shares a commonality with oral history as a method for narrativising the history of minority groups. Much of my work has been concerned with the notion that both women and the working class have been the prime casualties of exclusion from both television culture and the official annals of academia and I have drawn ethnographically on their previously unheard voices with a political need to value, legitimate and take them seriously. In this way, one can trace my early and continued interest in protesting against exclusions from official cultures that both women and the working-class have faced, as well as my interest in the cultural politics of textual strategies through art-making or academic writing which are interested in augmenting change and giving empowerment to women's lives. Inevitably, it is through my current location that I re-evaluate my work as a feminist in 1986 through the lens of memory.

Now back to the prints and to the present. My old artwork lay dormant in a fusty portfolio somewhere at home in the attic. When I first embarked on the idea of re-discovery, I readied myself for peeling open a past moment to see what might happen. Going into the attic, finding and unzipping the withered, crumbling-at-the-edges black portfolio, is emotionally treacherous. Stored things hurtle you back and trigger memories, unexpected sensations, daydreams and a sense of things that used to matter. Actually I was more pragmatic than I thought. Purposeful and intent, I bent over the portfolio: looking, assessing and angling my head to pull focus. Cognisant that the delicate act of leafing through would bring forth the musty smell of prints in their various 'states', I was surprised to find that they are intact, the ink well preserved. This is the first print I encounter (see Figure 2).[10]

Between 1984 and 1987 I studied English Literature major and Art minor for a BA (Hons) degree. The pieces I discuss here were made for the final show. The prints were

Figure 2. 'It was as if she had painted with the brush between her toes ... '
Source: Author's photograph.

intended to illustrate the arguments being made at the time about women's location in art history and how that position compared to the privileges male artists had enjoyed. In one case, I used the etching to visualise the witty turn of phrase used by the feminist writer to make a point. In Germaine Greer's introduction to *The Obstacle Race: the fortune of women painters and their work* she discusses the difficulties of researching female artists:

> The unreliability of the classic references when it comes to a woman's work is the consequence of the commentators' condescending attitude. Any work by a woman, however trifling, is as astonishing as the pearl in the head of the toad. It is not part of the natural order, and need not be related to the natural order. Their work was admired in the old sense which carries an undertone of amazement, as if they had painted with the brush between their toes.[11]

Cross about the patronising attitude of the male commentator,[12] I appropriated Greer's image with the intent of suggesting that the female artist, contrary to what might be implied in such histories, has the extra-ordinary talent to paint with her toes, should she so wish. Note too that the female artist in the role of the active subject has painted a male nude, with the aim of objectifying him. And if you look carefully his penis is erect; a deliberate move to serve (heterosexual) female sexual delectation. Challenging the idea of exclusive male artistic genius by giving visibility to the female artist; implying that female artistic talents are equal to men's; reversing the usual subject/object dichotomy by making her the active deciding subject were typical of the visual political tactics being utilised in feminist art at the time.

Speaking autobiographically of their first encounters with feminism, Hollows and Moseley suggest that attachments to feminism take particular 'routes'.[13] One possible journey might be through education, so that on an undergraduate course about visual culture one would encounter Laura Mulvey's notion of the male gaze in mainstream cinema for example.[14] Another might be through the interactive participatory pleasure gleaned from strong popular feminist female role models in popular culture such as Madonna or The Spice Girls.[15] For me it was both. In my case, as a working-class girl who had passed the 11-plus entrance exam to the local grammar school in the late 1970s, I was in a position to make a liberal move to self-improvement through education. It was predominantly the passage through university where I encountered the women's writing and feminist art that were finding a foothold in the humanities curriculum, within an atmosphere where popular culture was beginning to make women's stories, beamed out through a lens of popular feminism, apparent. So for pleasure I read Alice Walker's *The Color Purple*[16] and I also saw Steven Spielberg's 1986 adaptation of the film at the cinema.

The 1980s was an exciting time to be a humanities literature and art undergraduate interested in cultural politics. One of the necessary strategies of the time was the act of both celebrating and making visible women's cultural production with the ultimate aim of placing women on a more equal platform of cultural recognition. This trend was bubbling in literature circles. Ferment for feminist publishing had started out in the 1960s. *Spare Rib* began in 1973 and, somewhat typical of the time, the story goes that the magazine's founders Carmen Callil and Rosie Boycott had leafed through a book of goddesses in 1978 to find the name *Virago*, 'a war-like woman' for their new publishing house.[17] While publishers had specific ambitions, often fuelled by a desire to embrace the marginal, for example *Sheba* published writing by black, working-class and lesbian writers, most were united, 'by the conviction that women's writing should be taken as seriously as men's, and, as a result, should have the same chance of remaining in print and becoming part of the canon'.[18] And indeed there was a groundswell of action: by 1988 there were eleven feminist publishers in the UK.[19] There was a spirit of excitement about both the acts of uncovering and re-naming using strong inspiring new labels which served our interests. I can remember the excitement of wandering through my university library in search of the distinctive brand symbols at the base of book spines, for example the black and white iron that stood for *The Women's Press*. This type of contagious spirit informed feminist art of the time but, as I show, feminist art circles in both the US and the UK were divided.

Feminist art practice in the 1970s

If in the Anglo-phone West in the 1970s the feminist art scene of critics, commentators and art-makers was about female artists mutually and practically supporting each other's work in a bid to mitigate against discrimination in the art world, the 1980s were categorised by a shift to 'strategic practices' which came out of an emergence about debates about 'representation and a critique of modernism'.[20] Feminism is a broad umbrella category and during this period there were a range of positions taken up by women artists in both the US and the UK. While there were many practitioners who eluded easy categorisation, broadly artists could be seen as either occupying, or at least being influenced by, two existing camps. The first was politically feminist, anti-essentialist and theory-based which drew on Marxism and/or post-structuralist ideas from deconstruction, semiotics and psychoanalysis. Some artists who positioned themselves at this side of the debate were characterised by the use of avant-garde and experimental practice and at times they were referred to as being 'radical' in terms of form. Artists and filmmakers such as Mary Kelly, Laura Mulvey and Peter Wollen were identified with this group.[21] Key differences in American and British feminist approaches to art history are starkly drawn in Griselda Pollock's response to Thalia Gouma-Peterson and Patricia Mathews' survey 'The Feminist Critique of Art History'.[22] For Pollock the emphasis placed by the American writers on the generational and geographic differences between feminist writers across the Atlantic served to miss the salient objectives of the work of British feminists and depoliticised it in the process.[23] The insistence on using the term 'methodology' to describe the job of art criticism tended to gloss over the illuminating power of the nexus of theories being used to produce a feminist politics with which to question art history as an ideological practice. Pollock argued that Foucault's ideas about discursive formations enabled an understanding of the historical oppression of women; Althusser's Marxist notion of ideological state apparatuses helped to explain the role cultural representations have in reproducing relations of difference and power; and the dialogues between semiotics, psychoanalysis, feminism and post-structuralism were important for thinking about how meaning is made in power relations and for theorising the subject; such that representation, power, difference and desire become objects of study from a feminist standpoint. The decision to exclude Althusser's notion of ideology and Foucault's theory of discourse is also significant in that the text becomes 'structured by what it absents';[24] by refusing to grapple with ideology the text reproduces the 'dominant discursive formations of an academic narrative' of art history; by ignoring Foucault's genealogy, the story of feminism and art history becomes a 'typical art-historical narrative of development and progress'.[25] Worryingly, the American authors charge the use of theory itself as exclusive and authoritarian; this served to masculinise difficult theory, hence robbing feminism of the tools it required to grapple with complex dilemmas.

The other camp, with its celebration of an all-encompassing women's experience of 'herstory' was seen as feminine and humanist.[26] The most well-known practitioners who occupied this position were North American artists drawing on physical body imagery, such as Judy Chicago and Mariam Schapiro, although, as I show, there were artists in Britain who also drew on their strategies.[27] The former were seen as intellectually esoteric and somewhat difficult. The latter were conceived as more accessible, not just to feminists, but to a more general female audience; but they were also attacked as essentialist and non-political.[28]

With a view to challenging the art school discrimination they had undergone and which they believed female artists still experienced as prevalent, Judy Chicago and Miriam Schapiro set up the Feminist Art Program in 1971 at the California Institute of the Arts.[29] Disseminating their ideas through public lectures and writing, their work was based on the idea that patriarchy distorts, breaks-down or denies women's access to an authentic, true sense of self. They advocated the notion of a female sensibility via 'central-core' visual motifs where vaginal imagery acted as iconography which was designed to positively symbolise an intrinsic essence of womanhood.[30] For example, *Female Rejection Drawing* (1974) by Judy Chicago from the *Rejection Quintet* clearly depicts the female vulva. She claimed the work was an expression of her sexuality, while insisting that the combined strategy of using flower and genital imagery was used to express dualisms. Chicago's method involved hand-writing underneath her painting in a move to express the feelings which motivated the work; it also shows her intention to include audiences unfamiliar with abstraction. These artists argued that female creativity can only be fully realised in a separatist women's culture. 'If it is not perceived that my work is about the nature of women', she told Lucy Lippard in an interview in 1974, 'then all the other things that are in my art are invisible'.[31] In the same year, Schapiro admitted that her abstract geometrical painting in the *OX* series of drawings and paintings which she had previously claimed as shapes reminiscent of the California landscape *OX* (1967), was a 'cunt painting'.[32] While this term acts as one kind of descriptor, these abstract forms express a relationship to the female body. Works under-girded by similar beliefs, which aimed to capture a universal sense of the power and nobility of femaleness, were being exhibited across the Atlantic. In Britain in 1978 a touring exhibition 'Womenmagic', a show concerned with the celebration of the power and creativity of women's fertility and sexuality, contained paintings and batiks by artists such as Monica Sjoo and Marika Tell. The ethos of the show was to celebrate the spiritual, universal and biologistic creativity of women across history, race and culture. Its strategy was to, 'reach back through ignored traditions, religions, and mythologies to goddess worship'[33] in a bid to generate a specifically female aesthetic. One can understand the powerful appeal of work which hopes to celebrate femaleness and which foregrounds with pride the unique specificity of the fabric of 'everywomen's' life experiences. In relation to the use of vaginal motifs, Tickner argued that such images promoted 'self-knowledge (like the self-examination health groups by which it has probably been influenced)' and it 'refutes at least rhetorically both the

Freudian concept of penis envy and the notion of woman as "The Dangerous Sex"'.[34] Indeed, to some extent my decision to use naked bodies in my own practice came out of a need to both express femaleness and re-define it as more powerful by combining it with satire and illustrative commentary about how the female artist was located. But the problem with creating an essence of womanhood is that it re-enforces existing oppressive patriarchal definitions of femininity, thereby defining and reducing women to their bodies and their biological destiny.

For Mary Kelly the importance of Marxist, psychoanalytic and semiotic theory was central to her development as a practitioner. She was a member of the History Group formed in London in 1970, where she worked alongside feminist theorist/activist Laura Mulvey.[35] Interested in the sexual division of labour she collaborated with the Berwick Film Collective to make *Nightcleaners Part 1* (1970–75). Non-realist, self-reflexive and aesthetically experimental in terms of its form, the film's main narrative charts the material conditions which prevent a group of night cleaners from organising politically, the reluctance of the Trades Unions to help and the impossibility of organising meetings due to working conditions and a lack of economic resources. It shows the efforts of Women's Liberation members to provide them with resources and sign them up to Trades Unions to enhance their pay and conditions. The film offers an account of feminist activism against the political and economic backdrop of attempts to contain the power of trade unions. It shows how the women's conditions were cast outside mainstream regulations into casualised employment by the contract system. Offering, 'a rare insight into the experiences of a group of women who even within the working-class have little visibility as historical subjects',[36] the film visualises an unrelenting sense of the exhausting, nerve-racking, boring and gloomily isolated domestic work undertaken by the women. Collectively made and regarded as one of the most important radical British documentaries to date, it disrupts audience passivity and insists on hailing viewer participation, 'in a process of consciousness-raising'.[37] Filmed largely in fragmented sequences and drawing on various aesthetic devices including frozen shots, the unexplained cut off, as well as using black leader between shots such that the viewer is left with a pause pregnant with the meaning just conveyed, it attempts to, 'jolt a new consciousness in to being'.[38] In an interview, Marc Karlin described *Nightcleaners* as a 'film about distances'.[39] What the film conveys are the gulfs of differences of class and political hope between the middle-class campaigning women and the cleaners. As Johnston observes:

> We hear Movement women on the soundtrack discussing the notion of sexuality, while we see an image of a cleaner working alone in a high office block shot at a distance and from below ... too often these contradictions are repressed by filmmakers ... THE NIGHTCLEANERS presents an honest vision of what such political work really entails.[40]

Feministo (1975) a 'visual communication network by post' was a British cross-country women's group which aimed to develop visual relationships which explored the lives of domestically located mothers and artists.[41] In 1978 a travelling mixed media exhibition entitled Mother's Pride: Mother's Ruin (1977–78) was organised by two leading members of the group Trisha Davis and Phil Goodall, who came together in a socialist reading group. Drawing on austere objects and materials from women's quotidian domestic lives—toys, collage, photographs, clothes—the tour set out to look at how education, work and domesticity structured women's lives differently because they are 'cut across by class'. In *Cot* a doll-sized woman lies on pink satin sheets, confined next to a medicine bottle which says 'Drink Me' in a crib painted black. The artists attest, 'behind the bars is not a baby but a doll woman, reduced to size by the lack of adequate socialized child care'.[42] The exhibition itself caused controversy because it ends with a final positive note for future resistance; *Badges Women* a silhouette of a woman—hands on hips—covered with campaign symbols, quotes and badges. The tour was clearly an attempt to lay bare the socially constructed, material conditions of women's lives while identifying points of political action. Davis and Goodall stress the need for a feminist politics to focus on 'points of tension':

> Without exploring these complexities is to beg a crucial question of how class cuts across women's experience. It is to place women's experience within a universal and a-historical context, to deny it the specificity which allows us to analyse the contradictions and organise from the reality of our oppression and exploitation.[43]

Both positions deploy strategies to uncover events of women's lives which have been under-valued—hidden away in the mundanity of domesticity or, in the case of giving birth or menstruation—swathed in silence. I would argue that it is more useful to position experience within a socially and historically specific framework so that strategies of resistance can be calibrated to the conditions of oppression affecting women's lives, so that real change can be both envisaged and acted upon.

Looking back: the feminist scholarship which influenced my practice

Revisiting the scholarship and journalism about art in circulation in the mid-1980s, and the writing which precedes it from around 1970, reveals a distinctive set of concerns. First, emotion emanates from the pages. There was anger: an explosive energy or what Nancy Fraser terms an 'insurrectionary spirit'[44] which fuelled the atmosphere: 'Underneath We're Angry' was the title of a *Spare Rib* article by Rosalind Coward about sexist underwear advertising which she argued degraded women.[45] And, at the age of 19, it felt good to get annoyed in amongst other older and wiser angry feminists, and to feel informed enough to form and be able to articulate an opinion. Actually, re-reading this collection of texts I realise that there was much to feel angry about. Second, historically entrenched male institutional privilege under-girding art practice was identified as a key causal problem; patriarchy pervaded the art establishment and acted as a bulwark which barred, in a myriad of ways, women's artistic production. In a bid to unpack such privilege was a fierce polemic which set out to de-mystify skewed gendered power relations. Artistic genius as a gender and class neutral category was punctured.[46] Male art critics and their sexist commentaries and refusals to take women's art seriously were outed. Take for example the press response to Mary Kelly's 1978 exhibition of the *Post-Partum Document* shown at the 1978 Hayward Annual, a piece which publically announced an 'unacceptable combination of roles mother/artist',[47] which by exhibiting the documents and objects (perhaps most famously a baby's vest and nappy liners) refused to visualise a public portrayal of a conventional figure of the mother and child. The exhibition was attacked for its content: it belonged, the critics asserted, in a maternity ward or a woman's magazine, but not in an art gallery.[48] It was further attacked, Pollock and Parker believed, because it dared, by using intellectually challenging materials from psychoanalytic theory, to tread on masculine territory.[49] Furthermore, this writing exposed the systematic male dominance which structured art teaching, artistic patronage, exhibition, employment, prizes and publicity practices.[50] Sexist art, for example the *Women As Furniture* series sculpted by Allen Jones, which famously used life-size mannequins of women in exploitative sexual positions as tables and chairs, was deconstructed psychoanalytically by Laura Mulvey (1973) in her seminal *Spare Rib* article 'You don't know what is happening, do you, Mr Jones?' as demonstrative of male fear of castration anxiety.[51] Third, some Feminist critics argued that Feminist art practice of the 1970s marked a political rejection of Modernism, which at the time was the most dominant institutional art movement in Britain. In the USA, Lippard argued that feminism was actually anti-Modernist.[52] If as Pollock claims:

> Modernism refers to the criticism and art history which classifies paintings, sculpture and other art forms according to stylistic innovations and reactions (Cubism, Abstract Expressionism etc.) embodied in the masterpieces of great individual geniuses (for instance Picasso, Matisse, Pollock, Johns).[53]

then feminist art-making, with its concerns for the everyday and the experiential, formed a reactive rejection to the Modernist ethos of artistic production. And running alongside these challenges was a spirit of collective organisation through which feminist initiatives started: for example Griselda Pollock and Rozsika Parker were two of the founders of the London Women's Art History Collective, formed in 1972, which aimed to organise group teaching and research; and during the period 1972–85 there were a number of all-women exhibitions. Back then, I felt outraged to read that it was nigh-on impossible for women to source an exhibition space which would agree to an all-female show![54] I remember reading at the time Parker's review of the exhibition Women's Images of Men shown at the Institute of Contemporary Arts, London, in 1980. The exhibition featured a variety of ways in which women chose to represent men; indeed it contained portraiture of famous men and images of male violence, but what Parker's review focused on was the predominance of work about weak, vulnerable or 'invalided' men. I recall not being able to help but feel a small sense of glee in the fantasy of a power balance in re-dress:

> male invalids are so gratifyingly grateful for attention ... the sick man clearly takes on the virtues associated with women ... once a man is desperately ill he can sympathise with women's sufferings.[55]

Tracing a historical line of incapacitated men through fiction as well as art from the seventeenth century, she asks: what is so powerful about the idea of pitiable, blind, literally muscle-bound, pallid, sick and suffering men? She argues:

> It is perhaps inevitable that women's images of men in art as much as literature should be about the effects of differences of power between the sexes; about the fear and hatred it can generate, and about the desire to reveal, challenge, transform or destroy the imbalance.[56]

As I argue later, this exhibition had some influence on how I chose to depict the male figures in my etchings, based no doubt on the fantasy of evening out the power imbalance. The men in my prints are vulnerably naked: the tilted head of one of the men renders him feminised and rather coy; and in the case of the other there is something ludicrous and pathetic about the male figure desperately penetrating the canvas. Parker and Pollocks' (1987) edited collection *Framing Feminism: art and the women's movement 1970–1985* is illustrative of the flavour of the mid-1980s. Deliberately diverse, it gathers periodical and journalistic writing of the time: it features feminist responses to the regime of sexist images in art and popular culture, feminist art collective manifestos, reactive press cuttings which show the institutional outrage which feminist art provoked; women's accounts of the difficulties of being a female artist; writing about difference by Black women artists; feminist reviews of feminist art exhibitions; feminist onlookers considering the politics of the types of textual strategies informing art-making exhibitions as well as writing by women artists about their own work.

Pollock posits that her approach differed markedly from American feminist art criticism which argued that women were 'hidden from history' and subject to sexual discrimination in contemporary art practice.[57] Rather, her position offered an historically specific approach which argued that women have 'always been present as artists', but that they had been ascribed 'positions' such that their 'ways of getting in to art practice have varied and been affected by different historical factors'.[58] Theorising art and art history as a discursive and ideological practice she suggested two strategies:

> The first is to recognise the significance in art writings of an insistent assertion that all women's art is homogenous and 'feminine' by definition, and the second is to retrieve a knowledge of consistent but diverse, heterogeneous and historically specific work of women artists, to retrieve it from the discourses of art history and criticism, which are either silent on the subject of women artists, or submerge their work in to the 'feminine' category of 'women's art' and set it apart from both the rest of art history and from history itself.[59]

Rather than being excluded, Pollock argued that female artists have 'occupied and spoken from a different place within it'.[60] I wanted my work to illustrate women's vexed and difficult locations. Pollock identified that women's art was systematically acknowledged in the literature until the nineteenth century, but it is in the twentieth, at the very moment when women's gains in education, employment, contraception and reproductive management enable women to increasingly participate in cultural life, that a pall of silence falls on the history of women's art. They assert that it is a set of particular systemic ideological assumptions which under-gird the silence. Pollock recognises that the system which writes them is dominant and she isolates how they are expressed: female artists are assessed according to their sexual attractiveness; women are associated with childbearing as opposed to cultural production; female art is associated with craft fashioned in the home rather than with public 'art' and women's art is accused of aping the art of men.[61] But even more consistently, women have been associated with a feminine touch which, in comparison to a man's, is theorised as weak.

The influence of the Women's Liberation Movement

Feminist art making was firmly fastened to the historical backcloth of women's liberation —'a powerful, exciting and vibrant social movement'[62]—which hit the Western hemisphere in the late 1960s. Offering a history of aspects of the movement is crucial for understanding the personalised narrative of my artistic production; here I draw on the factors which created the movement, with particular reference to education, events which foreground differences within feminist positions and to the significance of consciousness-raising as a political practice. Accounts of the period, some of which are autobiographical, credit the New Left and those radicalised into collectivity by the student movement as factors which urged women to turn inwards to their own consciousness to ask: 'What have we been putting up with?' While social activism did take the form of public demonstrations, such as the National Joint Action Campaign Committee for Equal Rights in London 1969, women's liberation was also emerging as an informal, un-coordinated practice in women's groups. Indeed as Pugh argues the 'devolved character' of the movement was not a weakness, indeed, 'it gave full scope to the energy, enthusiasm and originality of a wide range of women who effectively adapted the board principle of women's liberation to the needs and ideas of their own communities'.[63] Some were led by those circulating in left-wing organisations such as the International Socialists; further groups came from women who were home-based and who simply shared similar life experiences. And despite being subject to derision, for example the contemptuous ridicule with which Sheila Rowbotham's suggestion for a women's history conference was met by male colleagues at History Workshop,[64] this event was hailed as the starting point of Women's Liberation, the first conference at Ruskin trades union college took place in 1970. 'It was not just about voting', Rowbotham recalls:

> or belonging to parties, or about state power or the art of the impossible. It was about direct action, participatory politics, about transforming daily existence and all aspects of relationships, about demanding the impossible and living against the grain.[65]

Indeed there were a number of direct action campaigns where women used their vociferous presence to make their voices heard: the unruly women's protest at the 1970 Miss World competition; and radical feminists, who identified themselves as a separatist revolutionary faction formed Women Against Violence Against Women who, angered by police advice to stay indoors as a response to violence and rape in the streets, organised the 'Reclaim the Night' protests through the prostitution district in Leeds. The National Abortion Campaign of 1975, formed to successfully re-secure the imperilled 1967 Abortion Act, was heralded as the most fruitful campaign in the period; it succeeded in gathering a huge demonstration of 100,000 march supporters.[66] These early years were infused by optimistic energy and the decade witnessed important gains: there was the Equal Pay Act of 1970 and the Sex Discrimination Act of 1975. There were significant gains in education during the period too. Pugh argues that texts devoted to writing a specific women's history, such as Rowbotham's *Hidden from History* (1973),[67] 'stimulated a vast range of research, and for some women the very work of research became an important expression of their feminism'.[68] The decade saw a rise in women's studies courses, some of them appended to literature and history, though growth in the area saw the subject promoted to postgraduate studies. In 1982 the first Women's Studies MA was launched at Bradford University and by the 1990s women's history was firmly embedded in most history courses throughout the UK.[69]

But it is important to stress that women's liberation during the 1970s and beyond was shot through with division. For example, the anti-nuclear protests at Greenham Common became women-only in 1982.[70] The campaigns drew much media attention partly because the women on the base used a range of creative and highly resourceful visual strategies for making their protest visible. Women, some of whom had devoted months to living and protesting on the camp, pinned baby clothes to the camp's fence and invaded the base with a huge serpent's tail sewn by 2,000 peace women.[71] Factions of the movement were critical of the separatist, maternal and essentialist flavour of the protest, arguing that universalist, 'transhistorical' calls for the natural nurturing powers of women to overcome the naturally warring, violent characteristics of 'men' was fixed, biologistic and reductionist. Sasha Roseneil, who moved to the camp when she was sixteen years old, uses retrospective auto-ethnography as a method to construct a fascinating and highly detailed ethnographic account of the lived experience at the camp.[72] She argues that claims of essentialism and maternalism were assumed rather than investigated. For Roseneil, Greenham was a site of extraordinary experimentation, where gender and sexual identities and the practices which characterise their expression were thrown into question.[73] Women learned a great deal about practices such as collectivity and caring for the environment. Domestic routine practices, such as washing up were challenged and women were afforded some liberation. Heterosexuality was de-normalised and 'queer'—as opposed to the static identity of lesbianism—became 'normal'.[74] But for socialist feminists, who argued for the social construction of gendered identities, it diverted attention away from what they considered to be the real issue: an equal rights feminist politics. The virtual collapse of the national conferences around 1978 is attributed to the violent disagreements between these two feminist factions. And there were yet further divisions which became more concretised by the mid-1980s. While white feminists during the period were protesting against the family as a sexist institution which perpetuated gender divisions and oppressive practices such as housework, black and Asian feminists wanted to preserve the family as a sanctuary against their experience of racism; and while white feminists wanted to preserve the right to abortion, black feminists claimed that the British State was urging them to have abortions to keep the black birth rate under control.[75]

One recently re-evaluated dimension, which undoubtedly played a part in fuelling the social activism documented here, was the vastly important role of consciousness-raising to the movement. While often attributed to the early 1970s, feminist historians argue that the 'small group process' among women lasted far longer. Defined as 'the process by which women come together, talk about their experiences, try to put them into some sort of context and develop a feminist orientation and *practice*',[76] feminist historians have used oral history to investigate its value; in the process they have made apparent the voices of women who felt marginalised from academic, middle-class feminist circles, for example working-class women, who often lack the resources to disseminate, write or publish their views. Sue Bruley interviewed women from the Clapham CR group of which she herself had been a member. Consciousness-raising, she argues, was intimately and necessarily entwined with campaigning activities. What was crucial about the process was that the women she interviewed were able to forge new politicised identities as feminists while enjoying the nourishment of female friendship and support. Bridget Lockyer used oral testimonies of women who participated in Bradford WLM during the 1970s and early 1980s to argue that there was something distinctive about the group who produced *Irregular Periods*, the title of the newsletter the group used when they realised they could not meet regularly.[77] Split across a number of groups, for example the Bradford Dykes and the Bradford Women's Health Collective, Lockyer found that the group was made up of a large working-class and lesbian constituency. While regrettably the group failed to recruit South Asian or African-Caribbean members, Lockyer argues that the cultural diversity of Bradford at the time—10% of Bradford's population in 1971 comprised of non-UK citizens—actually forced collaboration and collective activity across conflicts of political ideas, hierarchies of oppression and personal rivalries within the Bradford scene. Consciousness-raising had been central to the group Lockyer studied; several of the oral testimonies she includes talk about the 'profound personal transformation' that taking on a feminist identity involved for them. Consciousness-raising was certainly important to me back in the 1980s—there was an ecstatic personal unravelling about my experience of gendered politics that was occurring in the student houses and seminars I was attending. It became an energy propelling my art practice—itself a form of feminist activism—in its drive to inform and educate its audience about how women had been located in art history.

And now back to the prints

As I curled each print back I couldn't help flashing back cinematically to dipping and inking the etching plates, of working the printing press (and you needed some brawn for that). There was a relationship between the type of satirical art I wanted to make and the etching process itself. To etch you need a copper, zinc or steel plate. The plate comes covered in an acid resistant resin. Using an etching needle (and some pent up fury!) you draw out the first state, then dip the plate in to the acid; the acid bites the lines on the plate, corroding it back. The plate is then inked, paper is placed on to the plate, and the wheel is turned to put the plate and paper through the press. And then there were the things I wore which were also symbolic statements of what I wanted to say about my gendered position: that white leather jacket, those black patent Doc Martens, the bleached blonde short spikey hair and of course the unshaved legs …

Figure 3. Series 2: the female artist paints appropriately 'feminine' material while he depicts a nude. Source: Author's photograph.

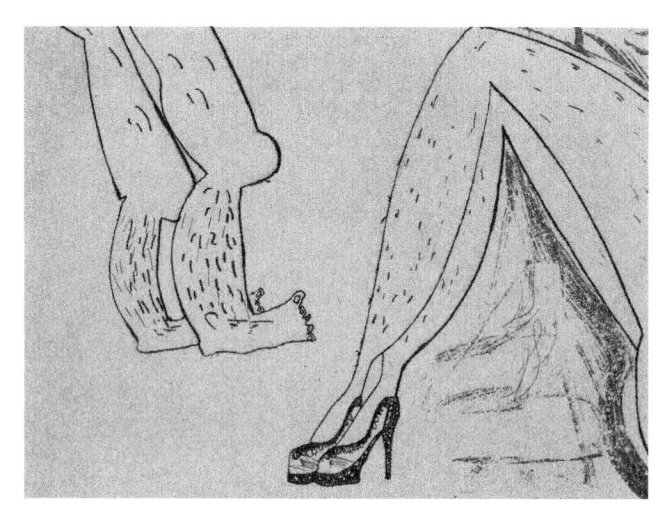

Figure 4. Close up of Series 1: both male and female artists show their sexual virility through their body hair. Source: Author's photograph.

The female bodies here are as erotically unshaved and hairy as the men (see Figure 4). My friendship group back then begged each other to maintain our body hair as an act of irreverence that was especially aimed at challenging the boyfriends of the time. And I remembered some of the reactions to the final show. My mother, herself at that time discovering impressionism through the University of the Third Age, thought they were 'aggressive'.[78] I was pleased about that; I wanted them to cause some upset. That was one of the reasons I had made them 'rude' by blowing up genitals and body parts that western culture had sexualised (in particular in my work, women's breasts). They are quite cross, fuming actually, about the women's oppression that I was seeing around me across a range of gendered practices which related to the feminist mantra that was on the lips of my politicised friends, that 'the personal is political'. For example, the labour of making a feminine appearance and the expectation that body hair was to be removed. I had read and enjoyed *The Female Eunuch* and as Greer put it:

> hairiness is like furriness, an index of bestiality, and as such an indication of aggressive sexuality. Men cultivate it, just as they are encouraged to develop competitive and aggressive instincts, women suppress all the aspects of their vigour and libido. If they do not feel sufficient revulsion for their body hair themselves, others will direct them to depilate themselves.[79]

Then there were the reproductive and sexual inequalities; we had talked a lot as students about whether 'he' took responsibility for the contraception. These everyday concerns about sexual politics were not unrelated to women's 'body art', an attempt to deal with how to communicate feminist concerns about the female body. One of the concerns of the literature of the time was the idea that women lacked the tools to speak authentically and powerfully about their own bodies given that language and images seemed like masculine tools. As Lisa Tickner argued, 'we are saddled with men's view of us and cannot find our true selves—in art, in literature and often in life'.[80] And there was a sense that we lacked corporeal ownership of our own warm bodies, 'breasts, the womb, ovarian secretions, menstruation, pregnancy and labour, as de Beauvoir has reminded us, are for the benefit of others and not ourselves'.[81]

Undoubtedly, the vaginal imagery I had seen in the work of Chicago and others made me bold enough to use nude figures. They are also a reaction, an attempt as much feminist art was doing at the time, to 'decolonise the female';[82] to re-claim a female-authored version of ourselves, to contest representations made by men for their pleasure with the added aim of generating pleasure for us as women. I was responding to calls made by feminists such as Tickner:

> women artists have only two consistent courses of action. One is to ignore the whole area as too muddled or dangerous for the production of clear statements; the other is to take the heritage and work with it—attack it, reverse it, expose and *use* it for their own purposes. The colonized territory must be reclaimed from masculine fantasy, the 'lost' aspects of female body experience authenticated and reintegrated in opposition to its more familiar and seductive artistic role as raw material for the men.[83]

I wanted to reverse, expose and use it, just as Tickner described but whether I had successfully 'reintegrated it in opposition' is a debateable point to which I return later.

I had also read Rozsika Parker's *The Subversive Stitch* (1984)[84] and of course Griselda Pollock and Rozsika Parker's *Old Mistresses* (1981) (see Figure 5). From those books I had discovered some startling revelations: some works surveying western art history, such as E. H. Gombrich's *Story of Art* (1961)[85] ignored women artists completely. I was also enraged that by the late seventeenth and eighteenth century with the founding of official academies of art in Europe, women were given limited access, or as in 1706 in the case of the *Paris Academie*, had excluded them all together. Women's exclusion from the life class in the academy schools which persisted until the nineteenth century meant that women were

Figure 5. Series 2: ransacking art history with curious juxtapositions ... the story of Rosa Bonheur. Source: Author's photograph.

barred from contributing to the most highly regarded form of painting.[86] I wanted to use print-making, and etching in particular, because of its historical relationship to satire. There is a long history of print-making and political satire: Hogarth's work for example.[87] I wanted to use the bite and excoriating tone of the piss-take. It was fun to immerse these metal plates only to see it bubble as it eroded the metal. I liked the idea of the reproductive nature of the print—it was useful for the work of consciousness-raising; the idea that many prints, with their messages about women and art, could be widely disseminated. I wanted to pluck some of the things I had learned about the skewed gender politics of how men had flourished and been encouraged while women had been ignored or barred from making art, encouraged to do art that suited their sex or how they had had to resort to guerrilla tactics to be included. These 'stories' shaped the curious bricolage of the elements in these prints; I ransacked history in curious juxtapositions. In Figure 5 the female artist is dressed 'like a man' in a bid to 'gender pass' in a suit and brogues, yet she is centrally placed as the active maker of art. This alludes to the story of Rose Bonheur (1822–99) a utopian socialist who had won awards for her sculptures and paintings of animals.[88] Despite the growing popularity of this type of work and the easier access women like Bonheur had to animal models, she had to dress as a man to gain entry to the Paris horse market and obtain legal authorisation to do so. Such were notions of female propriety; women were consigned to the private and domestic sphere; they were highly regulated and required to deny their gender to do otherwise.[89] Note too that the female artist shown here is painting a floral arrangement which again alludes to sixteenth- and seventeenth-century European painters: 'flower painting demands no genius of a mental or spiritual kind' wrote one twentieth-century commentator.[90] By the late eighteenth century, flower painting was a common genre for women: Parker and Pollock write, 'the characterization of flower painting as petty, painstaking, pretty, requiring only dedication and dexterity is related to the sex of its practitioners'.[91] This was the kind of relegation to the 'feminine' category of 'women's art' that was in danger of being separated from art history that Pollock had alluded to. For as Leon Legrange wrote in 1860: 'Let women occupy themselves with those kinds of art they have always preferred … the paintings of flowers, those prodigies of grace and freshness which alone can compete with the grace and freshness of women themselves' (see Figure 5).[92] It was precisely grace, freshness and the idea of female propriety that I was out to quash in these prints.

In some cases I can't remember what story the imagery in my work is referring to. Certainly the men in these prints are critics, commentators, male artists or a metaphoric mixture of all three. There is an attempt at reversing the roles, fashioned no doubt because most kinds of reversal were infuriatingly impossible. As Tickner illustrates:

> There could be no role-reversal equivalent to Degas' and Lautrec's brothel scenes, no 'keyhole' art recording the intimate and perhaps homosexual moments of *male* prostitutes. It is at this moment impossible to imagine a woman artist in the situation of Picasso's late prints: 89–90 years old, recalling with affection and nostalgia both creative and coital moments of her youth. And what of the male muse, doubling as cook, housekeeper and emotional support system?[93]

Set to the side (made marginal), engaged in looking, but at the same time objectified; the female viewer of this print can gaze at the penis and scrotum here or relish the male body hair from the chest, arms or anus. If you look closely at Figure 3, the canvas held by the male figure, his penis bursts through and penetrates the canvas through the image of a female nude. This was an allusive dig at historical notions of the male artist as semi-divine creator, to which were appended associations of virile male sexuality and artistic excellence. The idea that the artist should divert their sexual energy into their art rather than expend it on sexual activity has a long history from the Renaissance. As Vincent van Gogh is alleged to have said to an artist from his social circle: 'Eat well, do your military exercises and don't fuck too much, and because of not fucking too much, your paintings will be all the more spermatic.'[94] The female bodies in these prints are deliberately asymmetrical, note the differently shaped and sized breasts; they were intended to be unruly, disobedient female bodies which refused the position of bodily insecurity (see Figure 6). The female being depicted in the canvas by the more central female artist in this piece is also an artist, her hands tied behind her back as she reaches for her tools—some of which I notice are etching tools; a further comment no doubt about the constraints and limitations on women's artistic production, while masculinity seemed to maintain its power in arenas of cultural production.

Of course there are problems with these prints. I was a naive undergraduate; I understood the arguments being foregrounded, but I struggled to make the connection between critical thinking and my own practice. It was only later, as the exhibition took place, that I realised I was caught in a conundrum. With the decision to represent these nude women with slim bodies and large breasts (which are also bodily traits highly valued in pornography) in an attempt to satirise pronounced gender differences, I also risked perpetuating the traditional sexual identity of women. The well-known saying, 'want to come up and see my etchings?' has some meaning here: while the female viewer gets to see 'cock and balls', the male viewer gets some 'tits and ass'. When a male friend who came to the show asked me, 'Why have the women in your prints got such big tits?' I was positioned to both feel and recognise the contradictions. There were problems with my representational strategies.

Ultimately though, the men in these works get annihilated by being literally crossed out or burnt out (see Figure 7). One way to do this was to paint resin over the plate for another acid dip to produce further tonal effects; both of these works went through four or five states. By making the decision not to protect the male figure with resin, he kept getting

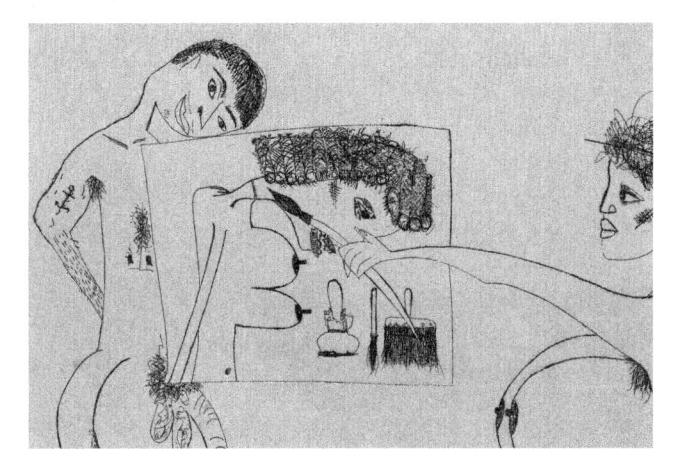

Figure 6. Close up of Series 1: the etching woman, her hands tied behind her back.
Source: Author's photograph.

Figure 7. Series 1: when in doubt – burn out the male art critic.
Source: Author's photograph.

violently burned out by the acid; such that in the end he becomes a ghostly blank. In the other print series the ink gets darker over further crossings out of the male figure shown fucking a canvas. The answer was relatively simple: when in doubt, just blank out, remove or annihilate the perpetrators of patriarchy. That was one of the answers being promulgated by radical feminists from North America.[95] And in my eclectic experimentation with a range of feminist arguments, I did not have a firm position at the age of nineteen, so I pillaged the bits that suited. In these ways, the prints tell of their contextual location in the 1980s, caught amidst a moment of contradictory positions. Looking back, these prints were full of an outraged, bubbling energy, with a voice that wanted to say 'hey—listen to some of the things that have happened to women who wanted to be artists!' I miss the art-making and the courage to take risks even though in my theoretical naivety I had also made images which could be dangerously misunderstood.

And what, if I went back to satirical print-making today, would I make prints about? In literature circles data suggests that female authors have to be careful about the content of their work. Women do want to read about men's lives in the novels they read, while men certainly want to read about other men. Yet, men are not especially interested in reading about women's lives and female authors must perish the thought of including children in the narratives they weave.[96] Recently a Canadian professor made the news with his refusal to teach books by Chinese or women authors:

> 'I'm not interested in teaching books by women' he told *Shelfesteem,* a blog by Random House publishers, 'What I teach is guys. Serious heterosexual guys. F Scott Fitzgerald, Chekov, Tolstoy. Real guy-guys. Henry Miller. Philip Roth.'[97]

This kind of material is ripe for a send-up; a print could hold a mirror up to this type of sheer narcissism.

A final anecdote: when I'd finished the show in the summer of 1986 I felt a need to thank and pay homage to one of the feminist writers and researchers who had made my work possible. Sisterhood, and the power of strong and articulate role models, like the female art lecturers I had encountered in higher education,[98] were important to me. In my naivety about an author's private security, I telephoned Virago publishers and asked if they would send me an address. No they replied, they would not give out her address, but they would be happy to send a communication on to the author. So I rolled up the print of the women with the paint brush between her toes (see Figure 2) and sent it to Virago through the post. Several weeks later I got a postcard from her, a postcard that I still have, but which eluded me in the attic. 'Dear Lisa', it read 'Thanks for the print. I'm looking forward to receiving it back from the framers. Kind Regards, Germaine Greer.'

Notes

1. It was argued by feminists in the US that women artists had been neglected. See Linda Nochlin (1971) Why Have There Been No Great Women Artists? in Elizabeth Baker & Thomas Hess (Eds) *Art and Sexual Politics* (New York: Collier Books), pp. 1–43.
2. Elizabeth Meehan (1990) British Feminism from the 1960s to the 1980s, in H. Smith (Ed) *British Feminism in the Twentieth Century* (London: Edward Elgar), pp. 187–199.
3. This conference was organised by Jo Hassall, Casey Orr and Liz Stirling. My thanks to them for inviting me to contribute. According to popular myth, bras were burned at the Miss America Pageant on 7 September 1968 which was attended by civil rights protesters and feminists. Symbols of femininity, for example false eyelashes, were burned and thrown into a rubbish bin, but no bras were burned.
4. Special thanks to Jo Hassall for encouraging me to re-visit my art-making.
5. Lisa Taylor (1995) From Psychoanalytic Feminism to Popular Feminism, in Joanne Hollows & Mark Jancovich (Eds) *Approaches to Popular Film* (Manchester: Manchester University Press), pp. 151–171.
6. Lisa Taylor (2005) It Was Beautiful Before You Changed It All: class, taste and the transformative aesthetics of the garden lifestyle media, in David Bell & Joanne Hollows (Eds) *Ordinary Lifestyles: popular media, consumption and taste* (Maidenhead: Open University Press), pp. 113–127; (2008) From Ground-Force to Garden-Making: how ordinary gardeners consume television lifestyle aesthetics, in David Hussey & Margaret Ponsonby (Eds) *Buying for the Home: shopping for the domestic from the seventeenth century to the present* (Aldershot: Ashgate), pp. 183–197.
7. Lisa Taylor (2011) 'I'm a girl, I should be a princess': gender, class entitlement and denial in *The Hills*, in Helen Wood & Beverley Skeggs (Eds) *Reality Television and Class* (London: Palgrave Macmillan/BFI), pp. 119–131.
8. Ann Gray (1997) Learning from Experience: cultural studies and feminism, in Jim McGuigan (Ed) *Cultural Methodologies* (London: Sage), pp. 87–105.
9. Lisa Taylor (2008) *A Taste for Gardening: classed and gendered practices* (Aldershot: Ashgate).
10. For a fascinating account of the historian's experience of both the psychological and physical experience of encountering artefacts and documents see Carolyn Steedman (2002) *Dust: the archive and cultural history* (Manchester: Manchester University Press).
11. Germaine Greer (1979) *The Obstacle Race: the fortunes of women painters and their work* (New York: Martin Secker & Warburg), p. 4.
12. See Clive Burrell, 'Police See Women's Lib Art Show', *The Times*, 19 Apr. 1973.

13. Joanne Hollows & Rachel Moseley (2006) (Eds) *Feminism in Popular Culture* (Oxford: Berg), pp. 2–3.
14. Laura Mulvey (1975) Visual Pleasure and Narrative Cinema, *Screen*, 16, pp. 6–18.
15. Cathy Schwichtenberg (Ed) (1993) *The Madonna Connection: representational politics, subcultural identities, and cultural theory* (Oxford: Westview Press).
16. Alice Walker (1982) *The Colour Purple* (London: The Women's Press).
17. Kira Cochrane, 'Has Virago Changed The Publishing World's Attitudes To Women?' *theguardian.com*, Friday 24 May 2013.
18. Ibid. See also Laurel Forster (2010) Printing Liberation: the women's movement and magazines in the 1970s, in Sue Harper & Laurel Foster (Eds) *British Culture and Society in the 1970s* (Cambridge: Cambridge Scholars), pp. 93–106; Deborah Chambers, Linda Steiner & Carole Fleming (2004) *Women and Journalism* (London: Routledge).
19. Cochrane, 'Has Virago Changed'.
20. Rozsika Parker & Griselda Pollock (1987) Fifteen Years of Feminist Action: from practical strategies to strategic practices, in Rozsika Parker & Griselda Pollock (Eds) *Framing Feminism: art and the women's movement 1970-1985* (London: Pandora), pp. 3–78.
21. Lisa Gabrielle Mark (Ed) (2007) *WACK! art and the feminist revolution* (London: The MIT Press), p. 294.
22. Thalia Gouma-Peterson & Patricia Mathews (1987) The Feminist Critique of Art History, *Art Bulletin*, 69(3), pp. 326–57.
23. Griselda Pollock (1996) The Politics of Theory: generations and geographies in feminist theory and the histories of art histories, in Griselda Pollock (Ed) *Generations and Geographies in the Visual Arts: feminist readings* (London: Routledge), pp. 3–21.
24. Ibid. p. 16.
25. Ibid.
26. The need for the histories of women's lives was being argued for by feminist historians. See Sheila Ryan Johansson (1976) 'Herstory' As History: a new field or another fad?, in Berenice A. Carroll (Ed.) *Liberating Women's History: theoretical and critical essays* (London: University of Illinois Press), pp. 400–430.
27. Artists such as Monica Sjoo, Beverley Skinner, Liz Moore and Marika Tell exhibited at the Swiss Cottage Library.
28. See Parker & Pollock, *Framing Feminism*, for the arguments against using figurative nude paintings of women.
29. Mark, *WACK*, p. 223.
30. Ibid. p. 224.
31. Lucy R. Lippard (1976) Judy Chicago, Talking to Lucy R. Lippard, in Lucy R. Lippard (Ed) *From the Center: feminist essays on women's art* (New York: Dutton), pp. 214–230.
32. See also Judy Chicago (2006) *Through the Flower: my struggle as a woman artist* (New York: iUniverse).
33. Parker & Pollock, *Framing Feminism*, p. 28.
34. Lisa Tickner (1978) The Body Politic: female sexuality and women artists since 1970, *Art History*, 1, pp. 236–49, 241.
35. Siona Wilson (2006) From Women's Work to the Umbilical Lens: Mary Kelly's early films, *Art History*, 31(1), pp. 79–102.
36. Sheila Rowbotham (2008) Jolting Memory: *Nightcleaners* recalled, in Maria Ruido (Ed.) *Plan Rosebud: on images, sites and politics of memory* (Santiago de Compostela: CGAC), pp. 1–19.
37. Claire Johnston (1976) The *Nightcleaners* (part one): Rethinking political cinema, *Jump Cut*, 12/13, p. 56.
38. Sheila Rowbotham, 'Jolting Memory', p. 4.
39. Ibid. p. 15.
40. Johnston, 'The *Nightcleaners*', p. 56.
41. Tricia Davis & Phil Goodall (1979) Personally and Politically: feminist art practice, *Feminist Review*, 1, pp. 21–35.
42. Ibid. p. 22.

43. Ibid.
44. Nancy Fraser (2013) *The Fortunes of Feminism: from women's liberation to identity politics to anti-capitalism* (London: Verso), p. 4.
45. Rosalind Coward (1980) Underneath We're Angry, *Time Out*, 567, pp. 6–7.
46. See Griselda Pollock (1987) Feminism and Modernism, in Parker & Pollock, *Framing Feminism*, pp. 79–122; Sally Potter (1980) in Parker & Pollock, *Framing Feminism*, pp. 290–292.
47. Laura Mulvey (1976) 'Post-Partum Document' by Mary Kelly, *Spare Rib*, 53, p. 40.
48. See journalist Kenneth Robinson's response in Griselda Pollock & Rozsika Parker (1981) *Old Mistresses: women, art and ideology* (London: Routledge & Kegan Paul), p. 161.
49. Pollock & Parker, *Old Mistresses*, p. 45.
50. Anthea Callen, Mary Crockett, Wendy Holmes & Linda Newington (1979) A Beginning, *Spare Rib*, 44, pp. 38–39.
51. Laura Mulvey (1973) You don't know what is happening, do you, Mr Jones?, *Spare Rib*, 8, pp. 1–16, 30.
52. Lucy R. Lippard (1980) Sweeping Exchanges: the contribution of feminism to the art of the seventies, *Art Journal*, 40(1–2), pp. 362–365.
53. Pollock, 'Feminism and Modernism', pp. 102–103.
54. Ibid. p. 185.
55. Rozsika Parker (1980) Images of Men, *Spare Rib*, 99, p. 6.
56. Ibid.
57. Linda Nochlin (1971) Why Have There Been No Great Women Artists?, in Elizabeth Baker & Thomas Hess (Eds) *Art and Sexual Politics* (New York: Collier Books), pp. 1–43.
58. Griselda Pollock (1979) Feminism, Femininity and the Hayward Annual Exhibition 1978, *Feminist Review*, 2, p. 33.
59. Ibid. p. 34.
60. Ibid.
61. Pollock & Parker, *Old Mistresses*.
62. Sue Bruley (2013) Consciousness-Raising in Clapham: women's liberation as 'lived experience' in south London in the 1970s, *Women's History Review* 22(5), pp. 717–738.
63. Martin Pugh (2000) *Women and the Women's Liberation Movement in Britain* (Basingstoke: Macmillan Press), p. 320.
64. Sue Bruley (1999) *Women in Britain since 1900* (Basingstoke: Palgrave), p. 149.
65. Rowbotham, 'Jolting Memory', p. 3.
66. Bruley, *Women in Britain since 1900*, p. 152.
67. Sheila Rowbotham (1973) *Hidden From History: 300 years of women's oppression and the fight against patriarchy* (Pluto Press: London).
68. Pugh, *Women and the Women's Liberation Movement in Britain*, p. 320.
69. For a discussion of how history has been theorised by feminist historians between 1969 and 1999 see Johanna Alberti (2002) *Gender and the Historian* (London: Pearson Education).
70. Bruley, *Women in Britain since 1900*, p. 154.
71. There are competing accounts of what happened at Greenham which demonstrate that there are different ways of making history. See Elaine Titcombe (2013) Women Activists: rewriting Greenham's history, *Women's History Review* 22(2), pp. 310–329.
72. Sasha Roseneil (1995) *Disarming Patriarchy: feminism and political action at Greenham* (Buckingham: Open University Press).
73. Sasha Roseneil (2000) *Common Women, Uncommon Practices: the queer feminisms of Greenham* (London: Cassell).
74. Ibid., p. 279.
75. See Beverley Bryan, Stella Dadzie & Suzanne Scafe (1985) *The Heart of the Race: black women's lives in Britain* (London: Virago); Pratibha Parmar (1990) Black Feminism: the politics of articulation, in Jonathan Rutherford (Ed.) *Identity: community, culture, difference* (London: Lawrence & Wishart), pp. 101–114.
76. Bruley, 'Consciousness-Raising in Clapham', p. 718.

77. Bridget Lockyer (2013) An Irregular Period? participation in the Bradford Women's Liberation Movement, *Women's History Review* 22(4), pp. 643–657.
78. U3A is an interesting parallel to Women's Liberation educational strategies.
79. Germaine Greer (1979) *The Female Eunuch* (London: Granada), p. 7.
80. Tickner, 'The Body Politic', p. 238.
81. Ibid. p. 239.
82. Griselda Pollock (1977) What's wrong with 'images of women'?, *Screen Education*, pp. 24, 25–33.
83. Tickner, 'The Body Politic', p. 239.
84. Rozsika Parker (2012) *The Subversive Stitch: embroidery and the making of the feminine* (London: IB Taurus).
85. E.H. Gombrich (1995) *The Story of Art*, 16th edn (London: Phaidon).
86. Pollock & Parker, *Old Mistresses*, p. 37.
87. Vic Gatrell (2006) *City of Laughter: sex and satire in eighteenth century London* (London: Atlantic Books). In particular Gatrell discusses the various ways in which gender was represented in the period: see ch. 12, 'What Could Women Bear?'
88. Pollock & Parker, *Old Mistresses*, p. 35.
89. Ibid.
90. M.H. Grant (1952) *Flower Painting Through Four Centuries*, p. 21, quoted in Pollock and Parker, *Old Mistresses*, p. 53.
91. Ibid. p. 54
92. Ibid.
93. Tickner, 'The Body Politic', p. 238.
94. Quoted in Pollock & Parker, *Old Mistresses*, p. 83.
95. See for example Andrea Dworking (1981) *Pornography: men possessing women* (New York: Perigee).
96. Cochrane, 'Has Virago Changed'.
97. Liz Bury, 'Canadian Author David Gilmour Sparks Furore Over Female Writers', *theguardian.com*, 21 September 2013.
98. Thanks to Dr Sue Malvern for imparting her knowledge and for all her encouragement.

Women's Liberation at the Grass Roots: a view from some English towns, c.1968–1990

Sue Bruley

ABSTRACT
Historical scholarship on the women's liberation movement (WLM) across the UK is as yet underdeveloped. This article argues against the commonly held assumption that London socialist-feminist accounts speak for England as a whole. This article examines the history of the WLM in England as refracted through a range of different English urban localities, specifically Bristol, Brighton, Norwich, Bolton and Leeds/Bradford. It attempts to show the importance of local studies to appreciate the diversity of the English women's liberation movement. The movement had very many unifying characteristics, but how they played out across the country differed according to local contexts.

It has been noted that within historical studies the women's liberation movement (WLM) is as yet underdeveloped. Natalie Tomlinson has described the historiography of the WLM as 'threadbare' as we do not as yet have even one full-length historical monograph for the UK.[1] There have been many autobiographical accounts from WLM activists. These have been very London focused and coming mainly from socialist-feminists.[2] This tendency has been reinforced by the media which has given a great deal of attention to WLM events in London such as the disruption of the Miss World Competition November 1970.[3] This article attempts to counter this tendency by outlining the history of the WLM in England as refracted through a range of different urban localities.[4]

Over the last fifteen years or so a great deal of oral testimony has been collected relating to the history of the WLM in England, funded largely by the Heritage Lottery Fund (HLF). Whilst community based oral history projects have proved to be a very valuable resource for 'recovery work' with marginalised groups, the oral testimony generated needs to be handled with care and sensitivity.[5] Kalwant Bhopal argues for the need for interviewers to be empowering and reflexive, allowing women space to make their voices heard.[6] Moreover, researching the history of women's liberation through documents of the self is problematic. Sasha Roseneil and Margaretta Jolly have acknowledged the 'conundrum of how individuals can represent a necessarily collective process'.[7] Valuable though accounts are, there are limitations to the autobiographical/life history approach.[8] As Lynne Segal has noted 'memory is not history'.[9] Although many autobiographical works are historically aware and thus provide fascinating insights into the period in question this is not the same as accounts by academic historians who have put the material into historiographical context and assessed its overall historical significance. Moreover, the WLM was characterised by a widespread network of local autonomous groups which eschewed both centralised control and any notion of leadership. There is a danger of elevating individual lives into personalities who somehow speak for the movement and are regarded as 'leaders'. The recent British Library 'Sisterhood and After' Oral History Project, funded by the Leverhulme Trust, created a data base of fifty 'core activists' who were said to 'power' the WLM.[10] This is misleading as it will be taken by many to mean 'leaders'.

We need historical accounts to create a record of the WLM as a key feature of post-war British society, culture and politics. As the movement was politically libertarian, deliberately choosing to avoid the 'vanguardism' current on the far left, which many WLM activists had escaped from, this research necessarily involves a 'bottom up' approach, paying particular attention to local communities and 'lived experience'. Early studies of the WLM described the movement as in decline in the late 1970s, particularly after the national WLM Conference in Birmingham in 1978 in which a major split emerged between socialist feminists and revolutionary feminists.[11] This has been shown to be inaccurate due to a failure to appreciate the diversity of the WLM and the fact that the movement had always contained divisions.[12] Jill Radford drew attention to the national and London focus, writing that 'local, autonomous women's liberation groups, great in number and diversity, have almost been written out of Women's Liberation histories'.[13] It is only in the last few years however that scholars have begun to address the issue of regional diversity within the UK WLM and significant work has been done by Sarah Browne in Scotland and Jeska Rees in West Yorkshire.[14] This article will aim to contribute to the ongoing historiography of the WLM by tracing the social and cultural history of the movement in England from the late 1960s to the early 1990s by examining the work of a selection of local groups and women's centres. It will show how women pursued feminist campaigns, challenged sexism and built feminist counter cultures in their own communities and in the process changed their own lives. It will point to a sense of regional diversity within the movement whilst acknowledging that much more in depth research will need to be conducted to fully comprehend the complex regional variations within the English WLM.

In a single article which seeks to foreground local activism it is not realistic to look in detail at the whole of England. Instead the focus will be on five urban centres which were chosen because of their geographical spread, variation in socioeconomic make up, variety of engagement with the women's movement and availability of sources. A combination of oral and archival sources has been used based on material held in the Women's Library, the Feminist Library, Feminist Archive North (Leeds) and Feminist Archive South (Bristol).[15] Bristol developed as a key English sea port, second only to London. Situated in southwest England it played a major role in colonial trade. The city's undoubted affluence is directly related to the role that Bristol played in the slave trade. By the late twentieth century it had a strong manufacturing sector and something of a reputation for innovation, technology and the arts. Brighton is a large town situated on the south coast. With easy access by rail to London, it developed a thriving tourist trade and is sometimes referred to as 'London by the sea'. The opening of Sussex University in 1961 as the first of the 'new' universities had an important impact on the town. Brighton and the surrounding area, including the nearby town of Lewes, developed a distinctive identity and reputation for radicalism, counterculture and the gay movement and also a strong interest in the arts. Norwich is a small historic city and the regional centre for the county of Norfolk in Eastern England. In the late twentieth century the Norwich area was a significant base for a diverse collection of light industries, some of which were known for low wages and poor conditions. Bolton is a former cotton town. The Lancashire cotton towns were significant employers of women and known for their organised working class women, in both the suffrage movement and the weaving industry.[16] Like many urban centres in the late twentieth century, Bolton developed a range of service industries. Leeds and its smaller neighbour Bradford are two closely connected northern cities which dominate West Yorkshire. This area was traditionally known for the woollen industry and for the mass production of clothes, both large employers of women. This area too gave way to service industries and public sector employment. In the late twentieth century the area was transformed by immigration from the West Indies and the Indian sub-continent. Leeds and Bradford had important distinctions. Bradford, for example, became known in the 1970s for its very strong gay movement which continued to be united, long after gay men and lesbians had split elsewhere.[17] There was, however, a strong regional identity and this was carried over into many joint WLM initiatives between the two cities. There is not space here to examine each town in detail. In any case this would become repetitive. Instead the intention is to provide a counter balance to the domination of London socialist-feminist accounts of the WLM, paying attention to both national characteristics across England as a whole and local/regional distinctions.

Establishing women's liberation

We consider first modes of organising––how did women's liberation establish itself in these English towns and cities? As has been said women's liberation was not a single organisation but an amorphous network of loosely affiliated local groups with no formal membership or hierarchy. As word spread about the new movement women's liberation groups sprung up in the early 1970s. In larger towns and cities a whole network of local groups quickly formed, including university WLM groups.[18] In Bolton three women, Gay Bennett, Vicki Turbville and Gaby Lewis came together and secured a piece on women's liberation in the local press and the first women's liberation group in Bolton was formed.[19] For many women it was a big step to attend their first meeting. In an interview recorded in 1983 Barbara Gray admitted that she was 'shaking like a leaf with nerves' when she attended her first WLM meeting in a pub Norwich, but she came away feeling that 'I've come home'.[20] Most groups met weekly and were for women only unless there was a special reason to invite men. Meetings were informal and often chaotic although Bolton appears to have adopted a much more conventional approach with a chairman (who was given guidance notes), secretary and minutes taken. Such formality was very unusual and may have been a result of the tradition of women working in industry and participating in the formal apparatus of the labour movement in Bolton. Bristol was more typical, described by Caroline New as 'shambolic at times, but by god we got things done'.[21]

Women's liberation had to be negotiated at a local level, the first challenge being the need for women only physical space. To create a sense of identity the new movement needed women only safe spaces to hold meetings and collectively develop ideas. Feminist geographers, notably Doreen Massey, have pointed out that the spatial organisation of society is crucial for the production of gender relations and not just the result of it.[22] Frequently there was no choice but to hold meetings in women's houses. In Leeds much of the housing stock in the 1970s was of poor quality with small rooms and often with no indoor sanitation. When Al Garthwaite decided to buy a flat she consciously chose one with a large living room which would be suitable for meetings.[23] The second problem was one of communication. In the pre digital age communication was by face to face contact, letter or home phone and many women did not have a phone. To find out what was going on women had to attend weekly meetings or subscribe to a monthly newsletter which was sent in the post. By the mid 1970s most towns and cities produced a monthly WLM newsletter with notices of events and articles on a range of topics. Following the WLM conference in Manchester in 1975 the national WLM newsletter WIRES (Women's Information and Referral Enquiry Service) was launched with a group of women in the Chapeltown area of Leeds taking on the task of producing the bimonthly newsletter. This group produced WIRES for over two years before handing over to another collective in Nottingham at the end of 1977. The Chapeltown WIRES group made an important contribution to the WLM in Britain. The WIRES workers (who were paid from subscriptions) often had to type up copy from handwritten drafts, sometimes adding personal comments from their own experiences. Frequently, articles in WLM newsletters were not signed as women regarded themselves as acting collectively not individually and did not want the media to latch on to particular feminists and attempt to elevate them to any sort of leadership role. There is also the added problem for the historian that WLM leaflets and other material were frequently not dated, often making detailed local chronologies difficult to establish.

The third challenge in establishing the movement was to develop a language of empowerment. Women were swept into women's liberation in considerable numbers, but were often unable to find a narrative structure to verbalise their innermost feelings. Many women, especially isolated full time mothers, were often felt lacking in confidence and self-esteem. Left wing women were accustomed to activism, but became increasingly angry as they were unable to persuade male leftists to take women's issues seriously.[24] Pen Dalton was active on the left with her husband in Brighton in the 1970s. Meetings were held in their house. Whilst the men talked about equality and liberation she was 'reduced to the role of tea making'.[25] Consciousness raising, sometimes known as 'the small group process', developed as a response to these needs.[26] Through CR women could learn to trust each other in a supportive environment, reflect on their experiences of sexism and collectively develop ideas for change; the personal became political. It is clear from the many examples of personal testimony we have on the WLM in these towns and cities that CR was a vitally important aspect of the movement. Elizabeth Shorrocks said 'it gave me an analytical framework into which I could try and fit my life'.[27] Barbara Gray recalled that it took one woman six weeks in her group in Norwich before she could speak, finally blurting out 'I know … that's it … that happened to me' and then bursting into tears.[28] Many groups were very long running, often lasting for several years. Helen Taylor belonged to a Bristol CR group for about five years. In her interview she recalled that there were 'some very intense times … but it was also a very happy time … it felt like a safe space to talk about how we felt about being women'.[29]

CR could be very emotionally draining. Meetings were very emotional with women expressing anger, but also euphoria, for some it was like finding a new life.

Consciousness-raising was not restricted to dedicated CR groups. In smaller towns and cities many WLM groups were 'multi-purpose' undertaking CR, activism and sometimes theoretical work. The Norwich WLM was set up in 1970 after the first WLM national conference at Ruskin College Oxford. According to Barbara Gray, average attendance was about twenty and they worked their way through many CR topics. The group also seems to have undertaken other activities such as assigned reading. It was not uncommon for a CR group to develop into a study group. WLM activists became adult education lecturers through the WEA (Worker's Educational Association) and developed feminism through their classes aimed at women.[30] Brighton had a women's branch of the WEA which ran a very successful course on women's liberation in the autumn of 1978 which continued into the following term.[31] Feminist academics developed university courses aimed at women which also challenged the male bias of many university courses. There was often a CR element to these classes.

The movement also looked outwards and sought to symbolically occupy public urban space by setting up Saturday morning stalls in shopping precincts, distributing leaflets and organising petitions. Public meetings were held with visiting speakers and talks given in local schools and colleges. The Bolton group developed an educational play called *Sweetie Pie* about sex role stereotyping and a slide show both of which were shown to local school and college pupils.[32] Bolton also produced a manual on local health services for women. MPs were lobbied about local feminist issues. In the large cities of Bristol, Leeds, Bradford and Brighton multiple WLM groups were established and the women became very bold and assertive, sometimes engaging in direct action. In the more conservative cultures of Bolton and Norwich WLM activists initially tried hard to be polite and 'respectable'. In the mid 1970s Norwich WLM gave talks to church women's groups, the Housewives Register and the Women's Institute, but they had to tread very carefully. They were prevented from using such words as 'abortion' in the title, but had to refer to 'motherhood' instead.[33] Bolton activists attempted to embed themselves into local institutions such as the health authority and the trades council. In an effort to reach out to as many women as possible Bristol WLM initiated a series of 'Introductory sessions' to explain what the movement was all about. A rota was established and long-standing activists took it in turns to run the meetings. Nicola Harwin, who was involved, described these sessions as 'excellent'.[34] An article in WIRES stated that over a two-year period 1975–77, 248 women had come into the movement in Bristol via this method, leading to about twenty new CR groups.[35] Women also reached beyond their local area. Women's liberation conferences were a huge spur to activism. Besides the annual national conferences between 1970 and 1978 there was a multiplicity of regional and special interest conferences such as socialist feminism, radical feminism and sexuality. In the autumn of 1978 Bristol held an 'anti-rape' conference which was attended by 200 women.[36] Barbara Gray said that very few women from Norwich went to conferences 'because we were still living in the system', adding that when she did go, 'we came back mindless, blown out of our minds … it was so good'.[37]

The prevailing notion of 'sisterhood' in the movement meant that women strove very hard to be supportive of each other and hold the movement together. The years from 1968 to the mid 1970s were characterised by a huge surge of feminist energy and euphoria but, beneath the veneer of a universalising feminism, all kinds of tensions were soon evident. As Miriam David observed in an interview in Bristol, it was 'only obvious subsequently … just how white and middle class we all were'.[38] Although working class women did join the movement, their position was often problematic and marginal. This could perhaps be expected in the more affluent towns but it was also true of working class Bolton. Sheridan Homer wrote that although the group was 'very friendly' she felt 'uncomfortable as they were mostly middle class or highly articulate, well read, political types'.[39] In the early 1980s the Brighton women's centre struggled with this issue and designated Friday as 'working class women's day' when only working class women could use the centre, which somewhat underlines the fact that it was predominantly a middle class set up.[40]

Bradford is exceptional in the towns depicted here in that Bradford WLM did gain substantial numbers of very assertive working class women. Bradford Dykes were an informal grouping of mainly working class lesbians who became notorious within the WLM.[41] They acquired a reputation for being anti-intellectual 'rough and ready', 'heavies' and 'boozers'.[42] Bradford Dykes were a noticeable presence at WLM conferences, being particularly known for their drinking and impatience with feminist theory.[43] They complained that WLM conferences were too middle class and working class women were not listened to.[44] Individuals had to negotiate their own relationship with the movement. In the early years the great majority do not seem to have been very motivated by ideological discussions and debates about feminism and were keen to get on with practical activism. The Bolton minutes reveal that 'some members were worried about getting bogged down in theory'.[45] One of the key activists in Bolton, American born Elaine Glover, said in an interview that she found theory 'hard to understand'.[46] Women's liberation was never static but constantly in flux, evolving and transforming itself: particularly noticeable by 1976–77 was the growing lesbian presence in the movement with many women abandoning heterosexual relationships and conventional nuclear family life.

Women's centres

Attention has been drawn to the fact that much emphasis has been given in WLM historiography to biographical accounts, often in the form of oral testimony. For some aspects of WLM history these sources are not sufficient, women's centres being a case in point. Evidence from biographical narratives on women's centres in this period is fragmentary. Consequently this area is as yet very underdeveloped. A key aim of this article is to help to remedy this situation. As we have seen, a sense of physical space for women within urban centres was very important. Bearing in mind the traditional gendered concept of 'public and private' and the designation of much urban space as masculine, it is not surprising that many WLM activists sought to establish a local safe place for women. This women only space could be not only a place of support and information, but also empowerment and learning new skills. In seeking to provide a physical home for women's liberation women's centres were challenging the gendering of urban space.

Local WLM groups had varying degrees of success with this ambition. The Bolton archives have numerous references to the search for premises for a women's centre. Despite raising funds for a women's centre, suitable premises could not found.[47] Elsewhere, even when premises were found, women's centres had a precarious existence, often existing in rather squalid squats or very short life tenancies. Another option was for someone to give over room in their own home. In 1973 Ellen Malos' basement of her house in the Redland area of Bristol became the base for the Bristol Women's Centre. The centre was largely a resource and information service only. Women in Bristol preferred to put their energies into activism and the community rather than trying to build women's liberation by bringing the community to the Women's Centre. As we shall see other towns had more ambitious ideas for their women's centres. Bristol Women's Centre did carry out pregnancy testing however, with the aid of trained volunteers. This was a vital service when no self-administered kits were available. They also gave women post-test counselling and information. Around 1976/77 the Bristol Women's Centre found its own premises in a small hut in 'The Grove' which is between the river and Queen Square, central Bristol. Jackie Barron was new to Bristol in 1979 and found herself volunteering at the Grove, doing a rota slot, answering the phone, providing information and 'just facilitating a drop in for women new to the area or lonely or who had problems and who would come in and have a cup of coffee and a chat about their lives'.[48] The Grove was vandalised and the Bristol Women's Centre went through two further premises, eventually running out of steam and closing due to lack of funds and volunteers sometime in the mid-to-late 1980s.[49]

Despite the numerous obstacles, by 1979 over forty women's centres had been established in Britain all aiming to make a positive impact on women's lives.[50] The centres ran on a strictly 'women only basis' although in Norwich a room was allocated for men accompanying women to wait. Norwich and Brighton are both examples of cities which sought to build the women's movement around the women's centre. The Norwich Women's Centre began life as a room in an arts centre in the mid 1970s and from 1977 was housed in a grim licensed squat which was said to be off-putting to some women. In 1983 it moved to better accommodation and also adopted a formal constitution and charitable status. It had about 120 women using the centre a week, including black women, lesbians and disabled women, who all felt various degrees of exclusion from wider society.[51] Lesbians made use of the centre as they could freely express their sexuality, unlike other public places.[52] The centre ran consciousness-raising groups, training courses and provided a drop-in advice service, most often relating to maintenance/matrimonial issues, benefits, housing, health and the usual pregnancy testing.[53] In the years 1987 to 1990 the Norwich Women's Centre reached its peak. With help from the local council, the Equal Opportunities Commission and the Princes Trust, the centre acquired a four storey listed building close to the city centre with facilities including a crèche, coffee bar and courses on anything from women's rights to bricklaying.[54]

Women's centres were usually initiated by a collective who undertook to work a rota on a volunteer basis. In Brighton the WLM secured an abandoned maternity hospital in Buckingham Road in 1974 from social services with a £6,000 grant towards renovation with the idea that the women's centre would reduce the load of social workers.[55] This arrangement only lasted two years, consequently from 1976 until 1989 the centre went through several changes of premises, each time providing a home for a thriving mix of users, including groups for Jewish lesbians, woman and photography, the matriarchy network, women and health and women's self-defence as well as the usual prominent national WLM campaigns. Collective management could be chaotic. As Jen Murray in Brighton put it, 'it was never terribly well organised, as you can imagine'.[56] There were constant appeals for women to volunteer for the rota. In August 1978 Alison Hammer wrote that 'The centre seems to be perpetually on the verge of collapse ... the organisation of the place and the way the centre is run is in a mess or non-existent'.[57] Rosemary Lovatt was a volunteer in Brighton for nine years in the 1980s. When she arrived the women's centre 'did not believe in accounts, did not even keep cheque stubs'.[58]

If women's centres were to be largely the provision of information and resources, then it was possible to run on a voluntary and collective basis, as in Bristol. If education and training, and serious inter agency case work with social services, police, medical personnel etc. were to take place (as in Brighton and Norwich) then serious funding was required from local state or central government and for that the culture had to change.[59] In 1989, when Norwich Women's Centre acquired substantial financial assistance and a part-time paid worker, a management committee was adopted with monthly meetings and each member taking a specific responsibility, attended by two council officers and an elected councillor.[60] Not all WLM activists were prepared to go down this route. In Brighton there were opposing views on the question of a paid worker, with some arguing that it would establish unequal power relations which were not in the WLM spirit of collective self-management.[61]

Campaigns

Surveying WLM activism in this period it is apparent that there were some very big national campaigns which penetrated, with varying degrees, across the whole women's liberation community. The National Abortion Campaign (NAC) is a case in point, a 'woman's right to choose' being one of the first demands adopted in 1970. On the whole NAC activists were heterosexual socialist-feminists. By the mid 1970s there was significant opposition to the Abortion Act of 1967, most notably from the Society for the Protection of the Unborn Child (SPUC) which triggered the campaign to defend the Act. Along with several other NAC activists in Bristol, Betty Underwood became involved because of her own painful experience of back street abortion.[62] Bristol and Brighton both had very strong NAC groups. In Brighton a hundred women marched against the Corrie Bill to reduce access to abortion in 1980.[63] Campaigns were also raised against numerous other attempts to undermine the Abortion Act in the late 1970s and early 1980s. On NAC demonstrations women chanted 'not the church and not the state, women must decide their fate'.[64] In Brighton the NAC group aimed to do more than defend the 1967 Act, working towards improving access for abortion facilities locally and gradually becoming more involved in women's health generally'.[65]

It was often the case that the establishment of a women's centre was linked to other projects and campaigns. In Brighton in 1974 the building for the women's centre was next to another council property allocated for a Women's Aid refuge, with a convenient passageway between the two, allowing battered women a cover whereby they appeared to enter the centre but were actually entering the refuge, which was of course not made public.[66] When the Bristol Women's Centre was founded a bed was put in for occasional overnight use. It began to be used by women escaping violent relationships. When women began to sleep on the floor the Women's Centre started the Women's House Project for a women's aid refuge.[67] After a two-year campaign they managed to secure a tiny house which was soon overwhelmed, leading eventually to a local housing association granting them a larger property on the edge of town. Bolton feminists did not succeed in finding premises for a women's centre but they did open a refuge, which they named Fortalice, and a hostel for homeless young women, Radclyffe Hall.[68] One of the Bolton women remembered how hard it was emotionally to be involved in refuge, as women sometimes came to Fortalice straight from hospital with visible injuries inflicted by domestic violence.[69]

Central to the concept of the women's aid movement was the breaking down of the traditional divisions between 'client' and 'social worker'. However, as with women's centres, the movement gradually moved from collective to hierarchical management structures and cultures in order to secure funding. Inevitably this led to a degree of institutionalisation. In an oral history workshop in 2009 Jenn Bravo talked about Sahara, an organisation in Leeds which works with black women subjected to violence, which was founded in 1982. She spoke about the need for Sahara to adopt a much more professional approach in order to secure funding from social services, 'you've got to jump to different tunes'.[70] West Yorkshire feminists developed work in the area of both women's aid and sexual violence, with Leeds establishing a rape crisis centre in the late 1970s and Bradford in the early 1980s. Ruth Ingram worked on sexual violence and young women in Bradford providing support, counselling and a safe house called 'One in 4', referring to the fact that it was estimated that one in four young women were subjected to sexual abuse in their own families. The project was very successful and by the late 1980s was attracting substantial Department of Health grants for paid workers. Ruth Ingram eventually withdrew however, complaining that 'the values had changed' and the management was no longer feminist.[71]

With the notable except of Jeska Rees, little historical work has been conducted hitherto on radical and revolutionary feminism and the shift in the late 1970s towards a new focus on violence towards women.[72] By the mid 1970s many radical feminists had evolving towards revolutionary feminism, arguing that men were 'the enemy' and that the system of hetero patriarchy was maintained through violence or the threat of violence towards women. Around 1977-8 prominent revolutionary feminist Sheila Jeffreys moved from London to Leeds. Cheap housing and a thriving gay community made both Bradford and Leeds attractive places for lesbians at this time. Soon the area became known for its discussions on 'political lesbianism'.[73] They argued that women in the WLM should not 'sleep with the enemy' as they saw heterosexual women as 'collaborators'.[74] This paper created uproar in the WLM, not least because it was a direct challenge to the dominance of London based socialist-feminism.

To explain the extraordinary growth of revolutionary feminism in West Yorkshire and the rapid explosion of work around violence we need to look at the local context. Revolutionary feminism had been developing in Britain over several years, fuelled by blatant sexism in society, sexual violence and the inability of left wing groups to take feminism seriously. What gave it special poignancy in the late 1970s in West Yorkshire was the 'Yorkshire Ripper' Peter Sutcliffe who killed thirteen women between 1975 and 1980. The Chapeltown area of Leeds, where many of Sutcliffe's victims came from, was also home to many feminists. Police took very little notice of the first victims as they were prostitutes. Only with the fifth victim, who was not a sex worker, did the police begin to take serious interest. This outraged the local feminists. These events led Leeds Rape Crisis Centre to initiate a conference in 1980 in which Women Against Violence Against Women (WAVAW) was founded.[75] WAVAW organised 'Reclaim the Night' marches in which women would carry flaming torches through red light areas, chanting 'women unite, reclaim the night, wherever we go, yes means yes and no means no'. Sometimes this was met with opposition from local porn shop owners leading to scuffles and police intervention.[76] WAVAW spread to other areas of the UK, its reach going well beyond revolutionary feminist enclaves. Sandra McNeill estimates that there were about forty WAVAW groups across the country in the early 1980s.[77] Brighton WLM was quick to organise Reclaim the Night marches and also sent delegations to national marches, including two coaches for the London Reclaim the Night on 20 January 1979.[78] Bolton women were initially reluctant to become involved in WAVAW. In June 1978 Bolton WLM recorded that 'it did not feel able to do anything' for a Reclaim the Night, but in March 1982 they are recorded as having 'a wonderful march, marred slightly by the presence of men at the beginning, who were, with one exception, persuaded to go away'.[79] Bolton women also organised protests outside sex shops. During the 1980s Norwich revolutionary feminists similarly developed an interest in combating violence against women, which was taken to include pornography. In 1988–89 they undertook a spate of direct actions, including ripping porn magazines from shelves and tearing down posters for a theatre event which was deemed to be violent towards women. On the night the play was staged, the theatre received a bomb threat half way through the performance and the theatre had to be evacuated. In a press release a group calling itself WITCH (Women's International Terrorist Coven from Hell–Norwich branch) claimed responsibility.[80] This may have been one of the factors which led Norwich Council to cut their grant of £5,000 a year to the women's centre.[81] This event calls into question the idea that the feminist campaign against violence against women petered out after the early 1980s.

In the early years of the movement there were many 'all purpose' local WLM groups. Gradually, more specialist groups developed and the movement became hugely diverse moving from utopian imaginaries to more practical campaigns. This was accompanied by an increased awareness of difference. By the late 1970s black women were organising their own groups and there was a new recognition that women of colour had a different agenda from white women. In Bristol, mixed race Cristel became active in the WLM and was pleased to find a black women's group. Overall though Cristel felt that the WLM did not offer much for black and immigrant women because 'issues that were being addressed never included us, or if it did it was very much at a tokenistic level'.[82] In West Yorkshire Women's Aid the situation of Asian women gradually became apparent when large numbers began using the refuges, seeking to escape from violent relationships.[83] Asian families were prepared to pay 'bounty hunters' to secure the return of their women.[84] White feminists realised that they had to do more to combat passive racism. In 1986 Norwich women's centre developed an anti-racist policy which demanded a thorough review to ensure that the group became as inclusive as possible, including subscribing to the Asian women's magazine *Mukti*, buying African, Chinese and Indian dolls for the children's room and making sure that all women's centre publicity reached the local ethnic communities.[85]

Bristol had a large and extremely active women's movement covering many different national campaigns. Wages for Housework was particularly strong in Bristol although they were constantly in conflict with other feminists, leading to their expulsion from the women's centre by a majority vote.[86] Academic Hilary Land, based in Bristol, was a key player in the campaign for women's financial and legal independence. This movement, which sought changes to the taxation and benefit systems, became known in the late 1970s as 'YBA Wife'.[87] The peace movement was also strong in Bristol. Many Bristol women visited the Greenham Common peace camp and some stayed for extended periods. Juley Howard is a good example of a Bristol feminist peace activist. She was resident at Greenham for three and a half years and imprisoned nine times. In an interview she described in graphic terms the evictions she endured:

> The evictions had a terrible effect really, everything had to be mobile ... you couldn't leave your tent up. Even if it was pouring with rain you had to take your tent down and pack up all your bedding. Several times all my stuff got taken by the bailiffs, even when I was there ... they'd just thump you and take your stuff and shove it in the back of a dustcart ... it was awful.[88]

Besides national issues there were struggles based around local issues. Many WLM groups made serious attempts to reach local working class women based on their own particular needs. Sometimes this work was undertaken jointly with local left groups, for example under the umbrella of the Working Women's Charter, which had the support of the labour movement through local trades councils. The International Socialists (Socialist Workers Party from 1976) established local Women's Voice groups in the late 1970s, which tried hard to engage with issues such as women's low pay, inequality at work and abortion, but this initiative did not last.[89] Some local WLM initiatives never got off the ground. Bolton launched a campaign against Christmas, presumably on the grounds that it was such hard work for women, which flopped.[90]

A notable feature of the 1980s was the move towards 'municipal feminism' in local authorities as many WLM activists moved into the Labour Party. Labour-controlled Leeds was a good example of this trend which aimed to 'feminise' the local state. Leeds began serious work on equal opportunities in 1982.[91] Eventually four equal opportunities officers were in post and leader of the council George Mudie was keen to advance work with disadvantaged groups. Lots of grants were given for equal opportunities projects in the community, some of which proved controversial, most notably the black lesbian group.[92] Following on from Ripper murders it was clear that police attitudes towards women and violence had to change as the standard approach was not to take domestic violence seriously. A police women's unit was set up and with the aim of developing training programmes to challenge traditional attitudes. This was largely the work of feminist sociologists Sheila Saunders and Jalna Hanmer, who also encouraged inter agency work between the police, housing and social services on domestic violence.[93] These gains came at a cost. As Ruth Ingrams put it: 'I remember ... at "1 in 4" standing up in my dungarees trying to talk to councillors and not getting anywhere, learning to put a suit on before I did it.'[94]

Culture and personal life

Women's liberation was about more than meetings, conferences, formal demands and campaigning. Any historical account would be incomplete without mentioning cultural forms such as feminist art, literature and performance. Feminist cultural production celebrated femininity, but was also important for expressing feminist ideas and creativity. As Eve Setch has written, creative work is not a peripheral part of the WLM but 'needs to be understood as an integral part of the movement'.[95] This is evident in the towns and cities examined here. There were women's theatre groups, women's bands and discos, comedy, cinema screenings, performance poetry and many other feminist cultural activities. Sadly, WLM historiography has neglected this important area of women's liberation. In contrast to WLM conferences and theoretical position papers there are few sources relating to many performance and artistic aspects of WLM cultural forms. Bristol, which had a large number of feminist artists and writers, has addressed this issue with its HLF booklet on *Feminism in Bristol 1973–5* which focuses particularly on Sistershow. This was a feminist cabaret which was active in Bristol and elsewhere 1973–74.[96] Combining poetry, sketches, dance, song and mayhem Sistershow was 'unruly and anarchic, disorganised and confrontational'.[97] Sistershow was performed surrounded by feminist art works. Among the works on show was that of Swedish-born Monica Sjöö whose most famous work is 'God giving birth'.[98] This work was thought to be so shocking at the time that many art galleries refused to show it.[99]

Finally this article turns to personal life and changes in lifestyles. This comes over very clearly in the oral testimony relating to the movement. As Marilyn Porter said, she looks back to this period as 'tremendously exciting, lots of new ideas around the place and above all, fun fun, I can't believe we had so much fun'.[100] The archive relating to Bolton WLM can make the Bolton women appear rather straight-laced and earnest, but this was far from the case. In a Bolton celebration of International Women's Day, women did the 'conga' all linked together in a long line dancing and singing to 'We are family' by Sister Sledge.[101] WLM conferences were also a great time for social events. At the end of the Bristol National WLM conference in Bristol in 1973 women took off their clothes and danced together in a giant circle 'ecstatic and naked'.[102] No written record of this 'spontaneous gesture of trust and solidarity' was recorded at the time.[103] It exists only in the memory of the women who took part, but it is just as important to the social and cultural history of the movement as the conference resolutions which were debated. Women's liberation actively promoted communal lifestyles. In Brighton there were many women's collective houses, sometimes leading to accusation of cliques.[104] Revolutionary feminists established separatist collective households. Sadly, as yet little is documented about this aspect of the movement. In women's aid refuges it was standard practice for the women to cook and eat communally. In Bolton, six of the women jointly rented a set of adjoining terraced houses and enjoyed communal meals, shared childcare, cars, washing machines, social events and loaned each other money etc.[105]

Within heterosexual relationships the idea of monogamy was being challenged. Dorothy Sheridan lived for several years in a 'threesome' in Brighton with two men, living communally, sharing income and care of a child.[106] Among the bohemian feminist circles of Brighton in the 1970s and 1980s there was a belief in 'open relationships' and the idea that sexual partners should strive to overcome feelings of jealousy and possessiveness.[107] The shift away from heterosexual relationships has already been mentioned. In this period lesbians were able to 'come out' and openly celebrate lesbian sexuality, although discrimination was still rife. In the early 1970s Bolton WLM appears to be very much based on heterosexual women, but this had changed by the late 1970s and in the Bolton oral history project four women from the seventeen interviewed stated that they were lesbians. Lesbian feminists who were mothers offered different ways of being a family. This was fraught with difficulty however as the Family Courts tended to grant custody to fathers on the grounds that being a lesbian was incompatible with being a mother.[108] We have also noted that there were problems between revolutionary feminists and heterosexual women. A woman told Sarah Braun in the Bristol women's centre in the mid 1980s that she was a 'traitor and had no right to be in the centre' after she revealed that she was married with two sons.[109] There were also issues with boy children in women's centres and attending WLM events. Although in some cases attitudes were extreme, this was generally not the case as there was much overlap and fluidity between socialist feminists and radical/revolutionary feminist circles and thinking. Kate Page defined herself as 'a socialist and feminist' but spoke of the influence of radical feminist ideas on how she has lived her life; in a long-term relationship with a man but living apart, not allowing him to have power over her and not seeing herself as part of a couple:

> I think that for me the crucial thing was always about not wanting to be … about not believing the romantic model where you fall in love with one person and they fulfil your every need, and as a woman that's all you need, is to be satisfied through that one person.[110]

Conclusion

This article has demonstrated the importance of local studies for the history of the English women's liberation movement. It was very much a national movement, but there was no central organisation and few national structures except for some individual campaigns. As we have seen, local WLM groups had an informal communication network, mainly through WIRES, but local groups very much 'did their own thing'. Even national WLM conferences were organised locally on a volunteer basis by different local WLM groups and they ceased after 1978. It is unwise to take a 'top down' approach and see this as the beginning of the decline of the WLM. This is far too simplistic. We need to build the analysis from the bottom up. Only with detailed local histories can we appreciate the rich diversity of the movement and overcome the bias in the historiography towards London based socialist feminist intellectuals. We have hinted here at some of the regional variations in WLM activity. Bristol had a strong interest in peace and the arts. Brighton WLM also had a strong cultural dimension and it also developed a lasting interest in women's health care. West Yorkshire developed work around violence towards women which set off a surge of activity around the country. We need to be very wary of applying any kind of national chronology as local groups often had very individual trajectories. Women in Norwich, for example, appear to be pursuing direct action on violence in the late 1980s whereas previously it appeared that this aspect of the movement petered out by the mid 1980s. This case also illustrates the diversity of the movement even within cities as, at the same time as the WITCH group in Norwich was engaged in high profile direct action, the Women's Centre management was attempting to appear 'respectable' in order to qualify for local authority funding.

We have seen women's liberation as a *collective* activity which firmly rejected any concept of leaders. The movement had very many unifying characteristics, but how they played out across the country differed according to local contexts. The WLM has been seen as a widespread movement which embedded itself into the fabric of communities and brought about important social change.[111] There has been a tendency to over-intellectualise and over-categorise the movement rather than seeing it as 'lived experience'. Ideological differences were often not very significant to women who simply wanted to challenge 'traditional' sexist attitudes, behaviours and structures in their own communities and thereby improve the lives of women. Where significant differences did occur they were not exclusive as women usually accommodated difference and often friendships traversed ideological divides.

The role of women's centres has been examined, which has hitherto been overlooked in WLM historiography. Tension between putting energy into providing a safe physical space for women and taking campaigns into the community has been revealed. Ultimately the women of Bristol chose to keep their commitment to a women's centre contained and to focus instead on the wider aspects of the movement. Others, such as Norwich and Brighton, tried to build the movement around the women's centre. Feminists of the 1970s had an enormous amount of energy and utopian idealism. By the 1980s most WLM activists had learned that if they wanted to bring practical benefits to women they had to engage with local and national state agencies for funding and this entailed compromise. Perhaps surprisingly, revolutionary feminists were involved in this process by helping to change attitudes, policies and training in the police and social services regarding violence towards women. The WLM helped to bring about a profound change in society towards women in the late twentieth century, not least being the lives of lesbians which were transformed in this period. More research needs to be undertaken on the WLM in other English regions to build on this initial sketch. Hopefully more archive material and oral testimony will become available to fill the gaps. By writing accessible history we can bring these important changes to light and thus make women's liberation an essential part of our cultural memory of late twentieth century Britain.

Notes

1. Natalie Thomlinson (2012) The Colour of Feminism: white feminists and race in the women's liberation movement, *History*, 97, pp. 454–455.
2. Sheila Rowbotham (2001) *Promise of a Dream: remembering the sixties* (London: Verso); Lynne Segal (2007) *Making Trouble: life and politics* (London: Serpent's Tail); Michèle Roberts (2007) *Paper Houses: a memoir of the '70s and beyond* (London: Virago).
3. The BBC Radio 4 programme 'The Reunion', broadcast 5 Sep. 2010, on the disruption of the Miss World competition in 1970 is a good example.
4. I would like to thank the anonymous reviewers of this article for their detailed and constructive feedback.
5. Arthur McIvor (2013) *Working Lives in Britain Since 1945* (Basingstoke: Palgrave MacMillan), p. 5.
6. Kalwant Bohopal (2010) Gender, Identity and Experience: researching marginalised groups, *Women's Studies International Forum*, 33, pp. 188–195.
7. Margaretta Jolly & Sasha Roseniel (2012) Researching women's movements: an introduction to FEMCIT and Sisterhood and After, *Women's Studies International Forum (WSIF)*, 35, p. 128.
8. Margaretta Jolly (2012) Recognising Place, Space and Nation in Researching Women's Movements: sisterhood and after, *WSIF*, 35, p. 145.
9. Segal, *Making Trouble*, p. 367. See also Margaretta Jolly (2011) Consenting Voices? Activist life stories and complex dissent, *Life Writing*, 8(4), pp. 363–374.
10. See *Sisterhood and After* website: http://www.bl.uk/learning/news/sisterhood.html (accessed 4 Jan. 2015).

11. See, e.g., David Bouchier (1983) *The Feminist Challenge: the movement for women's liberation in Britain and the United States* (London: MacMillan), p. 147; Anna Coote & Beatrix Campbell (1982) *Sweet Freedom: the struggle for women's liberation* (Pan: London), p. 225.
12. Eve Setch, *The Women's Liberation Movement in Britain 1969–1979: organisation, creativity and debate* (PhD thesis, University of London, Royal Holloway), p. 8. See also Jeska Rees (2010) Look Back at Anger: the women's liberation movement in 1978, *Women's History Review*, 19(3), who argues (see pp. 337–356) that the enormous practical problems for local groups in hosting these large national conferences also contributed to their decline.
13. Jill Radford (1994) History of Women's Liberation Movements in Britain: a reflective personal history, in Gabriele Griffin, Marianne Hester, Shirin Rai & Sasha Roseneil (Eds) *Stirring It: challenges for feminism* (London: Taylor & Francis), pp. 43–44.
14. Jolly, 'Recognising Place', pp. 144–146. See also Sarah Browne (2014) *The Women's Liberation Movement in Scotland* (Manchester: Manchester University Press); Jeska Rees (2007) *Revolutionary All the Rage: feminism in England 1977-83* (PhD thesis, University of Western Australia). Similar work is being done in the USA: see Stephanie Gilmore (2013) *Groundswell: grass roots feminist activism in post war America* (London: Routledge). This exciting book examines the US WLM in the very different local contexts of Memphis, Tennessee, Columbus, Ohio and San Francisco, California and argues that 'the local story is much more complex than the dominant narratives suggest': p. 19.
15. Basic factual information on these towns can be gained from the local authority websites.
16. Jill Liddington & Jill Norris (1978) *One Hand Tied Behind Us: the rise of the women's suffrage movement* (London, Virago); Sue Bruley (1993) Gender, Class and Party: the Communist Party and the crisis in the cotton industry in England between the two world wars, *Women's History Review*, 2(1), pp. 81–106.
17. *The Women's Liberation Movement in Leeds and Bradford, 1969–1979*, Oral History Project Feminist Archive North, University of Leeds, see particularly the interviews with Yvonne Stringfellow and Julia Moore.
18. Bridget Lockyer provides an insight into the Bradford WLM scene in Lockyer (2013) An Irregular Period? Participation in the Bradford Women's Liberation Movement, *Women's History Review*, 24(4), pp. 643–657, p. 647.
19. June Corner, 'Women in Search of LIBERATION', *Bolton Evening News*, 4 Feb. 1971, press cutting in scrap book, Bolton Women's Liberation Group archive, Feminist Archive North (FAN), University of Leeds.
20. Barbara Gray, report of an interview, in *Norwich Women's Education and Resources Centre Newsletter*, n.d., c1983, Norwich Women's Centre Archive, Box 21, Feminist Archive North, University of Leeds, p. 5.
21. Caroline New, *Personal Histories of Second Wave Feminism* Vols 1&2, Summarised from interviews by Viv Honeybourne and Iona Singer, Feminist Archive South, Bristol University Special Collections, http://feministarchivesouth.org.uk/wp-content/uploads/2013/02/Personal-Histories-of-the-Second-Wave-of-Feminism.pdf, p. 30.
22. Doreen Massey (1994) *Space, Place and Gender* (Oxford: Polity Press), p. 4. Historians have also drawn attention to the importance of gender in defining urban space, see Fiona Williamson (2014) The Spatial Turn of Social and Cultural History: a review of the current field, *European History Quarterly*, 44(4), pp. 703–717, p. 713.
23. Al Garthwaite, The Women's Liberation Movement in Leeds and Bradford, interview with Louise Lavender and Lee Comer. Oral History project held at Feminist Archive North, Special Collections, University of Leeds. The fact that there was a joint oral history project covering both Leeds and Bradford underlines the close connection between the two cities.
24. There is no space here to develop the relationship between the left and the WLM, see Sue Bruley (2014) Jam Tomorrow? Socialist women and women's liberation 1968–1982: an oral history approach, in Evan Smith & Matthew Worley (Eds) *Against the Grain: the British far left since 1956* (Manchester: Manchester University Press), pp 155–172.
25. Pen Dalton, *Personal Histories*, Feminist Archive South, p. 76.

26. Sue Bruley (2013) Consciousness-raising in Clapham: women's liberation in south London in the 1970s, *Women's History Review*, 22(5), pp. 717–738.
27. Elizabeth Shorrocks, *WLM in Leeds and Bradford*, Feminist Archive North, Interview no 3.
28. Gray, *Norwich Women's*, Norwich Women's Centre Archive, Feminist Archive North, p. 7.
29. Helen Taylor, *Personal Histories*, Feminist Archive South, p. 42.
30. Bristol WEA Lecturer Miriam David was frustrated by the lack of material for women's studies classes. She organised a collective which produced Bristol Women's Studies Group (1979) *Half the Sky, An Introduction to Women's Studies* (London: Virago).
31. Brighton and Hove Women's Liberation Newsletter, Nov. 1978, Women's Library, LSE (henceforth Brighton WL newsletter), 5BW/survey/B/31 Box 16-17.
32. *Sweetie Pie: a play about women in society*, introduced by Eileen Murphy, copy in Bolton Women's Liberation Group Archive (BWLG), Box 2 A/3A Feminist Archive North.
33. Gray, report of an interview, in *Norwich Women's*, p. 7
34. Nicola Harwin, *Personal Histories*, Feminist Archive South, p. 99.
35. WIRES, monthly national WLM newsletter, Sep. 1977, available at Feminist Archive North, University of Leeds, and other archives.
36. Report back from four delegates from Brighton, Brighton WL Newsletter, 5BW/survey/B/31 Box 16-17, Nov. 1978.
37. Gray, report of an interview, in *Norwich Women's*, pp. 10–11.
38. Miriam (AKA Miki) David, *Personal Histories*, Feminist Archive South, p. 87.
39. Sheridan Homer, Bolton Oral History Project, Box 6, Bolton WLG, handwritten response to questionnaire, was not interviewed. Other women in this project, some of whom preferred to remain anonymous, also refer to it as a predominantly middle class group.
40. *Brighton WL Newsletter* 5BW/survey/B/31 Box 16-17, July 1984.
41. Lockyer, 'An Irregular Period?', pp. 649–650.
42. Jalna Hanmer, Interview no 9, Julia Moore, Interview no 17, Karen Griffiths, Interview no 20, *WLM in Leeds and Bradford* Feminist Archive North.
43. Karen Griffiths, Interview no 20, *WLM in Leeds and Bradford* Feminist Archive North.
44. Karen Griffiths, Women's Liberation in Leeds and Bradford, Interview no 20; Lockyer, 'An Irregular Period?', p. 650.
45. *Minute Book 1*, 23 Feb. 1972, Box 1, BWLG, Feminist Archive North.
46. Elaine Glover, Bolton Women's Liberation Oral History Project, Box 6, BWLG, Feminist Archive North.
47. Anon, interviewed 23 Jan. 2009, Bolton Oral History Project, no 12, Feminist Archive North, BWLG, Box 6. She says the campaign 'just fizzled out eventually'.
48. Jackie Barron, *Personal Histories*, Feminist Archive South, p. 61.
49. Angela Rodaway, *Personal Histories*, Feminist Archive South, p. 32.
50. WIRES, 20 July 1979.
51. *The Future of the Norwich Women's Centre: a briefing document*, Dec. 1990. This document was a defence of the women's centre, in the light of council proposals to cut funding: Box 21, Norwich Women's Centre Archive, Feminist Archive North, p. 3.
52. Ibid. p. 4.
53. The Norwich Women's Centre Day Book for 1977–81 is available: Box 9, Norwich Women's Centre Archive.
54. City Treasurer, Evaluation, *Norwich Women's Education and Resource Centre*, 1990 Norwich Women's Centre Archive, Box 3. There are also various leaflets for the centre.
55. Various authors (1999) *A Woman's Place 1974–1999: a celebration of women's lives in Brighton over the last 25 years* (Women's Words: Brighton), Jen Murray, p. 52, also p. 109.
56. *A Woman's Place*, Jen Murray, p. 52.
57. Alison Hammer (1978) writing in Brighton WL Newsletter: 5BW/survey/B/31 Box 16-17, Aug. 1978.
58. *A Woman's Place*, Rosemary Lovatt, p. 95.
59. Both Leeds and Bradford had women's centres but as yet there is little archival material or oral testimony which relates to this, which has limited the analysis which can be made here.

60. Norwich Women's Centre AGM, 8 Mar. 1989, Box 21, Norwich Women's Centre Archive.
61. Alison Hammer (1978) writing in Brighton WL newsletter: 5BW/survey/B/31 Box 16-17, Aug. 1978.
62. Betty Underwood, *Personal Histories*, Feminist Archive South, p. 44.
63. *A Woman's Place*, p. 9.
64. Personal memory of author.
65. Both Kate Page and Dorothy Sheridan were involved in NAC and went on to promote women's health facilities in Brighton: Kate Page, interview, Dorothy Sheridan interviewed by Sue Bruley in Brighton, 2 Aug. 2011 and 18 Sep. 2011, transcript (TS), pp. 5–10.
66. *A Woman's Place*, p. 110.
67. *Personal Histories*, Feminist Archive South p. 8 (Sarah Braun), pp. 66–67 (Janet Brewer).
68. Hilary Eastham refers to her role in helping to set up Fortalice, Bolton Oral History Project, Box 6, BWLG, Feminist Archive North. Limited information on Radclyffe Hall is in Boxes 2A/3A, BWLG, FAN.
69. Anon, no 5, Bolton Oral History Project, Box 6, BWLG, Feminist Archive North.
70. Jenn Bravo, The UK Women's Liberation Movement, Violence Against Women, History Workshop, British Library, Leeds, 31 Jan. 2009, TS, p. 7.
71. Ruth Ingram Violence Against Women Workshop, TS, pp. 53–54.
72. Rees, *All the Rage*.
73. Leeds Revolutionary Feminists (1981) Political Lesbianism: the case against heterosexuality, in *Love Your Enemy? The debate between heterosexual feminism and political lesbianism* (London: Onlywomen Press), pp. 5–10. (originally a WLM conference paper, 1978).
74. Ibid. p. 7.
75. Sandra McNeill, Violence Against Women workshop, TS pp. 58–67. See also Rees, *All the Rage*.
76. Following the violence at the national Reclaim the Night March in London in 1978, warnings were given of the likelihood of hostility from both porn shops and police, Brighton WL newsletter, 5BW/survey/B/31 Box 16-17, 20 Mar. 1979.
77. S. McNeill, Violence Against Women workshop, p. 60. The idea for Reclaim the Night marches came from a similar event in Germany, but was originally thought to come from the USA: see Introduction.
78. Brighton WL newsletter, 5BW/survey/B/31 Box 16-17, Jan. 1979.
79. June 1978 and 1 Mar. 1982, Minute Book 3, Box 1, BWLG, FAN.
80. Reproduced in the Norwich Women's Centre Newsletter, n.d. c1989, Norwich Women's Centre Archive, Box 4, Feminist Archive North. The newsletter refers specifically to an Australian branch of WITCH. The use of the name WITCH also crops up among radical feminists in North America, e.g., Jill Vickers (1992) The Intellectual Origins of the Women's Movements in Canada, in Constance Backhouse & David H. Flaherty (Eds) *Challenging Times: the women's movement in Canada and the US* (Montreal: McGill University Press), pp. 39–60.
81. *The Future of the Women's Centre*: a briefing document produced in 1990 in response to council plans to cut the grant. Norwich Women's Centre Archive, Box 21, Feminist Archive North.
82. Cristel, *Personal Histories*, Feminist Archive South, p. 74.
83. June Butt, *WLM in Leeds and Bradford*, Feminist Archive South, Interview no 19.
84. Ruth Ingram, Violence Against Women workshop, TS p. 52.
85. *Anti-Racist Policy 2.10. 86*, Norwich Women's Centre, Norwich Archive, Box 3.
86. *Personal Histories*, Feminist Archive South, p. 55 (Harriet Wordsworth), p. 134 (Pat Roberts).
87. Hilary Land, *Personal Histories*, Feminist Archive South, p. 120.
88. Juley Howard, *Personal Histories*, Feminist Archive South, p. 115.
89. S. Bruley, 'Jam Today'; see also article by Laurel Forster in this volume.
90. Hilary Eastham, Bolton Women's Liberation Group, Oral History Project, BWLG, Feminist Archive North.
91. Frances Bernstein, Violence Against Women workshop, TS p. 103.

92. Ibid. p. 105.
93. Ibid. pp. 106–112; Jane McGill, Violence Against Women workshop, TS pp. 114–115.
94. Ruth Ingram, Violence Against Women workshop, TS p. 126
95. Setch, *The Women's Liberation Movement in Britain 1969–1979*, p. 103.
96. D-M Withers (Ed) (2011) *Sistershow Revisited: feminism in Bristol 1973–5* (Bristol: HammerOn Press), p. 18.
97. Ibid. p. 17.
98. For more details see Monica Sjöö, *Through Space and Time: the ancient sisterhoods spoke to me*, http://monicasjoo.com/index.php/god-giving-birth, accessed 22 July 2015.
99. Ibid.; M. Sjöö, *Personal Histories*, Feminist Archive South, p. 36.
100. Marilyn Porter, *Personal Histories*, Feminist Archive South, pp. 132–133.
101. Anon, interviewed 19 June 2009, Bolton Women's Liberation Group Oral History Project, no. 13.
102. M. Sjöö, *Personal Histories*, Feminist Archive South, p. 35. This testimony can be confirmed by other women at the conference.
103. P. Dalton, *Personal Histories*, Feminist Archive South, p. 78.
104. Brighton WL newsletter, 5BW/survey/B/31 Box 16-17, 25 Jan. 1978.
105. Dorothy Nelson, Bolton Women's Liberation Oral History Project, no 9, Box 6, BWLG, Feminist Archive North.
106. Sheridan interviews, TS, pp. 16–17
107. Ibid. p. 8.
108. Coote & Campbell, *Sweet Freedom*, p. 227.
109. S. Braun, *Personal Histories*, Feminist Archive South, p. 9.
110. Interview with Kate Page by Sue Bruley, 3 Jan. 2013, Brighton, TS pp. 29–36.
111. Joyce Outshorn has noted that establishing causality in relation to women's liberation and historical change is difficult: Outshorn (2012) 'Assessing the Impact of Women's Movements', *WSIF*, 35, pp. 147–149. Certainly there are strong indications of both attitudinal and structural change which there is not sufficient space to develop here. For a European perspective see Beatrice Halsaa, Sasha Roseneil & Sevil Sümer (Eds) (2012) *Remaking Citizenship in Multicultural Europe: women's movements, gender and diversity* (Basingstoke: Palgrave Macmillan).

The Women's Movement and 'Class Struggle': gender, class formation and political identity in women's strikes, 1968–78

George Stevenson

ABSTRACT
Women workers' industrial disputes were of fundamental importance to the WLM, reflected in the deeds of activists and early participant-histories. These disputes were sites of worker-employer conflict and conflict between feminists and the wider Labour Movement. This article considers how these differing interpretations related to the striking women themselves. It focuses on four key disputes and analyses contemporary reports and the accounts of those involved. It argues women strikers' particular experiences of trade unionism, class politics and feminism resulted in gendered, but still fundamentally class-based, identities, and concludes by considering the position of women workers' industrial actions in feminist histories.

Introduction

The industrial action for equal pay by working-class women at Dagenham in 1968 took place just as the nascent Women's Liberation Movement (WLM) was emerging in Britain. Dominated by socialist-feminists, the early liberationists saw the militancy of working-class women as a massively significant parallel development that had a 'formative' influence on the WLM's ideology, primarily through underlining the importance of 'cross-class alliances' between women.[1] This link remained fundamental to many feminists throughout the WLM's existence through its theoretical concerns, activism and press coverage. Indeed, women's strikes were frequently the subject of special issues or reports in publications like *Shrew*, *Spare Rib*, *Socialist Woman* and *Red Rag*.

The issue of class remained central in the original histories of the movement. As a result, the relationship between feminism and class politics in this period is part of a longer tradition that runs through from histories of Chartism to women's suffrage.[2] The early participator-accounts of the WLM made class central in both its origins and dissolution as class was understood as one axis of difference—alongside race and sexuality—the WLM was unable to recognise or address effectively as gender 'started to gobble up all other relations'.[3] Once brought into the open by black, lesbian and working-class women, differences around sexuality, race and class 'destroyed any notion of women's cosy unity'.[4] Black feminists in particular have critiqued the 'essentialism' of the WLM, arguing it was a 'liberationary' movement only for those within its primary demography; it offered 'sisterhood' only to the white middle-class women who dominated it.[5]

However, other perspectives have emerged that question the simplicity of the traditional narrative. Revisionists have argued that considerations of the local and grassroots activities of the WLM, rather than the academic participator accounts, reveal a more complex relationship with 'difference', where tensions over race, class and sexuality were discussed, debated and recognised.[6] Similarly, an analysis of the policy statement of publications like *Shrew*, reveals the movement's desire to 'take seriously individual voices without being individualistic while evoking collectivity between all women without assuming sameness'.[7] They argue the focus on difference in the traditional historiography also owes much to an analysis of the major texts of the movement, which privileges prominent individuals as well as following a form which encourages a distinctive theoretical outline.[8] Moreover, 'Far from destroying the movement, [disagreements and divisions] were indicative of organisations which could accommodate many different positions'.[9] Indeed, even the contentious issue of race within and around the WLM has been re-evaluated to assert that the 'commonplace' view that white feminists were racist ignored how the many attempts they made to address 'race', such as with Women Against Racism and Fascism (WARF) and Women Against Imperialism (WAI).[10]

The dominance of the original socialist-feminist histories of the WLM has also been challenged for over-emphasising the importance of class at the expense of other areas, which, far from being neglected, has dominated the academic discourse surrounding the WLM. When only socialist-feminists are heard, it is the voices of radical and revolutionary feminists, who rejected class analysis to lesser and greater degrees, that need to be recovered.[11]

Each of these authors has added required clarifications and complexity to the traditional essentialist narrative of the second-wave women's movement. However, in emphasising the experiences of the 'dominant' class/race of feminists in that period, there has been a cost to the understanding of how both working-class and black women constructed their identities. In particular, interest in the relationship between women workers and the WLM has fallen out of favour in recent histories of the movement as the traditional accounts are either left untouched or ignored altogether. Furthermore, the direction of travel is towards inward-looking histories of the WLM that consider the interactions between women within the movement, or at the least, between those identifying as feminists if not women's liberationists. This implies a perception of working women's struggles as separate and distinct from the WLM.

This article will re-engage with the relationship between working women and feminism through an analysis of four illustrative industrial disputes between 1968 and 1978: the Dagenham equal pay strike in 1968; the Night Cleaners' Campaign of the early 1970s; the Trico equal pay strike in 1976; and the 1976–78 Grunwick dispute. Each case study will analyse the narratives of the WLM and the Labour Movement against the views of the women workers involved and will ask two essential questions: first, how did women workers involved in industrial disputes during this period construct their political identities? Second, what does this mean for situating women's strikes within histories of the WLM and for working-class women's relationship within feminism more broadly? The first question shall be answered in relation to the Labour Movement and the Women's

Movement in this period due to their significance in each dispute and for women and workers generally. This article will argue that in spite of regular rejection from the 'class struggle' by male workers and trade unions, coupled with the WLM's support for them as *women*, the strikers founded their identities through the prism of class, not gender. The article will conclude by considering the second question and inquiring whether these disputes are rightly situated within the historiography of the WLM and their place in a longer tradition of histories of class and gender politics.

Dagenham

The 1960s was a period of substantial structural economic change for women as more jobs became available to them than ever before.[12] Female participation in the labour-force increased in unskilled, semi-skilled and skilled categories over the decade and the percentage of women active in the labour market continued to increase in the 1970s, reaching 64% by 1979.[13] The changes were particularly striking for married women and those with dependent children, with the percentage in employment more than doubling in both cases between the 1950s and 1980s.[14]

Nevertheless, women continued to have responsibility for childcare and domestic duties, which restricted their involvement in the labour force, with the vast majority of married women workers in part-time employment.[15] In the 1950s and 1960s, employer demand for part-time workers was attributed to labour market shortage but by the 1970s the situation had changed as employers utilised part-time work to extend overall labour hours and to develop a more flexible, and exploitable, labour force.[16] Married women's persisting roles as domestic labourers often made these 'flexible' hours their only employment option. More generally, what constituted 'women's work' outside of the home remained 'low paid, low grade and … unskilled' and there was a clear distinction between men and women's work; most male workers were employed in jobs with a 90% male workforce while female workers were employed in jobs that were at least 70% female.[17] Female dominated workplaces were characterised by weak trade union organisation, which was seen to reflect the patriarchal attitudes of local union officials and the trade union movement more widely.[18] These factors contributed to the level of inequality in women's rate of pay against men's staying constant in the mid-1960s, having actually fallen in the preceding decade.[19] Fundamentally, women workers remained 'economically disadvantaged' in this period.[20]

However, the period was also marked by other significant changes to industrial politics. After a lull in strikes and industrial conflict in the 1950s, the period after 1960 saw a revitalised 'shopfloor movement', including particularly heightened worker militancy between 1968 and 1974, with 1972 seen as a 'high point of class struggle' amongst an 'increasingly self-confident and militant' working class.[21] The 1970s also saw the re-emergence of 'political' strikes and a qualitatively different nature of industrial relations as 'a wide range of traditionally moderate and peaceful workers, many of them women, embarked on strike actions, many for the first time in their lives'.[22]

It is unsurprising in this context that the strike in 1968 by women sewing-machinists at the Ford factory in Dagenham was seen both at the time and subsequently as hugely significant by feminists and the Labour Movement. For the WLM, the strike's importance lies in its role in origin narratives of the movement. The strike has been said to have placed 'equality' on the political agenda, had 'a formative influence on the newly emerging women's liberation movement', and 'provided early role models' for second-wave feminism, all points reiterated in subsequent individual accounts.[23] In addition, it is seen as crucial in forcing the Labour Party to pass the Equal Pay Act in 1970, although this must be coupled with Britain's obligations after joining the European Economic Community and the necessary condition of equal pay in the Treaty of Rome.[24]

Trade union histories of the strike, by contrast, emphasise different elements of the strike. The TUC's learning resources on the strike, for example, illustrate less of a concern with the principle of equality in favour of the strike's symbolic significance for the solidarity of male and female trade unionists over a 'women's issue'. The resources focus on the 'unstinting support of their [the strikers'] union convenor [male]' and the difficulty of facing opposition from the company, rather than their status as women.[25] Moreover, problems of male solidarity with the women are concealed within the ambiguity of 'some' male colleagues opposing the strike.[26] That these problems were tied up with wider social and cultural understandings of 'women's work' is undeniable and is demonstrated by the parallel between the mainstream media's response to the strike and male workers' attitudes as recounted by the strikers.

The media's response illustrated a stark contrast to the TUC's interpretation, where a series of hysterical claims over losses to male jobs and damage to industry highlighted that the strikers had failed to understand their position as women rather than as workers. Taking *The Times* as an example, headlines included 'Ford talks failure threat to 40,000 [male jobs]' and 'Ministry acts as women threaten jobs at Ford', while an editorial discussed the need for 'Firmness' and considered the possibility of the company's acquiescence 'disastrous'.[27] This was significant due to the internalisation of the media narrative amongst some of the strikers' male colleagues. One woman recalled:

> The men would not come out, although we asked them to come out with us, and fight for us ... They thought we were working for pin money. Women's work is always pin money if you're married ... If they'd come out with us, it would have been over in days.[28]

Another underlined this point, stating they often faced questions from male workers: 'You did get a lot of people saying, "What are you doing this for? You only come to work for pin money, women."'[29] Indeed, another noted that her own husband had opposed the strike, highlighting the difficulty the strikers had simply being defined as workers as much as the direct conflict with the employer emphasised in the trade union history.[30]

Moreover, the agency for the strike lay with the women themselves; they voted for and led the strike, and eight women from the strike committee famously discussed the issue of equality with Barbara Castle at Downing Street.[31] Their commitment to the strike was demonstrated in votes and public statements and they dictated the terms of the dispute, focusing it on equality rather than the specific pay claim itself. In spite of smiles for the press, the women showed an obvious anger towards their employer on the one hand, and an awareness of the gendered dynamic to their struggle on the other, as illustrated in widely-used posters and banners reading, 'No surrender to Fords' and 'No sex discrimination'.[32]

Furthermore, Rose Boland, one of the strike leaders, was definite about sexual discrimination underpinning the motivations for the strike. Speaking about the original evaluation that sparked the dispute, she pointed out its gender-bias and when asked if she thought the strike was a struggle against sex discrimination she replied without hesitation: 'I do. Definitely.'[33] Another member of the strike committee also framed the dispute in gendered terms, recalling her feelings at the time: 'Well, we want C grade if the men are getting it. We want equal pay.'[34] Moreover, Boland and others on the strike committee affirmed their commitment to feminist politics of this type by subsequently playing roles in the development of the National Joint Action Campaign Committee for Women's Equal Rights.[35] It is impossible in this instance, and in others, to ascertain how representative these statements were of the overall mood of the strike body, especially since many of the available sources originate from spokespeople and prominent participants. However, the solidity of the strike suggests they were not detached from wider sentiments. Thus, to remove women who engaged in explicitly gendered struggles in the workplace from the narrative of the WLM, as many revisionist histories have, is to ignore important contributors to feminism in this period.

However, certain factors complicate a solely gendered perspective. For one, most of the women's accounts were clear that the strike was primarily concerned with equal grading rather than equal pay, as well as with being understood as skilled workers. One noted how the strike 'ended up' being about equal rights, having started as a grading issue.[36] Furthermore, while the strike was successful in forcing Ford to abolish the 'women's grade' and pushed the women on to the same 'B' grade as 'B' graded men, it was unable to achieve the 'C' grading that the women had desired, and therefore real pay equality.[37] Indeed, it took another strike sixteen years later to finally achieve parity.[38] The women's trade union had recommended that the women accept this offer and, although some voted against it, the majority of the strikers voted to return to work.[39] In so doing, they illustrated a disjuncture between the strike's female leadership—as opposed to the male-dominated trade union advising returning to work—and the strike body. Boland had doubted the desire of the majority of the women to move the strike beyond a traditional pay and conditions action towards one fighting for full equality in pay and grading, telling *Socialist Worker*:

> I don't think the women will go out for the 100 per cent equal pay in the C grade just yet. We're concerned with proving that we are skilled workers ... Personally I think that if a woman does the same type of work as a man she should be entitled to equal pay.[40]

Thus, while the situating of the strike within an 'equality' narrative undoubtedly resonated with many women involved, this was perhaps not its primary motivation for the majority. It was, then, as 'economistic' workers, rather than as women, that the strikers began and ended their dispute. Nevertheless, in framing the dispute in terms of equality, its leaders endowed the strike with enormous symbolic power that feminists were rightly conscious of.

The Night Cleaners' Campaign

The story was similar for those involved in the Night Cleaners' Campaign, with one important difference. Whereas the Dagenham strikers had only a trade union narrative of unified class struggle to call on in the absence of the developing but embryonic WLM, the night cleaners had feminist support from the very beginning of their campaign. Indeed the campaign, a long struggle for improved pay and conditions and union recognition for night cleaners between 1970 and 1973, was conducted by cleaners alongside women's liberationists.[41]

One outcome of this has been that, whilst the Dagenham strike has taken on equal significance within both feminist and labour histories, the Night Cleaners' Campaign has been of far greater importance to feminists at the time and subsequently. The campaign was covered widely by the contemporary feminist press, including special issues of *Shrew* and *Socialist Woman*, and Sally Alexander provided an activist account in a contribution to the feminist publication *Conditions of Illusion* in 1974.[42] Moreover, Sheila Rowbotham has maintained a strong interest in the topic and framed the campaign as 'part of a wider attempt to foreground women workers and challenge trade union complacency about women's subordination'.[43] Furthermore, as the cleaners were mostly married women balancing paid work with unpaid domestic labour, they personified the dual nature of working-class women's oppression. As a result, the feminist narrative was concerned with recognising both women workers' particular exploitation but also with the need for them to be recognised as part of the 'class struggle'. Thus, the WLM did not emphasise gender at the expense of class in their understanding of women's industrial disputes. This focus on class and the encouragement offered to working-class women to understand their actions in these terms were factors that distinguished the movement from its precursors, which had tended to 'dismiss' working-class women as external to feminism.[44]

The campaign began when one of the few union members, May Hobbs, sought to overcome the problems of unionising a disparate workforce by approaching the local International Marxist Group (IMG), and subsequently the Dalston women's liberation workshop, for assistance, resulting in the formation of the Cleaners Action Group (CAG), which was composed of cleaners, women's liberationists, and socialists.[45] The CAG picketed, distributed leaflets, and drew up a list of demands around wages and conditions and the right for the night cleaners to join trade unions.[46]

However, even with the aid of the IMG, the Communist Party and the Dalston women's liberation workshop encouraging union membership, the cleaners found it difficult to arouse the interest of male trade unionists and the trade unions.[47] These frustrations were evident when May Hobbs accused the TGWU of 'indifference' towards the female cleaners at the Workers' Control Conference in Birmingham in 1970.[48] Indeed, histories of the campaign have consistently noted the cleaners served as an example of how trade unions had to be 'force[d]' to recognise their struggles.[49] This contrasted with how a 'mutual relationship' could develop between women workers and the WLM, implying that second-wave feminist politics was more easily able to address issues affecting exploited workers than the trade union movement, which had also been historically poor in recognising working-class women's struggles.[50]

Trade union indifference did not prevent the CAG managing to unionise 75% of the cleaners by July 1972 but, although this work had been completed for him, the TGWU officer responsible for the cleaners remained 'very elusive'.[51] Local women's liberation groups and the socialist press reported that the TGWU's disinterest was apparent in their apathy towards further recruitment but also indicated that local trade unionists were strongly supportive of the campaign, illustrating the distinction between the rank and file and leadership that was present throughout the period.[52] However, the reluctance of the local *official* to respond suggested that gender was important as it reflected wider evidence that the attitudes of lower-level officials within the trade union movement offered only limited support for women's disputes.[53] The cleaners were, however, able to call on the support of the Civil Service Union more successfully in other buildings and, with the support of local workers, win concessions from specific employers, but the TGWU limited this level of support more broadly.[54] The campaign was consequently extended into an extremely long dispute that relied more on the support of feminists and socialists than the union movement the women were fighting to be a part of.

Thus, the women had varied interactions with industrial and political institutions during this dispute which impacted on how their political identities were constructed. To begin with, Hobbs' and the cleaners' desire to unionise against their employers, and her approach of an IMG rather than WLM, suggest that they sought to fight along traditional 'class' lines. The antagonistic interests they had as workers against their employer underpinned the campaign. However, their experiences with class politics problematised such a straightforward interpretation. The TGWU was reluctant to recognise their exploitation and their desire to, in effect, join a broader class struggle. For Hobbs and the cleaners it was apparent that this reluctance stemmed from their sex. In a repeat of those arguing the Dagenham women were working for 'pin money', the TGWU perceived the strikers as *women* before they were *workers*. Whereas this attitude had been infrequent and relegated to mostly grassroots union members at Dagenham, it was the union machinery which constructed this interpretation for the night cleaners. It was consequently unsurprising that those cleaners spoken to often attributed the successes of the campaign to the local WL group, rather than TGWU activists or the union itself.[55] Moreover, for their most prominent member, May Hobbs, the link with feminist politics became an increasingly important part of her political identity and she became directly involved with the WLM at conferences and meetings and traversed some of the class boundaries between herself and the women's liberationists who supported her, seemingly reflecting the greater ease of connections between women of different classes than workers of different genders.[56]

The implication for women's political identities is that, when rejected by the institutions of traditional class politics but validated by feminist politics, the more politically active cleaners like Hobbs and those interviewed gravitated towards a more sex- than class-based identity. However, this could again be unrepresentative of the majority of those involved. Indeed, the perspective of feminists active in the campaign reflected that it dissipated partly because of 'the yawning class gulf between the leafleters [WLM] and the cleaners'.[57] Moreover, it is important to qualify that even Hobbs tended to speak on the issues faced by women workers rather than *women* and was also critical of what she saw as the movement's failure to engage with the working class.[58] It is consequently apparent that the structures of class were still keenly felt in women's political identities, even when they perceived their struggle as being legitimised more greatly by feminist than class politics in ways that marked a point of departure from previous feminist incarnations.

Trico

The balance between class and gender politics was equally complex in the third case, the Trico equal pay strike. The strike took place over twenty-one weeks in summer 1976 at the

Trico windscreen-wiper factory in Brentford, Middlesex. It began after twelve months of 'exhaustive discussions'—over the payment of a higher rate to twelve men formerly on the night shift who had been moved to the same shift as 400 women on a lower rate—failed to resolve the disagreement.[59] On 24 May, all 400 women voted for strike action, supported by the twelve men and their AUEW branch.[60] Shortly after, AUEW's Southall District Committee endorsed the strike and the Executive Committee made it official on 15 June.[61] In contrast to the night cleaners' experience, on this occasion the trade union was immediately responsive to its members' wishes at all levels.

Nonetheless, in spite of its legitimisation, its place as the longest equal pay strike in British history, and its success, the Labour Movement's key institutions, the TUC and the Labour Party, were predominantly apathetic towards it. The strike was ignored at the 1976 Labour Party Conference, even though the events were concurrent, and while it did receive a supportive motion at the 1976 TUC Conference, action was thin on the ground.[62] However, for some prominent trade unionists like Jack Dromey, the strike was symbolic of both equality disputes and the trade union movement's strength and inclusivity—a parallel to the TUC's interpretation of the Dagenham dispute:

> We think this is the most important strike that is happening at this moment in the country. It is a struggle that we in the trade union movement cannot afford to lose.[63]

This view was supported by the *Morning Star* after the women's victory as the paper used its front page to note that, 'They have set an example to the whole labour and trade union movement'.[64]

Alternatively, the feminist narrative positioned the strikers as part of the women's movement and the strike as being as much concerned with the *idea* of equality rather than specific to the dispute, thereby deviating from the synthesis of class and gender propounded during the night cleaners' campaign. This was particularly prevalent in WLM press, such as *Shrew*, which asserted:

> If they don't win, then the Equal Pay Act will be shown to be what we have always found it was intended to be—a contemptuous and obvious nod and a wink in the direction of the feminist movement and part of the continuous co-option of radical politics that persists in liberal democracies as some kind of endemic disease.[65]

The strike was no less significant in *Spare Rib*, which featured various aspects in five consecutive issues.[66]

The women's actions and statements again offered evidence to support alignment with both perspectives. This was certainly true in one of the most ideologically insightful aspects of the strike, which was the women's decision to reject the Equal Pay Act and its accompanying tribunals in favour of emphasising the principle of equality and collective action. On the surface, this suggests that the women were demonstrating the sort of feminist consciousness evoked by the feminist press.[67] Indeed, the strike committee's statement on the legislation seemed to reflect *Shrew*'s interpretation: 'We are not prepared in this case to use a Tribunal that has allowed the Equal Pay and Sex Discrimination Acts to become a lawyer's paradise and cobweb of loopholes for the discriminator.'[68] Furthermore, individual women asserted their desire to 'defend the advances that women have made'; noted that 'We're carrying the rod for all women, let's see it through to the end'; and argued that 'A victory for us will be a victory for all women--so we *have* to win', statements which clearly aligned their actions with a gendered political project.[69]

However, an engagement with class politics was at least as powerful and foundational in shaping the women's political identities. First, the alternative the women saw to the legislation and its means of redress was not the women's movement, but 'strong Trade Union organisation' while there was also a clear class-based approach in what the strike committee's bulletins chose to emphasise.[70] The bulletins were regularly clear on the link to class politics, arguing: 'We are tired of hearing that, if they have to pay women more, they will have to lay men off. 'YOU CAN'T DIVIDE AND RULE US!' and, 'We shall say to the world—"OUR MOVEMENT WON FOR US THESE RIGHTS AND NOBODY WILL TAKE THEM AWAY FROM US—UNITED, WE WILL NEVER BE DEFEATED"'.[71] The capitalisation of these points showed a clear emphasis on situating their struggle in terms of trade unionism and perceiving a structural class antagonism between employer and workers rather than identifying with feminism. Moreover, a range of individual accounts support the contention that it was representative of the general mood with many women focusing on the importance of 'shop-floor organisation' and the unity of male and female workers.[72] Indeed, this was also apparent in the language the women chose to use to describe non-striking male workers, who were tarnished as 'scabs'.[73]

Thus, women's predominant understanding of the dispute tended to focus on the dynamics of class conflict rather than gendered divisions and this was reinforced through their experiences. It seemed therefore that feminist support had more impact on identities when the institutions of class politics were absent, such as for the night cleaners. However, as their simultaneous commitment to fighting on behalf of all women workers attested to, the class identity they developed was once more strongly gendered. Thus, as had been the case for the Dagenham strikers and the night cleaners, class and gender were inextricably intertwined. The final study, of the Grunwick dispute, is helpful for further developing the complexities of women's relationship to the politics of class, gender *and* race in this period.

Grunwick

The strike at Grunwick, composed of predominantly Asian women workers, took place from 20 August 1976 to 14 July 1978. Fuelled by underlying tensions over poor pay and conditions and a lack of grievance procedures, the strike was sparked by the sacking of Devshi Budia.[74] A number of workers walked out in protest and joined the Association of Professional, Executive, Clerical and Computer Staff (APEX), which made the strike official on 30 August.[75] The next two years featured mass pickets, enormous media coverage, and inquiry after inquiry, with the strikers' right to union recognition rejected by the House of Lords.[76] Increasingly desperate and facing defeat, some of the women resorted to hunger strikes against the wishes of APEX and the TUC, both of which threatened those involved with suspension.[77]

The role of Asian women workers, their receipt of trade union support and solidarity action from various white male workers have seen Grunwick stand as a symbol of the trade union movement's growing awareness and acceptance of the changing nature of the labour force at both the time and in many histories of the period.[78] It was, as Arthur Scargill, then President of the Yorkshire region of the National Union of Mineworkers (NUM), argued: 'a focal point in the history of our movement … if we are defeated at Grunwick, it is a terrible defeat for the whole movement.'[79]

In contrast to the other examples, feminist histories have tended to share this interpretation. Sue Bruley, for example, wrote in her history of women in Britain that, 'The sight of the diminutive Jayaben Desai standing up to the mass police ranks on the Grunwick picket line is one of the unforgettable images of the 1970s'.[80] Moreover, the recent *Striking Women* AHRC project agreed that:

> Although it was ultimately lost, this strike has become constructed as an iconic moment in the history of the labour movement: the moment when the trade unions recognised the rights of women and minority workers as equal to those of white working class men.[81]

However, it was certainly racial and industrial elements of the dispute that dominated its perception and this was reflected in the views of the women involved.

The women strikers situated their struggle in terms of 'class' through the use of traditional methods and the language of industrial disputes, particularly by its leaders, such as Jayaben Desai. Desai's comments often read as if they originated from a class struggle handbook:

> All this time I have been watching the strikes and I realised that the workers are the people who give their blood for the management and that they should have good conditions, good pay and should be well fed.[82]

However, this perspective was shared by others on the picket lines, such as one woman's 'them and us' characterisation: 'Bosses are bosses, to me, we are the workforce and without the workforce there would be no boss, and no work done.'[83] The idea of class solidarity was also key to another striker: 'It's every working-class person in this country and I can't just sit there and think about myself.'[84] Fundamentally, the strikers were motivated by the principle of demonstrating their position as an active part of the working class.[85]

However, throughout the dispute the trade unions acted as gatekeepers of class and political identity, alternating between accepting, challenging and rejecting the strikers' perspectives. To begin with and for much of the dispute, the strikers received the support of APEX, a range of other unions, and also huge crowds of male workers at the mass pickets.[86] These groups and processes legitimised and reinforced the development of a class consciousness amongst the women, which, over the course of nearly two years of struggle, had become internalised by a large cross-section of the strike body.[87] However, once the traditional routes of industrial struggle had been exhausted and some of the women used hunger strikes to extend the dispute, the full force of APEX and the TUC's definitional powers came into play. By rejecting alternative means of class struggle, the trade union movement undermined the identity the women had constructed as workers and made them distinct. In many black and Asian feminists' eyes the result was to break the 'unity of the working class' achieved during the strike.[88] Brixton Black Women's Group reported that the strikers were 'very upset' about the trade union movement's unilateral withdrawal from the struggle and their individual statements attested to this.[89] Desai, for example, was unequivocal in her condemnation:

> The union views itself like management. There's no democracy there ... The union says we have to accept everything that they say ... They have done the same thing to us as Ward [factory owner] did—they suspended us.[90]

Such sentiments ran through the Brixton report.[91]

Thus, in a parallel with the Night Cleaners' Campaign and working-class women's struggles in earlier periods, the Labour Movement played a key role in rejecting women workers' class identities.[92] Having felt assimilated into the broad class struggle during the dispute through the support of their union, the TUC, and rank-and-file workers at mass pickets, the legacy of this 'betrayal' later re-emphasised their identities along racial and gender lines alongside class and thereby challenges the strike's position in asserting the Labour Movement's developments in these areas.[93]

Conclusion

It is clear that in each case the women strikers' political identities had a relationship to class and gender, as well as race at Grunwick. At Dagenham, the women were conscious of their position as exploited 'workers' throughout their strike but were also aware of how this inherently challenged the dominant discourse of the way 'worker' was constructed. The media and attitudes of male colleagues situated them as separate to, and even in conflict with, working-class interests, thereby resulting in political identities that were founded in class but inflected inevitably by gender.

This was also true for the night cleaners who began by focusing on confronting their exploitation within the framework of class politics but came up against trade union apathy starkly contrasted with an engaged feminist movement offering an alternative identity structure. However, while some of its leaders interacted with the WLM and developed a feminist-inflected consciousness, the foundational power of class persisted and located their feminism strictly in the workplace. Moreover, class acted as an identity barrier that saw the cleaners remain critical of the WLM's lack of interaction with working-class women.

Similarly, at Trico and Grunwick the women originally formed class identities in opposition to their employer. Nonetheless, these identities had to be constantly renegotiated 'in situ'.[94] At Trico, the women were conscious their exploitation as workers was founded on their gender and distinguished them from higher paid male colleagues. Alternatively, those at Grunwick discovered that they were legitimised as part of the working class only so long as they followed the rules of acceptable class struggle defined by APEX and the TUC which, once rejected, saw them positioned as distinct sections of the working class.

Thus, while class-consciousness was developed by women workers on all four occasions, the process was complicated by the intersection of patriarchal and colonialist narratives within class-based institutions and amongst male workers. Their experiences thereby reflected many of their predecessors in the preceding 150 years.[95]

However, this period of working women's struggle should be distinguished from others in another respect. Whereas earlier feminisms had been as, if not more, likely to dismiss working-class women's concerns as the Labour Movement, women's class struggles were a fundamental concern of the WLM.[96] In each of these strikes bar Dagenham, which occurred alongside the WLM's development, the WLM offered physical, intellectual and financial support to the strikers. Strikes that were often unimportant or ignored by the trade union movement were recognised as possessing massive symbolic importance by feminists. As a result, the strikers were always conscious of the importance their strikes had not just for the class struggle but for women workers and women in society more broadly. Each of the strikes and campaigns were carried out by those who defined themselves as both workers and women and therefore, while class was fundamental to their political identities—and did therefore tend to distinguish them from their feminist supporters—their struggles should remain an essential part of feminist histories of the period.

Notes

1. Sheila Rowbotham (1989) *The Past is Before Us: feminism in action since the 1960s* (Boston: Beacon Press), p. 166; Lynne Segal (2013) 'Jam Today: women in the 1970s', in Lawrence Black, Hugh Pemberton & Pat Thane (Eds) *Reassessing 1970s Britain* (Manchester University Press), pp. 153–154; Anna Coote & Beatrix Campbell (1987) *Sweet Freedom: the struggle for women's liberation* (Oxford: Basil Blackwell), pp. 9–10.
2. See for example, Dorothy Thompson (1984) *The Chartists* (London: Temple Smith); Anna Clark (1985) *The Struggle for the Breeches: gender and the making of the British working class* (Berkeley: University of California Press); Jill Liddington & Jill Norris (1978) *One Hand Tied Behind Us: the rise of the women's suffrage movement* (London: Virago); Richard Evans (1977) *The Feminists: women's emancipation movements in Europe, America and Australasia, 1840–1920* (London: Croom Helm).
3. Sheila Rowbotham, Lynne Segal & Hilary Wainwright (1979) *Beyond the Fragments: feminism and the making of socialism* (London: Merlin Press); Sheila Rowbotham (1992) *Women in Movement: feminism and social action* (London: Routledge), p. 285.
4. Rowbotham et al., *Beyond the Fragments*; Segal, 'Jam Today', p. 160.
5. Hazel V. Carby (1997) White Woman Listen! Black feminism and the boundaries of sisterhood, in H.S. Mirza (Ed.) *Black British Feminism: a reader* (London: Routledge), pp. 149–166; Valerie Amos & Pratibha Parmar (1997) Challenging Imperial Feminism, in Mirza (Ed.) *Black British Feminism*, pp. 45–53; Pat Thane (2013) Women and the 1970s: towards liberation?, in Black et al., *Reassessing 1970s Britain*; Barbara Caine (1997) *English Feminism 1780–1980* (Oxford: Oxford University Press); Gerry Holloway (2005) *Women and Work in Britain since 1840* (London: Routledge); Sue Bruley (1999) *Women in Britain since 1900* (Basingstoke: Macmillan); Wendy Webster (1998) *Imagining Home: gender, 'race' and national identity, 1945–64* (London: UCL Press); Joni Lovenduski & Vicky Randall (1993) *Contemporary Feminist Politics: women and power in Britain* (Oxford: Oxford University Press).
6. Jill Radford (2003) A History of Women's Liberation Movements in Britain: a reflexive personal history, in Griffin, Gabrielle, Hester, Marianne, Rai, Shirin & Roseneil, Sasha (1994) (eds), *Stirring It: Challenges for Feminism* (London: Taylor and Francis), pp. 40–58.
7. Helen Graham (2003) 'New' 1970: 'I', 'we', and 'anyone else', in Graham et al., *The Feminist Seventies*, pp. 159–172.
8. Eve Setch (2000) *The Women's Liberation Movement in Britain, 1969–79: organisation, creativity and debate* (PhD thesis, Royal Holloway).
9. Eve Setch (2003) Women's Liberation Anti-Violence Organisation, in Graham et al., *The Feminist Seventies*, pp. 59–71.
10. Nathalie Thomlinson (2012) The Colour of Feminism: white feminists and race in the women's liberation movement, *History*, 97(327), pp. 453–475.
11. Sarah Browne (2009) *The Women's Liberation Movement in Scotland, c. 1968–c. 1969* (PhD thesis, Dundee University); Jeska Rees (2007) *All the Rage: revolutionary feminism in England, 1977–1983* (PhD thesis, University of Western Australia).
12. Coote & Campbell, *Sweet Freedom*.
13. Martin Pugh (2000) *Women and the Women's Movement, 1914–1999* (Basingstoke: Macmillan); Coote & Campbell, *Sweet Freedom*; Ken Coates & Tony Topham (1986) *Trade Unions and Politics* (Oxford: Blackwell).
14. Jane Lewis (1992) *Women in Britain since 1945* (Oxford: Blackwell).
15. Mandy Snell & Mary McIntosh (1986) 'Introduction', in Feminist Review (Ed.) *Waged Work: a reader* (London: Virago), pp. 1–11 ; Lewis, *Women in Britain since 1945*.

16. Ibid.
17. Snell & McIntosh, 'Introduction', p. 1; Anne Phillips and Barbara Taylor (1986) 'Sex and Skill', in Feminist Review (Ed.) *Waged Work*, pp. 54–66.
18. Ibid; Cynthia Cockburn (1986) 'The Material of Male Power', in Feminist Review (Ed.) *Waged Work*; Nicola Charles (1986) 'Women and Trade Unions', in Feminist Review (Ed.) *Waged Work*, pp.
19. Lewis, *Women in Britain since 1945*.
20. Ibid. p. 91.
21. Alan Campbell, Nina Fishman & John McIlroy (1999) 'The Post-War Compromise: mapping industrial politics', in Alan Campbell, Nina Fishman & John McIlroy (Eds) *British Trade Unions and Industrial Politics, 1945–79, Vol. 1: the post-war compromise, 1945–64* (Aldershot: Ashgate); John McIlroy & Alan Campbell (1999) The High Tide of Trade Unionism: mapping industrial politics, 1964–79, in Campbell et al., *Trade Unions, Vol. 2: the high tide of trade unionism, 1964–79*, pp. 326–352 ; James E. Cronin (1979) *Industrial Conflict in Modern Britain* (London: Croom Helm); Dave Lyddon (1999) Glorious Summer, 1972: the high tide of rank and file militancy, in Campbell et al., *Trade Unions, Vol. 2*.
22. Keith Grint (1991) *The Sociology of Work* (Cambridge: Polity Press), pp. 170–172; Sitnam Virdee (2014) *Racism, Class and the Racialized Outsider* (Basingstoke: Macmillan), p. 123; John E. Kelly (1988) *Trade Unions and Socialist Politics* (London: Verso), pp. 107–108; John McIlroy (1995) *Trade Unions in Britain Today* (Manchester University Press), p. 239.
23. Sheila Rowbotham (1999) *A Century of Women: the history of women in Britain and the United States* (London: Penguin), p. 349; Coote & Campbell, *Sweet Freedom*, p. 10; Segal, 'Jam Today', pp. 153–154.
24. Rowbotham, *A Century of Women*; Selina Todd (2014) *The People: the rise and fall of the working class, 1910–2010* (London: John Murray); Lewis, *Women in Britain since 1945*.
25. TUC Learning Resource, *Winning Equal Pay*, http://www.unionhistory.info/equalpay/TutorsPack.pdf, p. 10.
26. Ibid.
27. *The Times*, 14 June 1968, p. 22; *The Times*, 15 June 1968, p. 1; 'Editorial', *The Times*, 24 June 1968, p. 9.
28. TUC (2006) A Woman's Worth: the story of the Ford sewing machinists, *Recording Women's Voices* (The TUC and Wainwright Trust), http://www.unionhistory.info/equalpay/display.php?irn=619 (accessed 1 Feb. 2013).
29. Betty Crocker (2008) The Real Story of Made in Dagenham, *Workers Liberty* (14 July), http://www.workersliberty.org/story/2008/07/14/real-story-made-dagenham.
30. Ibid.
31. Staff Reporter, 'Heart-to-heart over cups of tea', *The Times*, 29 June 1968, p. 1.
32. R.W. Shakespeare, 'Union aid for Ford women', *The Times*, 19 June 1968, p. 19.
33. Rowbotham, *A Century of Women*, p. 349; Socialist Worker, 'Ford machinists' strike, 1968: an inspiring demand for women's rights', www.socialistworker.co.uk/art.php?id=15057 (accessed 24 May 14).
34. TUC, 'A Woman's Worth'.
35. Coote & Campbell, *Sweet Freedom*, p. 10.
36. Crocker, 'The Real Story'.
37. Sue Hastings (2006) *A Woman's Worth: the story of the Ford sewing machinists--notes by Sue Hastings* (London: TUC), http://www.unionhistory.info/equalpay/display.php?irn=651 (accessed 1 Feb. 2013).
38. 'Ford sewing machinists' strike, 1984', http://www.unionhistory.info/timeline/Tl_Display.php?irn=99 (accessed 24 May 14).
39. Crocker, 'The Real Story'.
40. SW, 'Ford machinists' strike, 1968'.
41. Sarah Boston (1980) *Women Workers and the Trade Union Movement* (London: Davis Poynter).

42. *Shrew: a magazine of the women's liberation workshop*, 3(2) (March, 1971); *The Nightcleaners Campaign: a socialist woman special* (Jan. 1971); Sally Alexander (1974) The Nightcleaners' Campaign, in S. Allen, L. Sanders & J. Wallis (Eds) *Conditions of Illusion* (Leeds: Feminist Books), pp. 309–325.
43. Sheila Rowbotham (2008) 'Jolting Memory: *Nightcleaners* recalled', http://www.workandwords.net/uploads/files/S._ROWBOTHAM_NightCleaners_-_ENG_.pdf, p. 2 (originally published in Maria Ruido [Ed.] *Plan Rosebud: on images, sites and politics of memory* [Santiago]).
44. Evans, *The Feminists*; Liddington & Norris, *One Hand Tied Behind Us*.
45. Alexander, 'The *Nightcleaners* Campaign'; Boston, *Women Workers*.
46. Ibid.
47. Alexander, 'The *Nightcleaners* Campaign'.
48. Norbert C. Soldon (1978) *Women in British Trade Unions, 1874–1976* (Dublin: Gill & Macmillan), p. 182.
49. Boston, *Women Workers*, p. 297.
50. Ibid.; Clark, *The Struggle for the Breeches*, pp. 264, 271; Liddington & Norris, *One Hand Tied Behind Us*, p. 263.
51. Soldon, *Women in British Trade Unions*, p. 182; Alexander, 'The *Nightcleaners* Campaign', p. 315.
52. *North London I.S. Women's Group Leaflet*, The Women's Library, LSE, 7SHR/D/1, Box 8; *Morning Star*, 11 August 1972; *Meeting at Longacre, 28/11/1970*, The Women's Library, 7SHR/D/2, Box 8; Lyddon, 'Militancy' 'Glorious Summer'; 'Introduction', in Feminist Review (Ed.) *Waged Work: a reader* (London: Virago), pp 1–10.; Colin Hay (2009) 'The Winter of Discontent Thirty Years On', *Political Quarterly*, 80(4), Vol. 80 (4), pp. 545–552.
53. Cockburn, 'The Material of Male Power'.
54. 'Conditions', *Shrew*, 3(9) (Oct. 1971); Arsenal Women's Liberation Workshop, 'Cleaners' Strike', *Shrew*, 4(5) (Oct. 1972); Sheila Rowbotham (2006) Cleaners' Organizing in Britain from the 1970s: a personal account, *Antipode*, 38(3), pp. 608–625.
55. 'Report on the Night Cleaners', *Spare Rib* (July 1972); *Unknown interview transcript with night cleaners, 'Ann' and 'Jean'*, The Women's Library, LSE, 7SHR/D/2.
56. 'Interview with May Hobbs', *Shrew*, 3(9) (Oct. 1971), p. 9.
57. Rowbotham, 'Cleaners Organizing in Britain', p. 615; Alexander, 'The *Nightcleaners* Campaign', p. 321.
58. 'Interview with May Hobbs'.
59. Roger Butler (1976) The Strike for Equal Pay––Trico-Folberth, Brentford, Middlesex, *AUEW Journal*, 43(7), p. 27; Geoffrey Sheridan, 'More Equal Pay', *Guardian*, 14 July 1976, p. 9.
60. Judith Cook, More Backing for the Equality Strikers, *Labour Weekly*, 6 Aug. 1976, p. 3.
61. Ibid.
62. National Executive Committee (1976) *Report of the Seventyfifth Annual Conference of the Labour Party, Blackpool, 1976*; Judith Hunt (1976), 'Equality for Women' Motion at Trades Union Congress, *Report of the 108th Annual Trades Union Congress, Brighton, September 6th to 10th, 1976* (London), pp. 467–468.
63. 'What Trico strikers need', *Morning Star*, 24 Aug. 1976.
64. David Turner & Helen Hewland, 'They've won!', *Morning Star*, 16 Oct. 1976
65. 'Trico Women Strike', *Shrew* (Autumn, 1976), p. 11.
66. *Spare Rib*, issue nos 49–53 (Aug.–Dec. 1976).
67. 'Trico Women Strike'; *Spare Rib*, issue nos 49–53.
68. 'Trico Women Strike'; *Trico Strike Committee Bulletin* (12 August 1976), TUC Library Collections, London Metropolitan University, http://www.unionhistory.info/britainatwork/emuweb/objects/nofdigi/tuc/imagedisplay.php?irn=1231&reftable=ecatalogue&refirn=781 (accessed 25 Oct. 2013).
69. Ibid.; Bel Mooney (1976) 'Trico Women's Strike', *New Statesman* (3 Sep.), p. 298; Helen Hewland, 'Say Equal Pay and Mean It': Trico call to TUC today, *Morning Star*, 7 Sep. 1976
70. *Trico Strike Committee Bulletin*; Hunt, '"Equality for Women" Motion', p. 467.

71. 'Trico Strike Committee Bulletin'.
72. *Photography: equal pay strike at Trico-Folberth*, Brentford (1976), TUC Collections, London Metropolitan University, http://www.unionhistory.info/Display.php?irn=7000151&QueryPage=AdvSearch.php (accessed 25 Oct. 2013); Monica Harvey, 'Victory at Trico!', *Socialist Worker*, 23 Oct. 1976.
73. 'Police Protect Unequal Pay', *Spare Rib*, 50 (Sep. 1976), p. 18; Jan O'Malley & Jill Nicholls (1976), 'We're out till we win', *Spare Rib*, 49 (Aug.), p. 20.
74. Ruth Pearson, Sundari Anitha & Linda McDowell, 'Chronology of Events', *Striking Women: Voices of South Asian women workers from Grunwick and Gate Gourmet*, http://www.leeds.ac.uk/strikingwomen/grunwick/chronology.
75. Ibid.
76. Ibid.
77. 'Indian Workers Solidarity Meeting, July 1978', in Brixton Black Women's Group, 'Britain-Africa-The Caribbean', *Women in Struggle* (London, 1978), Feminist Archive North, Leeds University, TUCRIC Box 1.
78. Bruley, *Women in Britain since 1900*, p. 168; Thane, 'Women and the 1970s', p. 181.
79. 'Get to that picket line!', *Socialist Worker*, 15 Oct. 1977.
80. Bruley, *Women in Britain since 1900*, pp. 167–168.
81. Ruth Pearson, Sundari Anitha & Linda McDowell (2010) 'Introduction', *Striking Women: voices of South Asian women workers from Grunwick and Gate Gourmet*, www.leeds.ac.uk/strikingwomen/introduction (accessed 8 Oct. 2013).
82. 'Grunwick Women', *Spare Rib*, 61 (Aug. 1977).
83. Brixton Black Women's Group, *Women in Struggle*.
84. Ibid.
85. 'Indian Workers Solidarity Meeting, July 1978'; Brixton Black Women's Group, *Women in Struggle*; Sheila Cunnison & Jane Stageman (1993) *Feminizing the Unions: challenging the culture of masculinity* (Aldershot: Avebury), pp. 107–108.
86. Philip Whitehead (1985) *The Writing on the Wall: Britain in the seventies* (London: Michael Joseph), pp. 216–219.
87. 'Grunwick Women', *Spare Rib*; Brixton Black Women's Group, *Women in Struggle*.
88. Amrit Wilson (1997) Finding a Voice: Asian women in Britain, in Mirza (Ed.) *Black British Feminism*, p. 35.
89. BBWG, 'Indian Workers Solidarity Meeting, July 1978'.
90. Ambalavener Sivanandan (1978) Grunwick (2), *Race and Class*, 19(3), pp. 289–294.
91. Ibid.
92. Clark, *The Struggle for the Breeches*.
93. Sivanandan, 'Grunwick (2)'.
94. Marc W. Steinberg (1996) Culturally Speaking: finding a commons between post-structuralism and the Thompsonian perspective, *Social History*, 21(2), pp. 193–214.
95. Liddington & Norris, *One Hand Tied Behind Us*; Clark, *The Struggle for the Breeches*.
96. Evans, *The Feminists*; Thompson, *The Chartists*; Liddington & Norris, *One Hand Tied Behind Us*.

Funding

This work was supported by the Arts and Humanities Research Council (grant number: AH/K502996/1).

White Women, Anti-Imperialist Feminism and the Story of Race within the US Women's Liberation Movement

Say Burgin

ABSTRACT
Histories are re-writing what Sherna Berger Gluck famously called the 'master historical narrative' of the US WLM, especially in historicizing the efforts of feminists of colour. This paper echoes this by exploring how white feminists embraced racial justice politics, particularly during the early 1970s, when it is often assumed that white feminists failed to enact racial justice. In historicizing the efforts of white anti-imperialist feminists in greater Boston, I maintain that the 'master historical narrative' wrote not only black, Chicana and multiracial feminisms out of history, but that it skewed our understanding of the race politics of white, US feminists.

One of the most significant debates amongst historians of the United States women's liberation movement concerns the ways in which race shaped this movement. In a 2002 special issue on 'Second Wave Feminism in the United States' in *Feminist Studies*, two of the movement's leading historians, Sara Evans and Becky Thompson, pointed out that newer histories reproduced problems associated with the movement's foundational accounts: they marginalized the ideas and activism of feminists of colour.[1] Even prior to this, in her widely-read 1998 article 'Whose Feminism? Whose History?', Sherna Berger Gluck lamented the continual telling of a stale version of the movement's history. A simplistic narration that highlighted an 'old litany' of feminist branches—liberal, socialist and radical—this 'master historical narrative' made little room for the work of feminists of colour, who were 'consequently left out of the histories of the early days of "the women's movement"'.[2] Beyond the eclipsing of much activism, though, many histories have been unable to impart a complex understanding of the racial implications of various feminist ideologies, strategies and goals, including those of white feminists. As Evans puts it, 'The fact that it took so long even to begin a widespread conversation among feminists about the meaning of differences of class and race is part of the story, too.'[3]

Over the past decade or so, numerous rich studies have appeared that have not only historicized black, Chicana, and multiracial feminist organizing in the 1960s, 1970s and 1980s, but have also provided a clearer sense of how race variously shaped women's paths to political activism, as well as their priorities, thinking and tactics.[4] This essay sees itself in concert with this important revisionist scholarship even while it works to problematize a particular trend within it. Exemplified through Evans' insistence that (white) women's liberationists 'took so long' to discuss class and race, newer histories now describe a movement in which white women spent a number of years unwilling or unable to recognize the importance of racial and class differences, only to be directly challenged on these points in the late-1970s by a growing number of feminist of colour. Winifred Breines, for instance, claims that Black Power drove a wedge between white and black women, and that 'contact' did not redevelop until the late 1970s and 1980s as powerful discourses around differences emerged.[5] While the story of race in the US women's liberation movement has grown in complexity and depth, it may also now be hardening into a simplistic narrative that pivots on a 'moment' of racial enlightenment and inclusiveness.

This article attempts to demonstrate that one of the ways in which the narrative of race relations within the movement remains problematic and simplistic is by inattention to anti-imperialist feminists. With the notable exception of Becky Thompson, most scholars of the movement have not taken seriously anti-imperialist analyses within the movement.[6] This is so despite the fact that such frameworks often allowed white feminists to connect issues of class, race and gender; to look beyond US borders; and to critique the racial politics of dominant feminist strands at the time. In this article, I attend to these dynamics through an examination of two groups—one, a loose group of white, anti-imperialist feminists in the Boston area in the early 1970s, and the other, women living underground as part of the militant group Weatherman (later, the Weather Underground) in the early 1970s. The first group converged around a number of feminist projects in Cambridge and Boston beginning in roughly 1970, including an International Women's Day demonstration that led to the occupation of a Harvard building and the creation of a feminist free school. Meanwhile, women in the Weather Underground began clearly articulating their feminist vision in 1973 within the pages of the Washington, DC-based feminist newspaper, *off our backs* (*oob*)—a city and a paper around which anti-imperialist feminists tended to coalesce. All of these women maintained links to anti-war and other New Left groups, and in fact they wanted to bring the anti-imperialist purview of the wider left to bear on the booming women's liberation movement, which meant they were sometimes dismissed as not 'real' feminists. Yet historicizing this groups of women and their feminist framework is not simply about insisting on the validity of their feminism or adding a new kind of feminist politics (to the 'old litany') that have been overlooked and ignored. These histories, in fact, help us complicate our understanding of the racial cognizance and concerns of the white-dominated women's liberation movement during its earlier years.

Boston-area women's liberationists were buzzing in the autumn of 1970. Already a hotbed of feminist activity with high-profile socialist feminist groups like Cell 16 and Bread and Roses, this city was beginning to attract a number of seasoned activists. Some, like Laura Tillem, who had organized within the Movement for a Democratic Society and had worked on the New Left-turned-feminist publication *The Rat*, left the bitterly divided New York feminist groups to participate in Bread and Roses. Others, like Laura Whitehorn, who had gone underground with Weather Underground, resurfaced in the Boston area. That fall, many women's liberationists were considering how to mark the tenth anniversary of the Vietnamese National Liberation Front. In addition, a number of activists had just returned from the Black Panther Party-hosted Revolutionary People's Constitutional Convention (RPCC). Taking place first in Philadelphia in early September and then two months later in Washington, DC, these conventions attracted large numbers of white women's liberationists from the East Coast, provided opportunities for the Panthers to demonstrate a commitment to women's and gay liberation, and, more generally, brought together a range of activists in order to re-imagine a more just and democratic United States. Though historian Anne Valk has argued that 'direct interaction at the RPCC' among white women's liberationists, gay liberationists, and Panther men and women 'exacerbated, rather than smoothed' the political differences among them, at least some Boston-area women's liberationists were buoyed by their participation in the events. They were inspired, in the words of women's liberationist Marla Erlien, to do 'something dramatic', and they set their sights on International Women's Day 1971.[7]

When the day arrived—Saturday 6 March—a rally was held at Massachusetts State House before the 150-plus crowd marched eastward towards Harvard University's campus in Cambridge. Most were not expecting what came next. Upon arriving at 888 Memorial Drive, the site of Harvard's Architectural Technology Workshop, the action's planners seized upon the building and declared it occupied. The building, organizers said in a statement, would serve as 'a women's center where women from all over will be able to meet with each other, exchange ideas and feelings, and determine what we need to do together'.[8] Among the hundreds of women involved in the ensuing ten-day occupation were members from Bread and Roses, Gay Women's Liberation, Weather Underground and other groups, but those few feminists who had planned the occupation necessarily did so in relative secrecy. Among them were Whitehorn and Erlien who carefully and surreptitiously met for months leading up to the occupation. They also canvassed women's groups in the area to let them know about an upcoming illegal action. Though organizers kept silent on most of the other details of the action, they knew that Boston feminists had been discussing the need for a women's centre for months. It had been difficult for women's liberation groups to find spaces for meetings and social gatherings. Area feminists were, thus, primed for this action, and their enthusiasm during the occupation came through via days of dancing, holding workshops, political organizing, childcare provisions for neighbourhood families and in providing support for lesbians.[9]

The development of a women's centre was the central goal for many, but for others, including at least one occupation organizer, the action served to connect the US women's liberation movement with larger anti-racist and anti-imperialist aims, including an end to the war in Vietnam. Upon arriving at the building, Laura Whitehorn provided a statement of solidarity with the people, particularly the women, of Vietnam, and she and the other organizers, who told the *Harvard Crimson* that they identified as 'feminists, anti-imperialists, socialists', had a list of demands directed at Harvard. The *Crimson* reported them as:

1. That Harvard build low-income housing on this, the Treeland site, in accordance with the demands of the Riverside community.
2. That Harvard provide a women's center to serve the needs of women in the Boston area.

3. That Harvard give us full use of this building, with full facilities (heat, plumbing, electricity, etc.), until it is necessary to tear it down in order to break ground for the Riverside low-income housing.[10]

Occupation organizers knew about the local Riverside community's ongoing struggle with Harvard to provide affordable housing for the largely black neighbourhood and, though some residents doubted the sincerity and effectiveness of this mandate, to organizers such a demand demonstrated solidarity with racial justice struggles and direct support for the needs of the local community.[11]

Tellingly, Whitehorn recalls that a fourth demand was made but quickly dropped—that Harvard cease any research connected to the US military and its war in Vietnam.[12] Arguably the most demanding of the mandates, to Whitehorn and undoubtedly to others it linked a fundamental institution within the US—academia—to the US's imperialist efforts abroad. As anti-imperialist feminists, she and others felt that they had a moral obligation to protest the US's war in Vietnam in whatever ways they could and that doing so must be a priority within the women's liberation movement. Though Whitehorn never expected the demand to be met, it was crucial to publicly link their local context to larger US imperialism:

> There we were in Boston, surrounded by MIT [Massachusetts Institute of Technology], Harvard. They both had war research facilities. I mean Henry Kissinger had been at Harvard.[13]

In fact, it had been Whitehorn who, setting her sights on Harvard as a target, had found 888 Memorial Drive for the occupation.[14]

For its part, Harvard was selective about which, if any, demands it would negotiate on, and its war research certainly did not enter into discussions. Only the second of the occupiers' demands, in fact, achieved a direct result from the Harvard occupation. Though Harvard had attempted to switch off the building's electricity and obtained an injunction in order to force the women to leave, several days into the occupation some women began to negotiate secretively with Harvard management. A few days later, occupiers voted on the options of persevering with their demands and occupation, or accepting a $5,000 donation from Susan Lyman, who was at that time the chairwoman of the Radcliffe College Board of Trustees. Though some, like Whitehorn, adamantly opposed taking the money—which was to be put towards the purchase of a building for a new women's centre—occupiers opted to do so, ending the occupation on 16 March. Several months later, in the autumn of 1971, 46 Pleasant Street was purchased and established as the Cambridge Women's Center, which is now the longest-running women's centre in the country.[15]

That the demand regarding Harvard's war research was readily abandoned by the larger group of (mostly) white women's liberationists signalled what, in the later life of the Cambridge Women's Center, became a clearer division between anti-imperialist and socialist feminists in the city. Feminists of both persuasions sought to challenge racism and sexism, supported nationalist groups like the Black Panthers, and felt that revolutionary change was needed in the US. However, they tended to differ in terms of their goals, the extent to which they included critiques of US imperialism within their political outlooks, and their general understanding of how revolutionary change would come about in the US.

Many, though certainly not all, white anti-imperialist feminists in the early 1970s maintained links with militant white groups like the Weather Underground. Reflecting on the work of one such woman, who left a similar group operating out of the Bay Area in the mid-1970s, Becky Thompson argues that white feminist participation in such groups 'reflect the reality that during the early 1970s, organizations in which white women could do anti-racist feminist work alongside feminists of color were scarce'.[16] Indeed, a lack of multiracial feminist coalition-building marked the early 1970s, but many militant white groups also attached great political value to whites organizing other whites against racism. In her research into feminist and black freedom activism in Washington, DC, Anne Valk found that, by the late 1960s, a number of the city's white feminists were 'heeding the message of SNCC [the Student Nonviolent Coordinating Committee] to concentrate their political skills on organizing against racism within white communities'.[17] A clear directive from SNCC, the Panthers and other nationalist groups, this was a key principle that guided anti-imperialist feminists, who were often frustrated by white women's liberationists' lack of attention to issues of racial injustice. Some, like Marilyn Buck, who served time in prison for assisting in Assata Shakur's escape from prison, preferred to remain within anti-imperialist groups that could sometimes be hostile to feminism rather than join women's liberation groups. Others, like Naomi Jaffe and Laura Whitehorn, participated in both kinds of efforts, and they saw their work within the women's liberation movement as attempts to organize other whites against racism, particularly by expanding feminists' purview to include an analysis of US empire and race.[18] Most feminists might articulate anti-racist positions, but, as Nancy Fraser has pointed out, the 'chief target' for the majority of (white) women's liberationists 'was the gender injustice of state-organized capitalism', which meant that race was often not central to their analyses.[19]

Anti-imperialist feminists, on the other hand, felt as though their political analyses centered on racism. As Marilyn Buck saw it:

> To be a serious anti-imperialist, one has to be antiracist. You can be an antiracist but not be an anti-imperialist. Anti-imperialist means trying to be an internationalist and believe in the right to self determination. To be an antiracist doesn't necessarily mean you believe in the right to one's own nation and the legal steps you might take to establish sovereignty. This is different than people who think that everybody has the right to be equal in society but that doesn't necessarily require major social change. I don't think you can be a very good antiracist and stay there because it is limited. It doesn't take on capitalist society.[20]

For white anti-imperialist feminists, then, the key was to put women's issues in the overall context of anti-imperialism, and they strove to connect issues of racism and sexism at home with the US's larger imperialist efforts to thwart self-determination for peoples of colour.

It must be stressed, however, that anti-imperialist feminism was not the creation of white feminists in the 1970s. Many African American women throughout the twentieth century provided gendered critiques of the racial injustices perpetrated within the US and connected their struggles with those of women struggling against colonialism around the world. Groups like the International Council of Women of the Darker Races linked issues of gender, imperialism abroad and white supremacy at home, while in the 1950s and 1960s women like Shirley Graham Du Bois and Lorraine Hansberry reflected on the significance of anti-colonial struggles in Africa for black women in the diaspora.[21] Meanwhile, given the US's colonization of indigenous lands, anti-imperialism was often the starting point for much American Indian and Chicana feminist organizing.[22] White anti-imperialist feminists, like those in Boston and in the Weather Underground, were influenced by the powerful critiques of black feminists like Angela Davis, as well as nationalist struggles in the US, Vietnam and elsewhere, but they consistently found themselves at odds with many other white feminists in terms of their feminist goals and strategies.

These differences in organizing principles and political ideology related to other important distinctions between anti-imperialist feminists, on the one hand, and socialist and other radical feminists, on the other. In particular, competing views on violence and its relationship to resistance almost always signified differing priorities and ideals. Often, such disputes highlighted rifts between feminists who viewed violence within the context of the state and those who analysed it in terms of gender norms. A case in point occurred when *oob* received an anonymous letter—one of several sent to a variety of news outlets—with information about plans to threaten the US government and corporations in order to secure the release of political prisoners. The letter left the editors at loggerheads. Received in January 1972, the letter explained that nine bombs had been planted in safe-deposit boxes in as many banks in San Francisco, New York and Chicago. Although one detonated early, all were constructed so as to detonate seven months after being set, a feat that, the letter said, could be used to 'kidnap property and offer it in exchange for the freedom of our people'.[23] *Oob* explained that it had not opened the letter until after they heard news of the bombs being found, but it had occasioned discussion 'in cheerful fang and claw oob style' on the 'bomb tactic'. In the end, 'two nearly opposite points of view' emerged. The first emphasized the risk to life involved in the use of bombs, insisted that 'it will be the clerks, the cleaning people, working people on their way to jobs' who would be hurt, and asked 'Why use the macho ego tactics of the past?'. The second underscored the idea that bombs might push an otherwise all-too-comfortable US public to 'make the choice that places humanity above property', and maintained that 'police department bomb squad' workers would be those most likely 'endangered', though they could 'refuse to dismantle' the bombs.[24] The latter point of view exemplified two key facets of anti-imperialist feminism: a nuanced and supportive view of armed resistance and an urgency around the release of political prisoners.

Similarly, while she was canvassing Boston women's groups to alert them to the upcoming occupation, Whitehorn recalls having multiple arguments with feminists about violence. Knowing that they could not divulge a great deal about the action, she and other occupation planners let others know that property damage and arrest were the key risks. She met with great resistance as she insisted that this property damage was not the same as armed struggle, but because 'the lines were drawn', most insisted that violent tactics were male-supremacist.[25] Having a more complex and supportive view of armed struggle stemmed from an understanding of how revolutionary change would take place within the US. Liz Horowitz, who moved to Boston in the early 1970s at the age of eighteen, got her bearings in the city by working first at the Cambridge Women's Center and quickly gravitated towards the anti-imperialist feminists connected to the Center. She remembers that she and others argued that, rather than taking place via 'a classical model of Marxism-Leninism', revolutionary change in the US would be led by peoples of colour, those who comprised what was often referred to as the 'internal colony' of the US.[26] She and other white anti-imperialist feminists, she recalls, 'felt that socialism in the way that Marx discussed did not fully take into account the way history, racism, and the nature of class had developed in the US'.[27] For them, then, any political action or analysis had to take into account the US's history of racism.[28]

Hence, many anti-imperialist feminists enthusiastically participated in establishing a feminist free school, the Women's School, out of the new Cambridge Women's Center. The Women's School opened in March 1972 and ran for twenty years, making it the longest-operating school of its kind in the country. Run mostly by feminist activists who donated their time to administer and teach the classes, the Women's School offered a huge range of courses over those two decades. A sampling includes: 'In Amerika They Call Us Dykes', 'Women and Their Bodies', 'The Middle East', 'Women's Literature', and 'Demystifying the Arms Race', as well as how-to classes in self-defence, nutrition, writing, auto mechanics, and general 'Fix It'.[29] Over the School's first few years—between 1972 and 1974—anti-imperialist feminists like Horowitz, Whitehorn and others were especially influential in the running of the school, and they staged a number of history-based classes that they hoped would, in Whitehorn's words, 'open white women's eyes'. Whitehorn recalls that they wanted to impart the lesson that:

> the key to making social change in the United States is for white people to act in solidarity with especially black people and other oppressed nationalities because the key things holding together the United States are its empire, which is based in white supremacy.[30]

Thus, their classes focused largely on African American history and included 'Black History', 'The Black Struggle and the White Radical Response', 'Resistance, Repression, Rebellion' and 'Women's History' classes that focused on black and working-class women.[31] When Whitehorn ran women's history courses with her comrades Jacqui Pine and Ginger Ryan, the readings included Friedrich Engels' *The Origin of the Family, Private Property, and the State*, Xeroxed excerpts from Gerda Lerner's collection *Black Women in White America*, various pieces from Toni Cade Bambara's *The Black Woman*, and Angela Davis' recently published and highly influential article, 'Reflections on the Black Woman's Role in the Community of Slaves'. Whitehorn remembers that many women who joined the classes expected to be learning about, for instance, suffragists, which exemplified why, through these classes, she and the others sought 'to redefine who we mean by women … because in those days, people would talk a lot about women's liberation and by women they meant white women'.[32]

Their other two key classes were more explicitly positioned vis-à-vis the problems that they perceived within the larger women's liberation movement. The description for 'The Black Struggle and White Radical Response' plainly linked it to anti-imperialist efforts and to general ignorance around racial justice struggles:

> We feel it is vitally important for the women's movement to study the history of black people and the roots of white racism for several reasons: (1) racism is one of the main props of the imperialist system; ([2]) black and third world people are the leading force today in the struggle against this system; and (3) sexism and racism reinforce each other and are closely linked in their origins.[33]

'Resistance, Repression, Rebellion' did not begin running until 1974, when Whitehorn first taught it with Susan Waysdorf in the spring and Horowitz taught it with Ryan in the autumn. Horowitz recalls that this course, in fact, grew alongside the 'burgeoning political line' of anti-imperialists who would later be involved with the Weather Underground's Prairie Fire initiative.[34] Focused specifically on the dialectic of repression and rebellion in US history, black history featured prominently within this class because, as the teachers wrote, this history 'provides some of the strongest and longest example[s] of a people in conflict with the state'. Yet, demonstrating the sure influence of Davis's article on enslaved women, they also sought to consider 'the role of women in maintaining the strength of the community and thus providing a base of resistance'.[35]

Perhaps unsurprisingly, over the years that these classes ran, many viewed the Women's School as peculiar within the larger sphere of the women's liberation movement. Though the Women's Center, in essence, hosted the Women's School, not many individuals spent their energies on both. The Women's School attracted 'most of the women who were more anti-imperialist', which goes some way towards explaining why the two institutions shared an acrimonious relationship. Horowtiz remembers that the Women's School folks 'were always kind of castigated' by the Center, whose organizers generally believed Women's School activists were not actually interested in 'women's issues'.[36] For their part, anti-imperialist feminists often felt frustrated with the Center's structure, and sometimes the School and Center became divided over race-related issues. Whitehorn thought that Jo Freeman's widely-read article 'The Tyranny of Structurelessness' could have been written about the meetings of the Women's Center committee, to which the School had to send a representative. She and others drifted away from the School in the mid-1970s—both to help with community defence efforts as the crisis over school integration took hold in Boston and to take part when the Weather Underground was redeveloped as the Prairie Fire Organizing Committee in 1975.[37]

But before they left the School, anti-imperialist feminists found themselves divided from the Women's Center committee over another issue—one that divided feminists across the nation and yet prompted a clearer picture of the contours of anti-imperialist feminism for white women's liberationists. In May 1973, white fugitive Jane Alpert wrote to *oob* asking that they publish her open letter to the women of the Weather Underground and a theoretical piece she had written called 'Mother Right'. Alpert had been living underground since skipping bail in 1970 when she had pled guilty to charges related to a number of bombings she had helped to carry out against military buildings in 1969. She wrote publically in 1973 to announce and explain her transformation from 'leftist' to 'radical feminist'.[38] It is no coincidence that Alpert wrote to *oob* and that doing so touched off a national debate over the politics of women's liberation. According to Anne Valk, Washington area feminists were known for their anti-war commitments and anti-imperialist politics. Many, including prominent members like Marilyn Webb and Charlotte Bunch, had years of experience with the New Left, via Students for a Democratic Society and the radical think-tank the Institute for Policy Studies. Like many of their counterparts in Beantown, feminists in the capitol city often identified as anti-imperialists and enacted such politics through a continued commitment to anti-war work, solidarity efforts with the Black Panther Party and other nationalist groups, and in maintaining their ties with the Weather Underground. *Off our backs* was a significant vehicle through which the city's feminist politics were broadcasted to the rest of the nation. In obliging Alpert's request for publication, it also provided a platform for one of the most high-profile contestations over anti-imperialist feminism.[39] Alpert's pieces yielded praise and critique alike. The rejection of the left and essentialist notions that undergirded 'Mother Right'—for Alpert believed 'that what basically unites us as women is our common biology'—drew a range of supportive and disbelieving letters.[40]

It was her open letter to Weather Underground women, however, that brought to the fore, unfolding across the pages of *oob*, a debate about anti-imperialist feminism around which questions feminism's relationship to the male left, and to wider critiques of US empire, were central. Speaking plainly to her 'Sisters in the Weather Underground', Alpert wrote that the crux of the problem was that 'you allow men to rule your politics'. She suggested that women in WU fooled themselves into believing that they had control of the organization and that their male comrades had changed their sexist ways. Alpert rejected their insistence that 'if I really practiced sisterhood I wouldn't make demands of you in the name of feminism, but would respect your political ... path as equally valid as my own'. Rather, she underscored the sexism of particular men in the organization, singling out individuals like Bill Ayers and Mark Rudd and detailing aspects of their chauvinism. In exposing information about individuals living underground, Alpert broke a cardinal rule of leftist fugitives—to never divulge *any* information about those living underground as the most innocuous details could jeopardize one's ability to elude authorities. Anticipating rebuke, Alpert insisted:

> I expose hitherto unknown information about the Weather Underground, not merely to shock but also to challenge other women to confront the oppression we face in the left. I urge women to leave the left and leftist causes and begin working for women.

To drive her point home, she shared much detail about her relationship with Sam Melville, the lover with whom she had carried out bombings. Melville had been horribly sexist and controlling, she contended, and he had threatened to leave her if she did not conspire with him. That he had died in the Attica prison uprising that took place less than two years previous made her now-infamous ending to this letter all the more bitter:

> And so, my sisters in Weatherman, *you* fast and organize and demonstrate for Attica. Don't send me news clippings about it, don't tell me how much those deaths moved you. I will mourn the loss of 42 male supremacists no longer.[41]

As with 'Mother Right', this open letter elicited a range of responses. Collectively, they point towards the serious debates being had, the country over, around the compatibility of feminist and anti-imperialist politics. Those folks at the Women's School, like many others around the country, were shocked with the callousness with which Alpert dismissed the Attica uprising and angered that she disclosed so much about people still living underground. Yet they found themselves in heated disagreement with their counterparts in the Women's Center.[42] Cell 16's Betsy Warrior and a group who identified themselves as 'X-Weatherwomen' indicated their pleasure in hearing of Alpert's public exit from the left, while 'three Bay Area lesbians' wrote to register their feeling that however difficult feminists find the left 'it is still wrong to discard all aspects of anti-imperialist, anti-racist thought'.[43] They likely concurred with another letter writer, Emani Thompson, whose partner had been shot multiple times during the Attica uprising. She spoke of the pain Alpert's letter caused her and defended her ability to be a feminist *and* supporter of the uprising:

> If you cannot 'mourn the loss of 42 male supremacists,' at least do not ask me to rejoice in the imprisonment and near death of my partner ... my ability to be a serious feminist and still relate to the struggle of the Attica Brothers is my struggle against my oppressions as I understand them.[44]

For their part, women in the Weather Underground offered a public response, printed via *oob* in the following issue.[45] Unsurprisingly, they were frustrated with Alpert's revelations but said they 'recognize[d] the need for a critical look at our herstory and our present practice––and to acknowledge our debt to the Women's movement'. Their letter was intended, in fact, 'to mark a change––to commit ourselves to the cause of women'. They had erred in the past in their denials of women's oppression (particularly white women's oppression) but had increasingly felt 'the need for women working and living together––the lesson of the women's movement'. They would, however, continue to struggle alongside men, though they knew that in doing so many women's liberationists might reject them and their brand of feminism:

> We realize that many women distrust us because we work with men. To some this puts into question not only our loyalties to other women but our very womanness. But the last few years we have both learned and suffered from our brothers in our family, struggled with and been passive to them, loved and been alienated and fought with them. We claim the integrity of our choice to work with them, and do not intend to either defend or reject them.

Thus, like Alpert, WU women confessed to a kind of conversion when it came to feminism and, like Alpert and many other white women's liberationists, experiences in the left had prompted this change, particularly widespread sexism. However, they pushed back against Alpert's either-or insistence with regard to feminism and leftist struggles. Much as Emani Thompson had, they rejected the idea that their participation in struggles against the war in Vietnam or political repression negated their feminism. To insist on such divisions could only aid in the repression of political movements, the WU feminists wrote, for 'If women come to deny the Attica brothers their full place as warriors, their beautiful humaneness in the liberation of the prison yard then we are turned against our comrades while our enemies laugh'.

As with Women's School feminists, this both-and approach (feminism should include *both* a dedication to feminism *and* commitment to ending racism and imperialism) was based in the knowledge that systems of oppression could not be viewed as separate dynamics. Racism, sexism and imperialism were connected, and WU feminists implied that the larger white feminist movement had not attended to these realities:

> We cannot liberate ourselves in some vacuum of our self-conception. The great majority of women in the world are bowed down by the questions of survival for themselves and their children's self-determination in their daily lives. The liberation of women cannot be realized while the U.S. empire remains the main consumer of the worlds food, resources, and energy. Our movement will have to take on the questions of state power. That is why our future is tied to the liberation of the Third World—for it is their struggles which, in our lifetime, have shaken the grip of empire ... Our feminist politics must embrace women of other cultures, learn from them the way they see the world, support in action their fight for liberation of their people, from repression, cultural penetration and genocide.

In attempting to demonstrate why the destruction of sexism necessarily entailed the destruction of the US's status as world super-power—a system based in racist exploitation—these women thus not only affirmed the compatibility of the left and feminism. They made clear their view that the liberation of women was inextricably bound to the liberation of peoples of colour the world over.

Clearly, many of the white feminists associated with both the Weather Underground and the Women's School demonstrated great racial cognizance and carried out important racial justice activity in the early 1970s. Their commitment to anti-imperialism prompted them to address what they felt were the political shortcomings of the largely white women's liberation movement: Euro-centric ideas and aims; a lack of understanding around the ways in which race and class underpinned the US's imperial efforts; an obliviousness to black history and its political importance for the present moment; and a denial of the connections between the left and feminism. These important interventions are overlooked, though, so long as the story of race in the US women's liberation movement is seen as one in which white women do not 'wake up' to racism until the late 1970s. Such an oversimplified narrative of redemption actually leaves much of the 'master historical narrative' intact. The dominant timeline prior to the mid-1970s—at which point, according to many, women's liberation was on the decline—goes largely unexamined. This narrative also falsely implies that there was a historical 'moment' at which racial divisions were overcome within contemporary feminist efforts.

Anti-imperialist feminists in Boston and in the Weather Underground help to demonstrate how much more complex ideas about race—indeed ideas about feminism—were in the movement. I am not merely trying to assert that that we should recognize that *some* white women's liberationists were active racial justice activists *too*. Rather, my concern relates to what may be a tendency within more recent historiography to come to a consensus about the story of race within the women's liberation movement, one that tells a *progressive* history of white women's consciousness around race. I am deeply sceptical of the notion that white feminists gradually gained critical race consciousness—not just because this is an overly simplistic narrative that collapses a great deal of infighting, denial and debate, but also because it relies on overly deterministic notions around nationalist movements like Black Power (and the hindrances they must have placed on women's relationships across race).[46]

For, in the end, the history of anti-imperialist feminists reveals that the 'master historical narrative' has skewed our understanding, not just of the rich histories of feminist organizing by Asian American, American Indian, African American, Chicana and other women of colour, but also by white women. It has written out of history the anti-racist interventions that *did* take place within many groups operating in the early years of the movement. That is, our misunderstanding of the racial politics of the Second Wave in the US includes not only a relative ignorance of feminist of colour organizing but also a distorted take on the work of many white anti-racist feminists.[47] In this way, the histories I have related here let us know that, in our attempts to overhaul the 'master historical narrative', we cannot simply 'add on' feminist organizing by women of colour and a subsequent willingness to address racism by white women. We must, in fact, deeply reconsider white feminist organizing, as well.

Acknowledgements

I would like to thank Kate Dossett, Simon Hall, Aviva Stahl and Anne-Marie Stewart for sharing their thoughts with me on the ideas in this paper, as well as Sue Bruley, Laurel Forster and two anonymous reviewers for their insights, suggestions and comments on an earlier draft of this paper. Thanks go, too, to the Feminist Archive North, its volunteers and excellent Periodicals Collection.

Funding

This work was supported by the Leeds Humanities Research Institute, the British Association of American Studies, the Economic History Society and the School of History at the University of Leeds.

Notes

1. Sara Evans (2002) Re-viewing the Second Wave, *Feminist Studies*, 28, pp. 258–268, p. 267; Becky Thompson (2002) Multiracial Feminism: recasting the chronology of second wave feminism, *Feminist Studies*, 28, pp. 336–361.
2. Sherna Berger Gluck (1998) Whose Feminism, Whose History?, in N. Naples (Ed.) *Community Activism, Community Politics: organizing across race, class, and gender* (New York: Routledge), pp. 31–56, pp. 31–32, 36.
3. Evans, 'Re-viewing the Second Wave', p. 266.
4. Benita Roth (2004) *Separate Roads to Feminism: black, chicana and white feminist movements in America's second wave* (Cambridge: Cambridge University Press); Kimberly Springer (2005) *Living for the Revolution: black feminist organizations, 1968–1980* (Durham: Duke University Press); Premilla Nadasen (2005) *Welfare Warriors: the welfare rights movement in the United States* (New York: Routledge); Anne Enke (2007) *Finding the Movement: sexuality, contested space and feminist activism* (Durham: Duke University Press); (2003) Smuggling Sex Through the Gates: race, sexuality and the politics of space in second wave feminism, *America Quarterly*, 55(4), pp. 635–667; Becky Thompson (2001) *A Promise and a Way of Life: white antiracist activism* (Minneapolis: University of Minnesota Press), pp. 113–170; Winifred Breines (2006) *The Trouble Between US: an uneasy history of white and black women in the feminist movement* (New York: Oxford University Press); Anne M. Valk (2008) *Radical Sisters: second wave feminism and black liberation in Washington, DC* (Champaign: University of Illinois Press).
5. Breines, *The Trouble Between Us*, esp. chs 3–5.
6. Though some scholars have briefly discussed anti-imperialist feminism, they have rarely discussed it in any detail or worked to distinguish it from socialist feminism. See for instance, Evans, *Tidal Wave*, p. 143; Barbara Epstein (1980) Thoughts on Socialist Feminism in 1980, *New Political Science*, 1(4), pp. 25–35; Nancy Fraser (2009) Feminism, Capitalism and the Cunning of History, *New Left Review*, 56, pp. 97–117. Thompson, on the other hand, explores 'white women activists who, in the late 1960s and early 1970s, chose to work in anti-imperialist, anti-racist organizations connected with Black Power groups rather than in overwhelmingly white feminist contexts', in her book *A Promise and a Way of Life*, p. 115.
7. Laura Tillem, phone interview with the author, 14 August 2011, Wichita, USA, and Leeds, UK; Laura Whitehorn, phone interview with the author, 27 July 2011, New York, USA, and Leeds, UK; George Katsiaficas (2001) Organization and Movement: the case of the Black Panther Party and the Revolutionary People's Constitutional Convention of 1970, in Kathleen Cleaver & George Katsiaficas (Eds) *Liberation, Imagination and the Black Panther Party* (New York: Routledge), pp. 141–155; Valk, *Radical Sisters*, p. 131; Marla Erlien interview in Susan Rivo (director) *Left On Pearl* (888 Women's History Project) Fine Cut edition, in author's possession.
8. Katherine L. Day & the *Crimson* Staff, 'Women's Group Seizes Harvard Building', *The Harvard Crimson*, 8 March 1971, http://www.thecrimson.com/article/1971/3/8/womens-group-seizes-harvard-building-brbrbdemand/. Whitehorn recalls that there were a couple of hundred women who arrived to take over the building: Laura Whitehorn, phone interview with the author, 21 December 2011, New York, USA, and Lincoln, USA. See also her remembrances: 'Laura Whitehorn on the Takeover of 888 Memorial Drive', *Left On Pearl Blog*, http://leftonpearl.blogspot.co.uk/2013/10/laura-whitehorn-on-takeover-of-888.html.

9. Laura Whitehorn, phone interview with the author, 21 December 2011; Rivo, *Left on Pearl*; and Day, 'Women's Group Seizes Harvard Building'. See also Daphne Spain (2011) Women's Rights and Gendered Spaces in 1970s Boston, *Frontiers*, 32(1), pp. 165–167.
10. Laura Whitehorn, email interview with the author, 26 March 2013; Rivo, *Left On Pearl*; Katherine L. Day & the *Crimson* Staff, 'Women's Group Seizes Harvard Building'. See also, Breines, *The Trouble Between Us*, pp. 101–102; Spain, 'Women's Rights', pp. 166–167.
11. Laura Whitehorn, phone interview with the author, 21 December 2011; J. Anthony Day, 'Graham Denies Alliance' *Harvard Crimson*, 10 March 1971, http://www.thecrimson.com/article/1971/3/10/graham-denies-alliance-psaundra-graham-president/ (accessed 30 Oct. 2014).
12. Laura Whitehorn, email interview with the author, 26 March 2013.
13. Interview in Rivo, *Left on Pearl*.
14. Ibid.
15. Rivo, *Left On Pearl*; Laura Whitehorn, phone interview with the author, 21 December 2011; Spain, 'Women's Rights', pp. 165–167. See also the Cambridge Women's Center website: http://cambridgewomenscenter.org/aboutus.html.
16. Thompson, *A Promise*, pp. 126–127.
17. Valk, *Radical Sisters*, p. 65.
18. Ibid. pp. 122–125. On the need for whites to organize against racism within white communities, see for instance, Stokely Carmichael & Charles Hamilton (1967) *Black Power: the politics of liberation* (New York: Random House). Many black feminists similarly argued that fighting racism was the responsibility of whites. See, for instance, The Combahee River Collective Statement (2000 [1983]) in Barbara Smith (Ed.) *Home Girls: a black feminist anthology* (New Brunswick: Rutgers University Press), pp. 264–274.
19. Fraser, 'Feminism, Capitalism and the Cunning of History', p. 104.
20. Thompson, *A Promise*, p. 130.
21. Scholarship on the organizing of feminists of colour has, thus, often paid much more attention to anti-imperialist politics than have histories of white-dominated groups in the women's liberation movement. See for instance, Kate Dossett (2008) *Bridging Race Divides: black nationalism, feminism, and integration in the United States, 1896–1935* (Gainesville: University of Florida Press), pp. 24–33; Gerald Horne & Margaret Stevens (2009) Shirley Graham Du Bois: portrait of the black woman artist as a revolutionary, in Dayo F. Gore, Jeanne Theoharris, & Komozi Woodard (Eds) *Want to Start a Revolution? Radical women in the black freedom struggle* (New York: New York University Press), pp. 95–114.
22. See for instance, Paula Gunn Allen (1986) Who Is Your mother? Red roots of white feminism, in *Sacred Hoop: recovering the feminine in American Indian traditions* (Boston: Beacon Press), pp. 209–221; Roth, *Separate Roads to Feminism*, pp. 129–177; Elizabeth Castle (2010) 'The Original Gangster': the life and times of Red Power activist Madonna Thunder Hawk, in Dan Berger (Ed.) *The Hidden 1970s Histories of Radicalism* (New Brunswick: Rutgers University Press), pp. 267–283, pp. 268–269); Thompson, 'Multiracial Feminism', pp. 338–341.
23. 'The 9th Key & Thoughts on Bombs', *off our backs*, January 1972, p. 14. In 1986, the former physicist and anti-war activist Ronald Kaufman, who had been living under a different name since 1971, was arrested by police in Los Angeles. See Steven Esposito, 'Time Bomber: The Forgotten Yippie', *The Freeman*, 17 July 2013, http://fee.org/freeman/detail/time-bomber-the-forgotten-yippie; John O'Brien, 'Bank Bomb Suspect from '70s Arrested', *Chicago Tribune*, 17 July 1986, http://articles.chicagotribune.com/1986-07-17/news/8602200779_1_bombing-charges-explosive-devices-ronald-kaufman.
24. 'The 9th Key'. By 1972, debates over the tactic of property bombing were as commonplace as bombings themselves. See also Wade Greene, 'The Militants Who Play with Dynamite', *New York Times*, 25 Oct. 1970, p. SM20.
25. Laura Whitehorn, phone interview with the author, 21 December 2011.
26. Liz Horowitz, phone interview with the author, 23 August 2011, New York, USA and Leeds, UK. On 'internal colony', see Carmichael and Hamilton, *Black Power*.
27. Liz Horowitz, email interview with the author, 25 March 2013.

28. Space constraints do not allow for a discussion of the limitations of such thinking here. However, see, Say Burgin (2013) *The Workshop as the Work: white anti-racism organising in 1960s, 70s, and 80s United States social movements* (PhD thesis, University of Leeds), pp. 190–191; David Gilbert, Laura Whitehorn & Marilyn Buck (2002) *Enemies of the State: an interview with anti-imperialist political prisoners* (Montreal & Toronto: Abraham Guillen Press & Arm the Spirit).
29. See Boxes 4 and 5, as well as *'Please come to a meeting of the Women's School, March 3'*, 1973 [1972]), 3 and 1, Box, 1, Folder 40: *History of Women's School: Background Information*: History of Women's School, Women's School Records, 1971–1992, M23, (Archives and Special Collection), Northeastern University, Boston (hereafter, WSR).
30. Laura Whitehorn, phone interview with the author, 27 July 2011.
31. Box 2, Folder 100: *Course and Teacher Lists 1972*; Box 2, Folder 107: *Course and Teacher Lists 1973*; Box 2, Folder 126: *Class Descriptions Spring 1974*; Box 8, Folder 339: *1972 Winter/Spring*, WSR.
32. Laura Whitehorn, phone interview with the author, 27 July 2011. Box 2, Folder 133: *Women in America Course Outline Spring 1974*; Box 2, Folder 92: *Black History Readings*; Box 2, Folder 117: *Black History Readings Summer 1973*, WSR.
33. *'Please come to a meeting of the Women's School'*: 3 and 1, Box, 1, Folder 40: *History of Women's School: Background Information*, 197?, WSR.
34. Liz Horowitz, phone interview with the author, 23 August 2011. Prairie Fire was a nation-wide anti-imperialist effort stemming from the publication of the same name by many Weather Underground members. See Dan Berger (2006) *Outlaws of America: the Weather Underground and the politics of solidarity* (Oakland: AK Press), pp. 183–198; Weather Underground (1974) *Prairie Fire: the politics of revolutionary anti-imperialism* (Communications Co.).
35. Box 2, Folder 126: *Class Descriptions Spring 1974*, WSR.
36. Liz Horowitz, phone interview with the author, 23 August 2011.
37. Laura Whitehorn, phone interview with the author, 27 July 2011. 'The Tyranny of Structurelessness' was originally published in 1970 under Jo Freeman's pseudonym, 'Joreen', and has been digitized and reprinted in many places. See, for instance, Duke University Libraries' *Women's Liberation Movement Print Culture* digitized collection: http://library.duke.edu/digitalcollections/wlmpc_wlmms01018/.
38. Jane Alpert (1972) Letter from the Underground, *off our backs* (May-June), pp. 6–7, 22, 26–28, at p. 6.
39. Valk, *Radical Sisters*, pp. 60–65; Alice Echols (1989) *Daring to Be Bad: radical feminism in America, 1967–1975* (Minneapolis: University of Minnesota Press), pp. 220–228
40. Alpert, 'Letter from the Underground', p. 6. For responses, see 'Responses to Jane Alpert', *off our backs*, July-Aug. 1972, pp. 24–26; 'Alpert Response', *off our backs*, Sep. 1973, pp. 30–31.
41. All quotes taken from Alpert, 'Letter from the Underground', pp. 6–7.
42. Laura Whitehorn, phone interview with the author, 27 July 2011.
43. 'Alpert Responses', pp. 30–31; 'Responses to Jane Alpert', p. 25.
44. 'Alpert Responses', p. 30.
45. 'Responses to Jane Alpert', pp. 2–3. All quotes from the WU women's response taken from this source.
46. Breines' narrative is a good example of such over-determined ideas: see *The Trouble Between Us*.
47. Thompson also makes this point: see Thompson, 'Multiracial Feminism'; *A Promise*, pp. 115–142.

'A Job That Should Be Respected': contested visions of motherhood and English Canada's second wave women's movements, 1970–1990

Lynne Marks, Margaret Little, Megan Gaucher and T.R. Noddings

ABSTRACT
This article focuses on the forgotten voices of marginalized feminist mothers—those active in welfare rights groups. These activists were primarily poor single mothers who understood motherhood differently from more mainstream feminists. Whilst they echoed mainstream feminist demands for childcare, they also supported women's right to stay at home with their children, emphasizing the role of the state. This presented a serious class-based critique in a society that increasingly saw stay-at-home motherhood as a middle-class option. This article focuses upon working-class mothers' groups, thus problematizing dominant feminist discourses and developing a more diverse history of second wave feminism in Canada.

Introduction: second waves

There are many ways to mother and many visions of how a society should support mothers. As scholars begin to explore the history of the second wave women's movement in Canada we are starting to recognize that there was more than one movement and more than one feminist understanding of motherhood.[1] Once the voices of women marginalized by class, race and indigeneity are more fully included in the history of the second wave women's movement many of the debates become more complex, and many assumptions questioned. While motherhood was not the only issue up for debate, it was a significant fault line between the mainstream women's movement and more marginalized activist feminist voices.

This article focuses on the voices of one particular group of marginalized feminist mothers—those active in welfare rights groups. These activists were primarily poor single mothers who tended to understand motherhood differently from more mainstream feminists. They echoed mainstream feminist demands for childcare and adequate retraining options, which would permit single mothers to enter the workforce if they chose to do so. However, they also very much supported women's right to stay at home with their children, if that was their choice, with adequate financial and institutional supports. The differences between these welfare rights activists and the mainstream women's movement were very real, since the latter argued that women's equality could only be realized if women left the home and entered into the paid workforce. Mainstream feminists were not a monolithic group, although they were predominantly white and middle class. For the majority the emphasis on paid work was rooted in support for a liberal 'equal rights' variant of feminism, while socialist feminists came at the issue with a different ideological lens, but nonetheless viewed paid work as essential to women's liberation. Mainstream and welfare rights feminists had very different understandings of motherwork and paid work, the meaning of equality for women and the role the state should play in improving their lives. The welfare rights activists were part of a long tradition of 'difference feminism' that focused on women's biological and or cultural differences from men, and often on their need for state support to accommodate these differences. This form of feminism attracted middle class support in certain contexts, but had particular resonance with many low-income mothers.[2]

For the low-income mothers discussed here, feminist activism around motherhood included perspectives we now find unfamiliar, but that were rooted in the realities of many poor women's lives. While some sought childcare and job retraining to enable them to find paid work, many rejected the low paid tedious work that left them with an exhausting 'double day' of labour. They also vocally challenged early provincial government attempts to declare mothers with young children 'employable', and fought for the right to remain at home to raise their children and to receive reasonable levels of state support to do so. If they sought childcare, it was to offer respite from what they viewed as their difficult but crucial role as mothers. They presented a serious class-based critique in a society that increasingly saw stay-at-home motherhood as an option only available to upper and middle-class married women. They were feminist activists, marching in International Women's Day parades and challenging patriarchy. Many mainstream feminists, both liberal and socialist, did not however see these mothers' struggles as fitting within second wave feminist paradigms. In the US context Rosalyn Baxandall has noted that low-income African-American mothers' activist groups were ignored by scholars of second wave feminism, because with their focus on their roles as mothers they did not fit dominant notions of feminism.[3]

In the context of recent Canadian history, the voices of the welfare rights mothers who lost out in the debates chronicled here have been largely forgotten. Indeed today's 'culture wars', in which feminism is associated with women's right to work outside the home and stay-at-home motherhood is linked to conservative Christian values, leave no culturally intelligible space for the perspectives of welfare rights activists who were able to avoid such binaries as they sought feminist solutions that worked for them as poor women and as mothers.[4]

Scholars have noted that the first wave women's movement both in the US and in English Canada had a very clear position regarding motherhood. The majority of first wave feminists were white, elite women who embraced a maternalist brand of 'difference' feminism in which their mothering role justified both their receiving the vote and their involvement in public policy. Because of the value maternalist feminists placed on the mothering role they believed all mothers should have the opportunity to stay at home and mother their children. As a result they were strong advocates for welfare programs for poor white, morally deserving mothers to permit them to remain in the home. At the same time, most maternalists were opposed to public childcare options because they drew mothers out of the home.[5]

American scholars note that mainstream second wave white feminists may have had a different vision than their first wave sisters but one that was equally limited.[6] Since mainstream second wave feminists understood stay-at-home motherhood as a major source of women's oppression, they focused on economic independence through participation in the paid workforce as the key to improving the lives of all women.[7] They promoted social policies that would improve women's working conditions (e.g., pay equity, employment equity, and childcare). However, American scholars have come to recognize that the mainstream white movement did not speak for all women. The African American women's movement, the Chicana women's movement, working-class feminism and the welfare rights movement looked very different from each other, and from the mainstream women's movement.[8] African American women and Chicana women viewed women's role in the family less as a source of oppression than as a source of pride, as well as a bulwark against a racist society.[9] Many of these women, particularly those in welfare rights groups, were very critical of employment as the only solution to women's problems. They recounted their experiences of poorly-paid jobs in which they faced sexual and racial harassment, while some spoke of their pride as mothers and their desire to mother full-time.[10] As a result scholars Nancy Fraser and Linda Gordon have cautioned feminists about embracing a popular discourse that views dependency as a negative for all adults, with the only legitimate option being economic independence through wage labour. What this has meant, according to Fraser and Gordon, is 'the occlusion and devaluation of women's unwaged domestic and parenting labour'.[11]

While we know a fair bit about these issues in the American context the tensions between mainstream second-wave English Canadian feminists and marginalized women during the 1970s and 1980s over questions of motherhood remain largely unknown.[12] This article takes an initial look at these issues by exploring differences and tensions between the National Action Committee on the Status of Women (NAC), the most visible representation of the Canadian mainstream women's movement in the 1970s and 1980s, and several welfare rights activist groups (the Mother-Led Union, the Mothers Action Group, the Family Benefits Work Group, BC's Welfare Rights Coalition, and Wages for Housework). All of these groups, with the exception of the last (WFH) were entirely or primarily composed of low-income mothers, and in some cases of those advocating on their behalf. The Welfare Rights Coalition was based in Vancouver, and Wages for Housework had locals in several Canadian cities, although its Toronto local appears to have been the most active. The other groups were Toronto-based, although some included locals in other Ontario cities.

Wendy McKeen has looked at earlier welfare rights activist mothers in the late 1960s and early 1970s, and the relationship between their perspectives and those of grassroots and mainstream feminist groups.[13] Both McKeen and Jill Vickers et al. have explored tensions between NAC and one of the groups we discuss here, Wages for Housework, but the other groups have remained largely invisible.[14] In finding sources about these groups we are indebted to the Canadian Women's Movement Archives in Ottawa which houses papers of a huge range of large and small feminist organizations. We have also examined mainstream and feminist newspapers of the period.[15] We realize the groups we have identified probably represent the tip of the iceberg in regard to low-income mothers' activism in Canada. As part of our larger project we will conduct oral history interviews with activists, but the current paper is based on the rich archival source base.

The National Action Committee on the Status of Women

The National Action Committee on the Status of Women (NAC) was formed in 1972 following the release of the report of the Canadian Royal Commission on the Status of Women. Its first objective was to monitor the implementation of the Royal Commission's recommendations. It began as a loose coalition of thirty women's groups from across the country and by 1982 had 230 affiliated women's groups. Annual general meetings were dynamic and often acrimonious events, where women's groups from across the country, representing many diverse interests and ideologies, attempted to develop a common feminist position on the leading equity issues of the day. There has been some scholarly attention to NAC's history, most notably Jill Vickers et al.'s *Politics As If Women Mattered*.[16]

While tensions between NAC and low income women's groups mirror similar American patterns, the Canadian movement was in many ways distinct. One difference is the greater impact that socialist feminists had on the ideology and politics of the mainstream women's movement in Canada.[17] While liberal feminists, who tend to focus on gaining greater equality for women in existing institutions (most particularly the workplace), played a central role in the creation of NAC, by the early to mid 1980s socialist feminists, who had always been active in the Canadian movement, took a more central role.[18] Socialist feminists have focused more attention on issues of unpaid work than have liberal feminists, providing an important analysis of women's unpaid work, including motherwork, housework and a range of other essential caring activities. While arguing for the need to recognize and value this work, socialist feminists also viewed the fact women did this crucial, unpaid, undervalued work as a major source of their oppression.[19] They therefore saw the solution to women's oppression in socializing caring work, for example through universal childcare, and by having women enter the paid workforce. As Lisa Pasolli's scholarship on the child care movement of this era makes clear, many socialist feminists saw childcare as a collective solution to what they viewed as the 'anti-social' privatized family of modern capitalist society.[20]

During this post-war Keynesian Fordist era characterized by welfare state expansion and an expanding labour movement, those fully entitled to state support as 'worker-citizens' were members of the paid workforce, thus further justifying a focus among both socialist and liberal feminists on encouraging mothers to move from the privatized home into the workforce.[21] Thus while socialist feminist analysis was in many ways distinct from that of liberal feminists, their solutions similarly focused on policies that challenged women's dependency and encouraged participation in the paid workforce. Thus, despite real ideological differences between English Canadian liberal and socialist feminists that could at times lead to bitter debates within NAC, they were able to develop clear policy recommendations to encourage women to enter the paid workforce, recommendations that they then lobbied the federal government to implement.

For example, NAC recommended changes to Canadian tax policy to eliminate the married exemption that married wage earners (usually husbands) could claim, because this promoted women's dependency upon a husband and discouraged women from seeking paid work. NAC wanted funds from the married exemption to be redirected to an increase in family allowances and the refundable child tax credit, and a childcare expense deduction.[22] While the latter was a benefit only for women in the paid workforce, increases in the child tax credit and family allowances would benefit both stay-at-home mothers and mothers in the paid workforce, while also recognizing the value of the unpaid, caring work of women. In addition, NAC recognized the serious poverty facing women on welfare, the majority of whom were single mothers at home. In 1979 NAC reaffirmed an earlier commitment to reducing women's and child poverty by advocating an increase in welfare rates.[23]

NAC was also concerned about the inequalities faced by older women who had devoted their lives to unpaid caring work. They were particularly supportive of pensions for homemakers, who were often left in poverty when their husbands died or left them. Nonetheless contentious debates over this issue reflected ambivalence about the role of women in the home. For example, NAC argued that the state should pay for pension contributions for women with children under seven and dependent disabled adults, but that the spouse should pay pension contributions for women in other cases. NAC activists clearly felt comfortable deciding when unpaid mothering work was socially valuable, and when it was not.[24] Freya Kodar has noted that, more generally, NAC tended to be unsupportive of pension proposals that might in any way encourage women's dependency within marriage, while supporting policies that encouraged women's greater participation in the paid workforce.[25] One of NAC's most outspoken advocates of pensions for homemakers, Louise Dulude, spoke out passionately about the need to provide protection from poverty for women who had done unpaid caring work throughout their lives, but for her the long term solution was that women be encouraged to work for pay since 'women themselves, as independent members of the labour force, could then build up their own security and stop relying on the protection now granted to them as a favour by their husbands and the state'.[26]

The majority of NAC's efforts, particularly by the 1980s, focused on questions of paid employment. NAC tracked the wage gap between men and women and often made reference to this gap and of the need for equal pay legislation.[27] Childcare was also central to NAC policy and became a major focus of lobbying efforts.[28] NAC also expressed strong support for paid parental leave, and led a major national campaign to lobby for the policy in the early 1980s.[29]

While NAC paid more attention to the problems facing stay-at-home mothers than mainstream institutions, their long term solution to women's inequality was their entry into the paid workplace. The liberal and socialist feminists of NAC saw themselves as working towards improving the lives of women, but with their challenge to women's dependency and their focus on women's equality through paid work they were also contributing to a larger cultural shift towards devaluing women's unwaged caring work in the home.[30] Given NAC's focus it is probably not surprising that low-income women, and mothers in particular, did not always agree with NAC's agenda.

Marginalized low-income women's groups

An alternative stream of the women's movement in Canada, as in the US, challenged this devaluation of women's parenting labour. In the 1970s and 1980s groups of mothers, many on welfare, had a different perspective from NAC on the value of motherwork, dependency and mothers' relationship to the paid workforce.[31] Below we explore in chronological order the platforms of five of these groups: the Mother-Led Union, Family Benefits Work Group and the Mothers Action Group in Ontario, the Welfare Rights Coalition in Vancouver and Wages for Housework, with locals in various Canadian cities. We do not claim that these groups represent all marginalized low-income women's groups during this era. Indeed the records of these groups, as well as other more limited records in the Women's Movement Archives, point to the existence of other groups of welfare rights mothers across Canada. Our archival and newspaper sources on these five groups suggest a leadership of predominantly Anglo women and women of Eastern European origin but there is also brief mention of indigenous and racial minority mothers' groups in several cities across the country. And at least one of these five activist groups wrote their literature in several languages. While these five groups were centred in Toronto or Vancouver, some of the Toronto groups also had affiliates in a range of smaller Ontario communities. We have chosen to focus on these five groups because they are fairly well represented in the archival records and provide a clear basis for arguing that there was another women's movement during this era. Activists within this movement, like liberal feminists but unlike many socialist feminists, supported the privatized family. Unlike either liberal or socialist feminists they defended the importance of full-time mothering, and challenged the view that only heterosexual women with well-paid husbands could choose this route, arguing that it was the state's responsibility to support their crucial motherwork. They used motherhood as a basis for demanding better living conditions for all low-income mothers and children.[32] While some groups used more explicitly feminist rhetoric than others, as poor women activists they all presented a clear class and gender-based challenge to the state which increasingly sought to force them into the paid workforce, and had little positive to say about mainstream feminists who also believed that poor mothers should enter the paid workforce for their own good.

Mother-Led Union

The Mother-Led Union (MLU) was established in 1974 when a group of low income women in Toronto left the Ontario Anti-Poverty Organization because they felt women's issues were being marginalized there. Their three key demands were:

(i) increase welfare rates to achieve parity with rates paid to foster mothers
(ii) the right to work part-time without having most of their income clawed back from their welfare cheques
(iii) the right to daycare for stay-at-home single mothers to give them respite

The MLU's position on daycare was distinct from that of mainstream feminists. The MLU stated that they were not:

> embracing the concept of institutional full time day care for their children as a solution to their needs. They *are* asking for the support and relief in their full time role as mothers to carry out their responsibility and maximize their potential as mothers alone.[33]

All three of these demands support a politics of mothering that envisions the state supporting low-income mothers who focus their energies on mothering. The MLU members articulated these goals in very explicitly feminist language. They argued that 'the whole system of deprivation for women seems to be designed by our self-glorified male legislators to "KEEP WOMEN IN THEIR PLACE"'. MLU advocated financial independence for women but it was a different independence than what the NAC supported. MLU wanted women to receive reasonable rates from the government to support their crucial mothering work.[34]

The MLU began with ambitious plans, including a plan to organize a strike of low-income mothers across the province in order to have their demands met.[35] As Joan Clark, the leader of the MLU stated, 'everyone else was striking for higher pay, except mothers'.[36] While the strike never materialized the MLU did claim victories. At their height they had twenty-five locals in Toronto, as well as groups in Hamilton, Ottawa, Sudbury and Chatham.[37] In 1976 they organized protest marches and they advocated a guaranteed income for all women and free daycare for everyone, regardless of whether they were doing paid work.[38] Through their efforts they claimed some success in winning two increases in the Ontario welfare rates.[39]

In 1976 the Ontario Government proposed that women with children be required to take any work that was available or be cut off welfare. The MLU protested vehemently against this policy, organizing rallies and sending out bulletins. They mocked the Ontario government's claims that efforts to push them into the workforce would promote sexual equality, arguing that the government:

> tries to rationalize these measures in the name of equality for women––to be equally forced to go to work as single males on welfare ... Rather than extending the welfare benefits to cover male sole support families, it has decided to force us to work in the name of Sexual Equality.[40]

They attack efforts to force sole support mothers into the workforce, so they can make 'useful contributions to society,' and clearly articulate the MLU's politics of mothering:

> It has been the Mother-Led Union's position all along that women who choose to remain at home to raise their children are making a useful contribution to society, that we are already working. We also hold that women who wish to go back to work should be given every assistance in this effort through the provision of adequate subsidized daycare and the availability of job retraining and other support services.[41]

At the same time Joan Clark was clear that, while the MLU supported retraining opportunities, that that was not their primary focus, because 'that's just laying two jobs on us. Would you want to work all day and have to do a second job at night?'.[42]

The MLU position on mothering is clearly distinct from that of NAC. The MLU lobbied the state to provide adequate financial support for women who chose to stay home full-time and mother, and battled efforts to force them into the workforce in the name of 'equality'. MLU policy proposals could be interpreted as accepting traditional roles for women, but by claiming the right to full-time reasonably paid motherhood for single, low-income women at a time when this option was only available to middle- and upper-class married women they were presenting a serious, class-based critique of the state oppression of poor mothers. Their demands reflect a form of difference feminism that advocated for the particular needs of women as mothers. But unlike first wave maternalists, they did not argue that stay-at-home motherhood was the only option for women.

These women eschewed the binary solutions that saw all mothers as either in the paid workforce or in the home.[43] They argued for solutions that fit their lives, such as daycare for respite, and part-time work as a real option. They were also clear that mothers themselves, not the state (and not middle-class feminists), should decide when it was appropriate for them to focus on full-time care for their children, and when it might work for them to enter the paid workforce (with appropriate supports).

Family Benefits Work Group

The Family Benefits Work Group (FBWG) was established in 1978, the same year that the MLU disappears from the historical record, and existed for at least five years. Since both groups were centred in Toronto, there may have been links between them. Certainly Joan Clark, who had been the chairwoman of the MLU, was active in the FBWG.[44] The FBWG was a coalition of welfare single mothers and social service groups who 'came together ... to fight against the deplorable conditions faced by parents and children now on social assistance [welfare]'.[45] Groups of mothers on welfare with links to the FBWG included the Sole Support Parents Group, Mothers Organizing Mothers, and Welland's Mothers' Group. By 1981 it boasted over one hundred individual active members and thirty-six organizational members.[46] The FBWG made strong efforts to ensure that its goals and recommendations for change came from mothers on welfare themselves.[47] The goals of the FBWG were:

(i) to increase welfare rates so that women did not have to raise their children in poverty
(ii) to have the state provide more 'incentives and supports for women trying to return to work or school'
(iii) to oppose the state forcing single mothers into the paid workforce.[48]

These goals recognized the value and importance of mothering and advocated that single mothers should have the choice to work as full-time mothers if they so choose. The FBWG advocated 'the importance that [sic] the parenting and homemaking role women play in the development of their children'. While they supported re-training options and universal childcare they argued for 'freedom of choice' regarding paid employment: 'Only the parent is in the position to decide when to enter the labour force, and she should not be forced into that decision.'[49] FBWG leaders told the *Globe and Mail* that government efforts to force mothers into the paid workforce 'undermines the value of parenting by implying that raising children full time does not contribute to community life'.[50]

The FBWG focused not only on low welfare rates but low employment wages. 'A woman who remains in the work force under these conditions not only deprives her children of the one full-time parent they had, but gains little financial reward for struggling to maintain her independence.'[51] In the late 1970s and early 1980s the FBWG organized a number of rallies and protests to try to increase welfare rates and to publicize other concerns of single mothers on welfare.[52] They produced a comprehensive sixty-page brief to the Ontario Government detailing the many problems with Family Benefits regulations and administration.[53] They attacked a government system that caused 'children and their mothers to suffer so unjustly when their only crime is that they are dependent and in need'.[54]

While the FBWG was less outspokenly feminist than the MLU, they clearly saw themselves as part of the women's movement. Leaders of the FBWG attended the feminist International Women's Day marches in Toronto in the early 1980s, singing songs about the challenges facing single mothers.[55] A focus on women's right to make their own choices permeates their documents. They argued that the government 'undervalues [mothers] work in the home and undervalues the welfare of her children'. They also note that the pressures of poverty both increase violence against women and have very negative impacts on children.[56] In recent years feminist scholars have argued that focusing on the needs of children as a rationale for improved welfare benefits is a problematic strategy, as it obscures the distinct needs of women.[57] However, the women of the FBWG did not see this as a binary choice. While part of their focus on children's welfare may have been a strategic one, their focus on the rights of both mothers and children reflected their perhaps more holistic approach to the issue.

Mothers Action Group

Another Toronto-based group, the Mothers Action Group (MAG) came together in the early 1980s, defining themselves as 'a group of sole support mothers on welfare united in its fight for educational incentives, affordable housing and a humanitarian welfare system'. The co-ordinator of MAG, Maria Ociepka, a welfare single mother herself, had been involved in the FBWG, and in that context had also attended International Women's Day marches. Ociepka, although only in her mid-20s, already had a history of fighting for welfare mothers' rights.[58] MAG had locals in at least two locations, Toronto and Weston, a suburb of Toronto. In 1981 they urged local government to develop a task force focusing on mothers on welfare. The government ignored their request, so in April of 1982 they put out a report themselves, 'Protecting our Own', which detailed their concerns with Ontario welfare policy, and proposed a series of recommendations for improvement.[59] One chapter of the report detailed their critique of the Ontario government's proposal to force mothers on welfare back into the workforce. They argued that the issue of forcing women into the workforce was 'not only a women's rights issue, but also a children's rights issue' and that the question that needed to be addressed was 'Should a mother be allowed to remain on benefits if she feels that her children will suffer without her being at home?'. They argued that:

> The decision to go to school or work and leave the children in the care of strangers is a very important one … the family unit should determine if and when the circumstances will permit the mother to seek upgrading or employment. This decision should not and cannot be left to bureaucrats whose decisions are directly affected by budget considerations.

They identified cases of child abuse which they linked to the pressures mothers faced as a result of the serious inadequacies of the welfare system, and the demands that they both work for pay and be 'good' mothers. The report continued by arguing that 'no one, especially the Provincial Government, can honestly say to us that children do not need their parents around', and they recommended that 'Protection for mothers wishing to remain at home with their children must be entrenched in the proposed new Social

Services Act'.[60] Another chapter detailed the many limitations of existing government policies around work and retraining for women seeking decent employment options. The recommendations relating to support for women seeking to enter the workforce noted the need for universal childcare, as well as the expansion of re-training programs and other educational options.[61] MAG supported the feminist demands for childcare, decent educational options and a focus on women's choices. But MAG situated these demands within the context of children's needs for adequate care, and the valuing of mothers' roles in the home. We can identify these demands as part of a long tradition of maternalist difference feminism, but many feminists today may see the former as feminist, and the latter as more suspect 'family values'. For the Mothers Action Group and the other welfare rights mothers these demands are integral parts of a coherent activist program emerging out of the realities of low income women's lives.

Welfare Rights Coalition

The Welfare Rights Coalition (WRC) was started in 1980 by a group of low income mothers living in a Vancouver public housing complex.[62] The WRC included 'seniors, handicapped, children, the unemployed and the underemployed', but low-income single mothers appear to have composed a majority of the coalition. WRC members were 'determined to take control over their lives'. Their political platform included the goals:

(i) to increase welfare rates
(ii) to increase the amount of affordable housing
(iii) to recognize domestic labour and the nurturing of children as legitimate work[63]

Again, in this list of demands, we see the importance granted to mothering work and the desire to advocate for state policies which would promote low-income mothers choosing to mother with dignity. 'Our work is not recognized', they argued. 'We are harassed into searching for often non-existent jobs … We are punished economically and socially for the work which we do, raising our families.'[64] In the early 1980s WRC organized a number of protests against the BC's government's cutbacks to welfare, including a major demonstration in November 1981 against plans to force mothers into the workforce when their babies were six months old. A single mother on welfare from the Sunshine Coast, north of Vancouver, who used 'a part of her food money' to attend the demonstration, argued that:

> raising a child is a job that should be respected in our society. If the government is the people, then the children are people too, and they need to be provided for properly.[65]

Wages for Housework

The most controversial group of this era that advocated a politics of mothering was Wages for Housework (WFH). Unlike the other welfare rights groups mentioned here, WFH groups in Canada have received some scholarly attention.[66] WFH emerged in Europe from Marxist feminist critiques of the failure of traditional Marxism to recognize the value of women's unpaid household labour.[67] Canadian WFH groups were well connected to WFH groups in the US and Britain.[68] The class background of WFH leaders differed from that of the other groups studied. Most of the other groups were led by low-income mothers who had personal understandings of poverty while the FBWG was a coalition of low income mothers and social service workers. Archival and newspapers sources suggest that the active leaders of the Toronto-based WFH group were predominantly middle-class women.[69]

WFH ideology was also distinctive with its clear Marxist feminist critique of capitalism that included a race, gender and class analysis of unpaid housework. For example, WFH activists argued that capitalism benefited enormously from the unpaid work of women in the home and advocated that the state needed to recognize the value of this domestic work and pay for it. In their words:

> We women are at the bottom because we labour without a wage, and that is both *our* fundamental powerlessness within the working class and the fundamental weakness of the entire working class vis a vis capital. The demand for a wage therefore, is *our* first fundamental level of power because it is our refusal to function for capital as unwaged reproducers of labour power, and it is *the* class demand because it puts an end to the division between the waged and unwaged.[70]

WFH argued that if the state paid for this caring domestic work, this would free women from dependence on men. They perceived this recognition of unpaid caring work as far more liberating than taking a paid job. Paid employment was a '"double slavery" of being expected to carry the burden of two jobs, one inside and the other outside the homes...'.[71] This message struck a chord with many of the single mothers and other low-income women whom WFH sought to organize. As a letter from a housewife in Thunder Bay, Ontario, stated in a WFH newsletter:

> Wages for Housework sounds like my kind of movement... All the 'women's liberation movement' has done is add more exploitation onto women by telling them to join the labour force.[72]

As part of their campaign for 'wages for housework' WFH made efforts to wring concrete concessions from the Canadian state to benefit low-income mothers. For example, in 1977 they launched a major petition campaign against the Liberal government's freeze on Family Allowances, a universal social program that provided at least some government support for unpaid mothering work. Petitions were distributed (in a range of languages) across the country 'to women's groups, welfare groups, Native people's groups and individual women'. They gained 10,000 signatures and WFH leaders met with the Minister of National Health in Ottawa to present the petition.[73] In addition to such national efforts, WFH worked with women at the local level. For example, in August of 1978 WFH in Toronto helped to organize a five-hour sit-in by fifty mothers on welfare to demand their welfare cheques, which were late.[74]

WFH also assisted a number of welfare rights mothers' groups. While it is obvious why the WFH message would resonate with these groups, who were fighting for the recognition of mothers' work in the home (and for decent welfare rates to support this crucial work), at times WFH's help veered towards efforts at control. For example, some WFH members in Toronto were involved in the Mother-Led Union. They tried to gain more control over the group to encourage a focus on the WFH message and tactics, but MLU leaders were wary of their motives, and WFH women ended up, in their own words, just 'doing the shit work' in the organization.[75] WFH also seemed to have some relationship with both the Family Benefits Work Group in Toronto and the Vancouver Welfare Rights Coalition.

Some mainstream feminists suggested that many welfare rights groups were simply puppets of WFH leaders and ideology.[76] However, the MLU experience and a comparison of the values of the welfare rights groups and of WFH suggest otherwise.[77] While WFH activists may have influenced some mothers' welfare rights groups, this influence reflected a shared belief in the need for the state to value and financially support women's mothering work in the home. For the welfare rights mothers, this belief emerged from a grounded analysis of what they perceived to be the needs of mothers and children, rooted in their own experiences, while WFH presented a much more radical analysis, demanding wages for all aspects of household work performed by women, as part of a profound challenge to capitalism, patriarchy and the state.

Nonetheless, given the shared focus on the need to value mothers' caring work, there was room for alliances. In Vancouver in the early 1980s WFH appears to have been central to the organization of activist Mothers' Day events in East Vancouver. The Welfare Rights Coalition participated in these events, as did immigrant women's and lesbian mothers' groups. These events celebrated the value of mothers' unpaid work, as well as recognizing the particular forms of oppression facing immigrant women and lesbian mothers.[78]

WFH's attention to marginalized women included a critical race politics. While in the US many African-American women organized through WFH, Toronto and Vancouver WFH groups focused their organizing efforts on a range of immigrant communities.[79] For their bigger campaigns, Toronto WFH ensured that their leaflets were in four languages: English, Italian, Spanish and Portuguese.[80] One major WFH campaign focused on the exploitative working conditions of immigrant domestic workers. They interviewed domestic workers, investigated complaints about their working conditions, and lobbied for their inclusion in the minimum wage law. In Toronto, WFH organized a one-day event entitled 'A View from the Kitchen: immigrant women speak out on the value of housework'. WFH newsletters argued that the immigrant mothers often 'carry the heaviest burden', are 'denied a basic sense of accomplishment for [their] role in the home', and are then further exploited through low paid domestic work.[81] In Vancouver, WFH allied with both South Asian and Japanese Canadian women's groups, who participated in their Mothers Day events, as well as speaking out on the issues facing immigrant domestic workers.[82] In Winnipeg WFH organizers were also involved in helping to organize indigenous mothers on welfare.[83]

WFH brought a class, gender and race analysis to their understanding of the value of mothering and the oppression of marginalized mothers. They also had a clear sexual politics. They organized a WFH Wages Due Lesbians group in Toronto, and held a conference to bring lesbians and heterosexual housewives together to recognize their mutual interests.[84] They also developed alliances with sex workers and lobbied for the decriminalization of prostitution.[85] As one feminist wrote to NAC:

> The WFH campaign has made a substantial gain among women who many of us have either failed to reach or have never attempted to reach. They have shown leadership with women on Mothers' Allowances [welfare], waitress (waitress' union), prostitutes, and immigrant women.[86]

Struggles with NAC

Not everyone was keen on Wages for Housework. Most socialist and liberal feminists involved in NAC viewed the tactics of WFH as divisive and disruptive and had major disagreements with their theories and policy platforms. In 1975 NAC resolved that they did not support the concept of wages for housework, because it reinforced women's oppressive roles in the home.[87]

In 1979 the tensions between NAC and Wages for Housework came to a head. Most analysis of this conflict has focused on WFH, although we have found that they were supported by a number of mothers' welfare rights groups. An understanding of the nature of these groups with their complex yet internally coherent mix of feminist and 'family' values gives more depth and poignancy to the conflict. In rejecting WFH, NAC not only rejected a divisive Marxist 'fringe' group, as they saw WFH, but a group whose basic message–that the state should financially support mothering work in the home–resonated with a range of low-income activist mothers who sought to make their own decisions around complex questions of paid work and motherhood. These women saw themselves as feminists, in ways that reflected their own lives and experiences. The NAC leadership felt otherwise.

In the spring of 1979 WFH organized a contingent of twenty-five women, representing ten political groups, including a number of low-income mothers' groups, to apply for NAC membership and to attend the NAC Annual General Meeting (AGM). The conference theme was 'Economic Realities for Women'. These WFH members and supporters particularly wanted to hear a talk at the AGM by Dorothy O'Connell, President of the Ottawa Tenants Council, and activist for low income mothers' rights. At first the NAC executive denied membership to WHF members and supporters, thus denying them the right to attend the AGM.

In justifying this decision, NAC President Kay Macpherson explained that while NAC and WFH agreed on short term goals such as childcare, job training, and improved services for women, the two organizations differed tremendously on long term goals. Macpherson wrote:

> What NAC is aiming for in the long run–equal opportunities, equal pay and end to sex role stereotyping, appears to be in contradiction to the basic goal of the WFH groups, since the aims of Wages for Housework–pay for housework, even the housework done in keeping oneself clean and fed … ultimately reinforces the stereotype of women in the home.[88]

NAC's refusal to permit WFH to attend the AGM sparked a major public conflict.[89] Middle class feminist lawyers, politicians, academics and artists from across Canada wrote letters to NAC defending WFH, noting the success of WFH groups in helping low-income, lesbian, immigrant and indigenous women to organize around issues of welfare rights and other concerns.[90] NAC received negative press both in Canada and internationally as 'elitist' 'well-off' women keeping out poor workers.[91]

A compromise was eventually reached and WFH members and allied groups were permitted to attend the O'Connell speech but denied NAC membership. In her speech O'Connell was very critical of NAC. She raised the question of why women on welfare were urged to 'get work' when this work meant low-paid dead-end work instead of being paid adequately for the work they were already doing in their homes. O'Connell accused NAC feminists of 'downgrading women in the home'. She concluded with a plea for women to lobby for more money for social services, including subsidized housing.[92] NAC leaders responded by saying that they were very active in addressing the concerns of poor and immigrant women but maintained that WFH were reinforcing women's oppressed role in the home.

The events at the 1979 AGM did not alter NAC's position. After the conference the new executive reaffirmed the earlier decision to deny NAC membership 'to any group explicitly affiliated or identified with the Wages for Housework Campaign'.[93] McKeen has argued that NAC ultimately went on to accept much of the analysis of WFH, particularly the need to value the unpaid work women did in the home.[94] NAC may have accepted this element of WFH analysis, as shown in NAC's 1990s campaign to have unpaid work acknowledged in the Canadian census. Nonetheless NAC leaders continued to believe that women should be discouraged from doing this unpaid work on a full-time basis. Throughout the 1980s NAC remained committed to challenging women's dependency, advocating their involvement in well-paid employment, with access to quality childcare. Stay-at-home motherhood was not accepted as a legitimate option.

This is most evident in a conflict between NAC and Mothers Are Women (MAW) in 1987. MAW was a group of middle class feminist women who were stay-at-home mothers. At the AGM, MAW brought a resolution advocating that parents should have the choice of staying home on a full or part-time basis to care for their children, and that therefore 'NAC's demands for government funding of daycare be extended to include equivalent financial support for parental daycare provided in the home'.[95] This resolution caused considerable discussion among the NAC executive. NAC President Louise Dulude was worried about diluting NAC's support for daycare with this resolution, and creating real divisions within NAC. At the same time, since R.E.A.L. Women (a right wing Christian 'family values' organization) was becoming an increasingly visible force and attacking NAC for not supporting women in the home, Dulude also wanted to avoid any conflict that would appear as a 'rejection of homemakers by NAC'.[96] She suggested NAC invite MAW members to speak at a family policy workshop at the AGM to try and develop a compromise position.[97] The President's request was denied by the panel organizers, the socialist feminist Organized Working Women. As a result, the fault lines between feminists who advocated government support for stay-at-home mothers and those who opposed it were again exposed at a NAC AGM. MAW's resolution created much dissention on the conference floor. Socialist feminists spoke against it, arguing that paid work was the only path towards true liberation for women. MAW's motion was voted down, and instead a socialist feminist motion affirming the need for the development of an integrated Family Policy 'based on the NAC principles of the equal responsibility of men and women for domestic labour and child-raising and of the equal right of women and men to work outside the home' was passed.[98]

Conclusion

Today some third wave feminists advocate for a form of feminist mothering that includes mothers' rights to choose to stay at home if that seems right for them and their children.[99] But the voices of earlier activist feminist mothers who sought to make their own choices about motherhood and paid work have been largely forgotten, particularly the low-income mothers on welfare who developed their own analysis of motherhood and dependency, and whose solutions were complex ones that reflected their realities, but did not fit easily with mainstream feminist discourse.

These voices have been forgotten in part because they do not fit into any familiar, or indeed comprehensible, feminist discourse. When we look at women's lives and discourses in the 1970s and 1980s, one sees increasing cultural power in the mainstream (both liberal and socialist) English Canadian feminist discourses that may have recognized that women's unpaid caring work was undervalued, but that saw liberation for women as only possible through the independence achieved through paid employment. As feminists like Louise Dulude had feared, this left support for stay-at-home motherhood increasingly within the discursive frame of conservative (and primarily middle-class) voices such as R. E.A.L. women, who saw stay-at-home motherhood as a positive choice, but very much as a conservative, Christian family values choice, only open to heterosexual families with the financial independence to afford to have a parent at home. The creation of this discursive dichotomy makes the voices of welfare rights activist mothers, who saw themselves as feminists with the right to childcare and adequate retraining, but simultaneously as stay-at-home mothers who were performing the crucial job of raising their children and deserved state funding to do so, increasingly culturally unintelligible.[100] This unintelligibility has of course been exacerbated by increasing state efforts to force low-income mothers into the workforce, in the name of 'independence', making strong powerful voices speaking out against such efforts in the name of feminism, class and motherhood hard to fit into any of our existing categories.[101] While these voices may be hard to understand in the current context of feminism vs family values, it is crucial that we recognize their voices and their realities as we seek to develop a fuller, more complex and diverse history of second wave feminism in Canada.

Notes

1. In using the term 'second wave women's movement' we acknowledge that there are issues with using a wave paradigm to describe different women's movements, as this paradigm ignores feminist organizing that was ongoing over the entire twentieth century. However, it is generally acknowledged that the late 1960s to early 1980s saw a particular flowering of feminist activism, which we still find useful to term the 'second wave'. Historical literature on this period of feminist activism in Canada is just starting to emerge. There are strong pieces on specific foci of activism. See, for example Jill Vickers, Pauline Rankin & Christine Appelle (1994) *Politics As If Women Mattered: a political analysis of the National Action Committee on the status of women* (Toronto: University of Toronto Press); Christabelle Sethna (2006) The Evolution of the Birth Control Handbook 1968–1975, *Canadian Bulletin of Medical History/Bulletin canadien d'histoire de la médecine*, 23(1), pp. 89–118; Nancy Janovicek (2007) *No Place to Go: local histories of the battered women's shelter movement* (Vancouver: UBC Press); Valerie J. Korinek (2000) *Roughing It in the Suburbs: reading Chatelaine magazine in the fifties and sixties* (Toronto: University of Toronto Press); Sean Mills (2011) Québécoises deboutte! nationalism and feminism in Quebec, 1969–75, in Michael D. Behiels & Matthew Hayday (Eds) *Contemporary Quebec: selected readings and commentaries* (Montreal: McGill-Queen's University Press), pp. 319–337; Cheryl Suzack, Shari M. Hudorf, Jeanne Perreault and Jean Barman (Eds) (2010) *Indigenous Women and Feminism: politics, activism, culture* (Vancouver: UBC Press). The best overview of the second wave Canadian women's movement remains Nancy Adamson, Linda Briskin &

Margaret McPhail (Eds) (1988) *Feminist Organizing for Change: the contemporary women's movement in Canada* (Toronto: Oxford University Press).

2. For some discussion of variants of 'difference feminism' particularly relevant to working-class women see Dorothy S. Cobble (2005) *The Other Women's Movement: workplace justice and social rights in modern America* (Princeton: Princeton University Press); Susan Pederson (2004) *Eleanor Rathbone and the Politics of Conscience* (New Haven: Yale University Press).
3. Rosalyn Baxandall (2001) Re-visioning the Women's Liberation Movement's Narrative: early second wave African American feminists, *Feminist Studies*, 27(1), pp. 225–245.
4. Some third wave feminists do argue for women's choice to remain at home, but they rarely do so from the perspective of low income women on welfare. See for example, Mielle Chandler (1998) Emancipated Subjectivities and the Subjugation of Mothering Practices, in Sharon Abbey & Andrea O'Reilly (Eds) *Redefining Motherhood* (Toronto: Second Story Press), pp. 270–286; Kristin Rowe-Finkbeiner (2002) Something is Bugging Me, *Hip Mama, the Parenting Zine*, 28, pp. 27–31.
5. Margaret H. Little (1998) *No Car, No Radio, No Liquor Permit: the moral regulation of single mothers in Ontario, 1920–1997* (Toronto: Oxford University Press); Sonya Michel (1993) The Limits of Maternalism: policies toward American wage-earning mothers during the Progressive Era, in Sonya Michel & Seth Koven (Eds) *Mothers of a New World: maternalist politics and the origins of welfare states* (New York: Routledge), pp. 277–320; Linda Gordon (1994) *Pitied but Not Entitled: single mothers and the history of welfare, 1890–1935* (New York: Free Press).
6. Gwendolyn Mink (1995) *The Wages of Motherhood: inequality in the welfare state, 1917–1942* (Ithaca: Cornell University Press); Nancy Fraser & Linda Gordon (1997) A Genealogy of 'Dependency': tracing a keyword of the US welfare state, in Nancy Fraser (Ed) *Justice Interruptus: critical reflections on the 'postsocialist' condition* (New York: Routledge), pp. 121–149.
7. For a discussion of motherhood as oppression see, for example, Jane Lazarre (1976) *The Mother Knot* (New York: McGraw-Hill); Adrienne Rich (1986) *Of Woman Born: motherhood as experience and institution, 10th anniversary edition* (New York: Norton); Betty Friedan (1963) *The Feminine Mystique* (New York: Norton); Ann Snitow (1992) Feminism and Motherhood: an American reading, *Feminist Review*, 40, pp. 32–51.
8. Benita Roth (2004) *Separate Roads to Feminism: black, Chicana, and white feminist movements in America's second wave* (Cambridge: Cambridge University Press); Becky Thompson (2002) Multiracial Feminism: recasting the chronology of second wave feminism, *Feminist Studies*, 28(2), pp. 337–360; Cobble, *The Other Women's Movement*; Premilla Nadasen (2002) Expanding the Boundaries of the Women's Movement: black feminism and the struggle for welfare rights, *Feminist Studies*, 28(2), pp. 270–301.
9. Patricia H. Collins (2000) *Black Feminist Thought: knowledge, consciousness, and the politics of empowerment*, 2nd edn (New York: Routledge); Premilla Nadasen (2005) *Welfare Warriors: the welfare rights movement in the United States* (New York: Routledge); Anne Valk (2008) *Radical Sisters: second-wave feminism and black liberation in Washington, DC* (Urbana: University of Illinois Press); Lisa Levenstein (2009) *A Movement Without Marches: African American women and the politics of poverty in postwar Philadelphia* (Chapel Hill: University of North Carolina Press); Marisa Chappell (2010) *The War on Welfare: family, poverty, and politics in modern America* (Philadelphia: University of Pennsylvania Press).
10. Mink, *The Wages of Motherhood*; Nadasen, Expanding the Boundaries of the Women's Movement; Annelise Orleck (2005) *Storming Caesars Palace: how black mothers fought their own war on poverty* (Boston: Beacon Press).
11. Fraser & Gordon, 'A Genealogy of "Dependency"'.
12. This article is part of a larger project that will look closely at the politics of motherhood among activist women's groups that have been marginalized by poverty, race, indigeneity, language and religion.
13. Wendy McKeen (2012) Seen But Not Heard: the construction of 'welfare mothers' in Canada's late 1960s/early 1970s 'war on poverty', *Canadian Woman Studies*, 29(3), pp. 107–123.

14. Wendy McKeen (1995) The Wages for Housework Campaign: its contribution to feminist politics in the area of social welfare in Canada, *Canadian Review of Social Policy*, 33, pp. 21–43; Vickers et al., *Politics As If Women Mattered*.
15. Feminist journals include *Kinesis, Upstream* and *The Pedestal*.
16. Also see Adamson et al. (1988) *Feminist Organizing for Change*; Ruth Roach Pierson, Marjorie Griffin Cohen, Paula Bourne & Philinda Masters (Eds) (1993) *Canadian Women's Issues: volume 1: strong voices* (Toronto: James Lorimer); Ruth Roach Pierson & Marjorie Griffin Cohen (Eds) (1995) *Canadian Women's Issues: volume 2: bold visions* (Toronto: James Lorimer); Sandra Burt (1990) Canadian Women's Groups in the 1980s: organizational development and policy influence, *Canadian Public Policy/Analyse de Politiques*, 16(1), pp. 17–28; Judy Rebick (2005) *Ten Thousand Roses: the making of feminist revolution* (Toronto: Penguin Canada); Constance Backhouse & David H. Flaherty (Eds) (1992) *Challenging Times: the women's movement in Canada and the United States* (Montreal: McGill-Queen's University Press); Susan D. Phillips (1991) Meaning and Structure in Social Movements: mapping the network of national Canadian women's organizations, *Canadian Journal of Political Science*, 24(4), pp. 755–782.
17. Adamson et al., *Feminist Organizing for Change*; Luxton (2001) Feminism as a Class Act: working-class feminism and the women's movement in Canada, *Labour/Le Travail*, 48, pp. 63–88; Vickers et al., *Politics as if Women Mattered*.
18. Vickers et al., *Politics As If Women Mattered*.
19. Jane Ursel (1992) *Private Lives, Public Policy* (Toronto: Women's Press); Meg Luxton (1980) *More than a Labour of Love: three generations of women's work in the home* (Toronto: Women's Educational Press); Luxton, 'Feminism as a Class Act'.
20. Lisa Pasolli (2015) *Working Mothers and the Child Care Dilemma: a history of British Columbia's social policy* (Vancouver: UBC Press). Also, these views were expressed by socialist feminist scholars of the era, most notably in Michele Barrett & Mary McIntosh (1982) *The Anti-Social Family* (London: Verso).
21. Pasolli, *Working Mothers*, p. 127.
22. *NAC Annual Report*: Women's Movement Archives (hereafter WMA) (1983), NAC Collection.
23. *NAC Recommendations from Workshops*: WMA (1979) NAC files, March 23–25.
24. Also see Margrit Eichler (1980) Family Income: a critical look at the concept, *Status of Women News*, 6(2), pp. 20–21, 24; debates between NAC and Vancouver Status of Women over pensions, *Kinesis* May 1983, p. 3, Oct. 1983, pp. 6., Feb. 1984, p. 5, Feb. 1984, pp. 33–34, May 1984, p. 5.
25. Freya Kodar (2012) Pensions and Unpaid Work: a reflection on four decades of feminist debate, *Canadian Journal of Women and the Law*, 24(1), pp. 180–206.
26. Lobby Group Has First Francophone Head, *The Gazette* (2 June 1986), p. C1; Louise Dulude (March 1979) What Are You Going To Live On When You Are Old?, *Status of Women News*, 5(3).
27. *'Economic Rights for Women' Memo*: WMA (1985), NAC newsletter, 10(3), p. 1.
28. See for example, *NAC Resolution*: WMA (1981–1982), NAC files.
29. *NAC Resolutions*: WMA (1981–1982), NAC files.
30. Fraser & Gordon, 'A Genealogy of "Dependency"'.
31. McKeen also notes the existence of this alternative stream of feminist welfare rights mothers groups as existing in the late 1960s and early 1970s in McKeen, 'Seen But Not Heard'.
32. Our findings on the way these groups defined motherhood as a politics rather than an individual experience is similar to how Baxandall understands the low-income mothers activist groups she examines : Baxandall, Re-visioning the Women's Liberation Movement's Narrative, pp. 225–245.
33. *Letter to Sandy Stienecker, Toronto YWCA, from Joan Clark, Chairwoman, MLU*: WMA (1974) box 57, Mother Led Union (MLU) file (Toronto, 1974–75), Dec. 6.
34. *Brief on Financial Independence for Single Support Mothers*: WMA (1974) box 57 MLU file, May.

35. *Letters from Joan Clark to low income mothers*: WMA (1974) box 57, MLU file, n.d., and 1 Oct.
36. *The Globe and Mail*, 24 Aug. 1974, p. 13.
37. *'Beware the Mother Led Union'*: WMA (n.d.) box 57, MLU file.
38. *MLU Comic Strip*: WMA, box 57, MLU file.
39. *Mother-Led Union Conference Poster*: WMA, box 57, MLU file.
40. *Special Bulletin to Our Members and Supporters, MLU*: WMA (1976) box 57, MLU file, 14 March.
41. Ibid.
42. *The Globe and Mail*, 10 Oct. 1974.
43. Also see McKeen, 'Seen But Not Heard.'
44. See, for example, FBWG Memo, *Re: 'What teams will say when contacting organizations and agencies'*: WMA (n.d.) box 26, 1978-83, FBWG records.
45. *Letter from Barbara Sands, Board Member, 1 November*: WMA (1981) box 26, FBWG.
46. *FBWG Annual Report, April*: WMA (1983), box 26.
47. *Memorandum, 'What teams will say'*: WMA (n.d.) box 26, FBWG.
48. *Welfare: A Poverty Trap: pamphlet*: WMA (1979) box 26, FBWG.
49. *Summary of Recommendations, of the FBWG Brief, 'Women and Children on Welfare: A Poverty Trap'*: 15 May WMA (1979), box 28.
50. *The Globe and Mail*, 25 Sep. 1979, p. 4.
51. *A Brief by FBWG*: WMA (1979), box 26, FBWG.
52. WMA (1981) box 26, FBWG, 1 November.
53. *A Brief by FBWG*: WMA (1979), box 26, FBWG.
54. *Welfare: A Poverty Trap pamphlet*.
55. *The Globe and Mail* (March 10 1980), p. 8.
56. *Brief, 1979 and Programme*: WMA (n.d.), box 28, FBWG.
57. Wendy McKeen (2004) *Money in Their Own Name: the feminist voice in poverty debate in Canada, 1970–1995* (Toronto: University of Toronto Press); Jane Jenson (1998) *Mapping Social Cohesion: the state of Canadian research*, CPRN Study no. F|03 (Ottawa: Canadian Policy Research Networks); Jane Jenson & Denis Saint-Martin (2003) New Routes to Social Cohesion? Citizenship and the social investment state, *Canadian Journal of Sociology*, 28(1), pp. 77–99.
58. *Toronto Star*: WMA (FBWG, FBWG clippings, 30, Welfare Mothers Protest, 7 May 1980), box 28; *Globe and Mail*, 10 Mar. 1980, p. 8; *Ottawa Citizen*, 16 Sep. 1985.
59. MAG brief (1982) *Protecting Our Own*, WMA, box 57, MAG file.
60. *Protecting Our Own*, p. 8, p. 9, p. 10, p. 12, p. 13.
61. Ibid. p. 21.
62. *Kinesis* (May 1981), p. 12.
63. *WRC pamphlet*, p. 4: WMA, Box 57, MLU file.
64. Ibid. p. 1.
65. *Kinesis* (Dec./Jan. 1982), p. 3.
66. McKeen, 'The Wages for Housework Campaign'; McKeen, *Money in Their Own Name*; Vickers et al., *Politics As If Women Mattered*; Kodar, 'Pensions and Unpaid Work'.
67. McKeen, 'The Wages for Housework Campaign'.
68. *WFH Letter to NAC*: WMA (1979) box 127, WFH Collection; *WFH Group II Statement*, 2 Mar.: WMA, box 127, WFH Collection.
69. While the archival evidence suggests that the Toronto WFH leadership were middle class in origin we have less evidence regarding the class backgrounds of the WFH leadership in other communities across Canada.
70. *WFH Group II Statement of Political Differences*: WMA, box 127, WFH.
71. *WFH Newsletter*: WMA (n.d.) box 127, WFH Collection.
72. Ibid.
73. *Wages for Housework Committee, letter from Frances Gregory*: WMA (1977) box 127, WFH Collection, 16 May.
74. *Money for Mothers*: WMA (1978) box 127, WFH Collection, 7 Aug.

75. *Notes on the Mother-Led Union*: WMA, box 127, WFH Collection.
76. See article by Kathleen Macleod Jamieson (May 1979), *Upstream*.
77. Oral history interviews, which will be undertaken at a later stage of this project, will provide more insights into the relationship between these groups.
78. By 1982 a range of these organizations had affiliated with the organization 'Women Workers in the Home', a 'group of women and organizations concerned about the status of women in the home'. It seemed to have been organized primarily by the local WFH group: *Kinesis*, Apr. 1982, pp. 14–15; 'Mothers Take Action', *Kinesis*, Apr. 1982, pp. 12–14; 'Mothers Day in the Park', *Kinesis*, June 1980, p. 3.
79. *Money for Mothers*: WMA (1978) box 127, WFH Collection, 7 Aug.
80. *MayDay in Toronto*: WMA (1975) box 127, WFH Collection.
81. *WFH Special Issue on Domestics* (Winter 1979), 4(2).
82. 'Mothers Take Action'; 'Mothers Day in the Park', p. 3.
83. *Letter from Sheila Ross (Boxer) to Kay Macpherson, President of NAC*: WMA (1979) NAC Collection, WFH file, 17 March.
84. *Lesbians Fight to Keep Kids*: WMA (n.d.) box 127, WFH Collection. Also see *Lesbians Join the Family Allowance Protest*: WMA, box 127, WFH Collection.
85. *International Women's Day Poster*: WMA (1978) box 127, WFH Collection.
86. *Letter from Chris Lawrence to NAC, 17 March*: WMA (1978) NAC collection, WFH file.
87. MacPherson, *What Does 'A' Do? NAC's dilemma*: WMA (1979) NAC Collection, WFH file, March.
88. Ibid.
89. *Newsletter from WFH Committee, 19 June*: WMA (1979), box 127, WFH Collection.
90. Ibid; *Letter from Sheila Boxer to NAC*: WMA (1979), NAC collection, WFH file, 17 March; *Letter from Ellen Murray to NAC*, 15 March 1979; *Letter from Dorothy Thomas to NAC*, 13 March 1979; and others in WMA (Mar. 1979) NAC collection, WFH file.
91. Article by Kathleen Macleod Jamieson, and editorial, *Upstream* (May 1979); MacPherson, *What Does 'A' Do?*.
92. *Recommendations from Workshops*: WMA (1979) NAC, 23–25 March.
93. *Letter from Lynn Macdonald to WFH*: WMA (1979) NAC collection, WFH file, NAC, 28 May.
94. McKeen, 'The Wages for Housework Campaign'.
95. *MAW resolution, received March 10*: WMA (1987), NAC collection.
96. For further discussion of R.E.A.L. Women (Realistic, Equal, Active for Life) see Karen Dubinsky (1985) Lament for Patriarchy Lost? Anti-feminism, anti-abortion and R.E.A.L. women in Canada, Canadian Research Institute for the Advancement of Women, *Feminist Perspectives*; Carol L. Dauda (2012) National Battles and Global Dreams: R.E.A.L. women and the politics of backlash, paper presented at the Canadian Political Science Association annual meeting, Edmonton Alberta, 13–16 June.
97. *Memo from Louise Dulude to NAC table officers, April 16*: WMA (1987) NAC collection.
98. *Resolution from Barbara Cameron, Chairperson, Social Services Committee, received March 10*. WMA (1987) NAC Collection.
99. Ariel Gore (1998) *The Hip Mama Survival Guide: advice from the trenches on pregnancy, childbirth, cool names, clueless doctors, potty training, and toddler avengers* (New York: Hyperion); Ariel Gore & Bee Lavender (Eds) (2001) *Breeder: real-life stories from the new generation of mothers* (Seattle: Seal Press); Rowe-Finkbeiner, 'Something is Bugging Me'; Chandler, 'Emancipated Subjectivities'.
100. For use of the term 'culturally unintelligible' see Judith Butler (1990) *Gender Trouble: feminism and the subversion of identity* (Oxford: Routledge).
101. Scholars have suggested that mainstream feminist discourse has been implicated in this neoliberal project. See for example: Mink, *The Wages of Motherhood*; Lynne Marks (2004) Feminism and Stay-at-Home-Motherhood: some critical reflections and implications for mothers on social assistance, *Atlantis*, 28(2): 73–83; Nancy Fraser, 'How Feminism Became Capitalism's Handmaiden––And How to Reclaim it', *The Guardian*, 14 October 2013; (2013) *Fortunes of Feminism: from state-managed capitalism to neoliberal crisis* (London: Verso).

Acknowledgements

We are grateful for the skilled research assistance of Drew Koehn and the editorial assistance of Emma Paszat.

Funding

This work was supported by Insight Grants 2012-13, Social Science and Humanities Council of Canada 4A Grant from Queen's University [File No. 435-2013-0480] and by work-study grants from the University of Victoria.

The 1944 Education Act and Second Wave Feminism

Phillida Bunkle

ABSTRACT
The women articulating Second Wave Feminism in Britain emerged from the environment created by the 1944 Education Act, which ensured that all girls completed secondary school, with a minority accessing academic girls' grammar schools. For some, the Act also provided a route to professional education in universities or teacher training colleges. A legacy of earlier feminist movements, such all-female residential institutions exercised control, but nevertheless encouraged women's achievements. This article explores the opportunities, tensions and contradictions created by this educational culture from 1945–65, reflected in the views of my contemporaries and the writers, Margaret Cooke, Anne Oakley and Margaret Forster.

Introduction

Most writers and researchers of the Second Wave of British feminism belonged to a generation of women born between 1938 and 1949.[1]

I explore connections between changes in post-war education and the articulation of Second Wave feminism by examining the autobiographical writing of three varied self-identified feminist writers: Margaret Forster born in 1938 and Margaret Cook and Ann Oakley born in 1944.[2] I also draw on the experiences, described to me by three readers of feminist texts, who were of similar age to the writers and willing to reflect in conversations with me about our education.

All six of these writers and readers (seven including me) were born to white British parents who were born before the First World War (WWI) and married in 1940 or before. In most of these families, childbearing was interrupted by the Second World War (WWII), often with a significant age gap between pre- and post-war siblings.

All six writers and readers supported equal pay, enlarged educational opportunities and employment opportunities for women and identified, sometimes with significant caveats, with the Second Wave Women's Movement. Yet none had significant engagement with feminist organisations.

Writing and reading women's liberation literature was their primary form of Consciousness Raising. It is true that Oakley participated in a face-to-face Consciousness Raising group, reader Jenni joined the Guardian newspapers 'Housewives Register' and reader Sal participated in one equal pay march. With these limited exceptions, none participated in public feminist events nor joined women's organisations or counter culture communities.[3] I avoid the distinction, utilised by Olive Banks, between activists and sympathisers[4] to suggest rather that a sense of identity with the women's movement, at least for those women who identified as straight, was largely generated from participation in a shared women's literary culture. It was through women's writing and reading that a sense of a common experience was generated and analysed. But this culture was itself a reflection of the greatly expanded educational environment created by the Welfare State in which selection was based on facility in the written word.

All six writers and readers attended publicly-provided grammar schools and universities. Like most of the women who articulated the Second Wave, they belonged to the 'lucky few' who passed the 11-plus, went to grammar school and obtained degrees.[5]

The unique culture of these post-WWII girls' grammar schools and tertiary institutions has had a major impact on the contemporary history of British women.[6] Education debate over the impact of the Act has been, however, dominated by concerns about the way it perpetuated class inequality. In particular, research focused on arguments against selection as a mechanism of transmitting class inequalities.[7] This paper seeks to explore the impact of this educational regime on the politics of the women who embraced the Second Wave of feminism.

Section 2 describes the provisions of the 1944 Act. I then describe the characteristic features of Second Wave feminism. In Sections 3 through 8 I discuss how personal life was analysed in terms of political power; how integral the written word was to Consciousness Raising; the centrality of the assumptions around harnessing the state to address women's issues; educational opportunity and the written word; career identity and sexual activity. The paper then identifies, in section 9, weaknesses of the Second Wave position and then in section 10 how they were reflected in the transition to present-day feminism. It ends by drawing some tentative conclusions.

Education Act 1944

The 1944 Education Act established free secondary education for all children according to 'age', 'ability' and 'aptitude'.[8] Six Local Education Authorities (LEAs) including the largest, London, began immediately to develop non-selective comprehensive schools.[9] The majority, however, established structures in which while the majority of children attended non-selective, usually co-ed, Secondary Modern schools or technical colleges, a select minority attended academically-oriented, single-sex, fully-'maintained' grammar schools.[10] By 1952, eight years after the passage of the Act, there were 3,480 Modern schools, 1,181 Grammar schools, 164 Direct Grant schools, thirteen Comprehensives, and a number of technical and hybrid schools, while 4,000 schools remained 'unreorganized'.[11]

Pupils, such as the three writers in this study, with exceptionally high marks in the scholarship examination (the 11-plus), and who had spent at least two years at a state primary school, might be offered a place at the older, more prestigious schools receiving a 'direct-grant' from central government in return for accepting at least 25% of scholarship pupils and which formed an elite tier within the grammar system.[12] Some,[13] but not all,[14] of these privileged schools for girls, such as those of the Girls Public Day School Trust, had their origins in nineteenth-century feminist activity.[15] By the early 1960s, 2% of all 14-year-olds in England and Wales were in direct grant and 17% in local grammar schools.[16]

The division on the basis of a competitive written examination into the separate educational paths of Secondary Modern and Grammar education was the anvil on which much of the class and gender culture of the Welfare State was forged.

The debate on the class implications of selection overshadowed recognition of gender as a source of inequality[17] until an influential generation of feminist scholars and educationalists, whose careers were often a reflection of the employment opportunities created by the expanding state,[18] drew attention to gender as a source of inequality and developed a gender analysis which has been very influential in challenging the curriculum, pedagogy and gender hierarchy of educational institutions.[19] However, since they also saw the existence of grammar schools and of selection as impediments to equality of opportunity, the culture of girls' grammar schools and their wider impacts received rather less attention, until later when concerns about girls' experiences in co-ed environments began to be raised. This papers aims to stimulate further analysis of the gender aspects of this selective educational regime by examining what a generation of 'grammar girls' have explicitly chosen to say about their education and its impacts.

The proportion of each age cohort of children attending grammar schools varied very widely (i.e., between 11 and 30%) between Local Education Authorities (LEAs)[20] but averaged about 20% across the UK.[21] Nevertheless, there were 2% fewer grammar places for girls, who had to attain much higher 11+ examination marks to gain a place.[22] These selective schools and colleges consciously cultivated a middle-class ambiance.[23] Far more middle- than working-class children entered them.[24] Class and gender differences increased the further up the system you progressed. Far fewer girls than boys continued to 'A level' and, in one sample, 69% of those girls that did came from middle class backgrounds.[25] Educational opportunities had to compete with the need and the allure of leaving school to earn money.[26]

The 1944 Education Act also removed financial barriers to higher education by establishing fee-free places for the children who reached University or Training College along with subsistence grants scaled to parental income.[27]

At the time of the Act, the biggest sex difference was in entry to higher education. Of the cohort of children born before 1910, ½% of girls and 2% of boys (or only 1 girl for every 4 boys) entered universities. The gender ratio of students accessing tertiary education changed very little through the first half of the twentieth century.[28] This inequality slowly began to change after 1944. By the mid-1950s, when girls affected by the 1944 Act began to apply to higher education, 2½% of all girls entered universities compared to 5½% of boys (or 5 girls for every 11 boys).[29] Many more girls than boys entered teacher training colleges.[30]

At reader Paulette's county grammar school for example, in 1961, 107 girls, mostly born between 1945 and 1946, obtained 0 level passes.[31] Two years later 38% of these girls took A levels and 11% went on to universities, while 20% entered teacher training colleges.[32] Thus 31% of these 'grammar girls' entered higher education immediately after leaving school.

Like girls in other autobiographical accounts, the six girls in this study were typical in that only one of their mothers, a teacher, had any higher education. All the readers and writers acknowledged that their state-supported education dramatically changed their lives compared with those of their mothers.[33]

Margaret Forster wrote that the Act:

opened the way for any child, however poor, to gain entry to the previously fee-paying grammar schools, since ability was now to be the only criterion. Universities and colleges would also be within their reach since means-tested grants would be available, as well as state scholarships, to cover all expenses.[34]

Very small numbers of girls attended these free grammar schools and universities but they exercised a disproportionately significant influence on their generation of women because at the time these schools were almost the only route to professional and public life. These were the public intellectuals and researchers who articulated second wave feminism, gave us the histories of First Wave Feminism and provided a sociological understanding of gendered culture.

Personal is political

For the tiny minority who went on to higher education the provision of free tertiary education and living allowances was life changing, not least because it would, with very few exceptions, take them away from home, into distant, usually single-sex residential institutions. This was a significant change. Before WW11 46% of women students at English universities other than Oxbridge and London, lived at home,[35] and many single women who yearned for independence found it difficult to find accommodation.[36]

Leaving home lessened the influence of parental class and gender regimes. It could be a way of escaping authoritarian fathers and subservient or distressed mothers. Forster wrote of her father:

> I'd hated the way he shouted, his need to dominate, his scorn for books, his insistence that everything should be done his way ... [37] [Forster had] ... wished him dead many times, but I'd just recently stopped wishing it. I didn't need him to die anymore, because I was going to leave home and him soon ...[38]

For her, like many others, university would prove to be a decisive break with the class culture and gender expectations of their families.

New opportunities produced tensions between parents and anxiety in their daughters. Some parents were both proud and resentful of their children as they moved into a world different from their own.[39] The living allowance enabled reader Paulette to go to university despite her mother's active opposition. Forster's mother could see only 'problems looming, a gulf emerging which would grow wider and wider. There had been no such gulf between herself and her mother ... '.[40] Forster's mother was clear that:

> I, as a girl, didn't need to be clever. It would do me no good just as it had done her no good. I would only marry and have children and share her own fate, whatever I said.[41]

While Forster's father complained that ' ... she was getting above herself '.[42] Autobiographical accounts by other feminists echo this theme of parental, especially maternal antipathy.[43]

The 1950s family had been almost off-limits to scrutiny; the expressionless public face of post-war British domestic culture. These girls were the unwilling witnesses to their mothers' frustrations and despair.

There is a slightly uncomfortable sense, explicitly explored in Oakley's recent account of her relationship with her father,[44] that the fathers prefer these clever, bright, successful girls. These daughters are the people their mothers might have been. But the daughter senses a sometimes subtle and sometimes overt disrespect for the clever wives who have been so easily reduced to a painfully limited domesticity. Oakley details the slow increments by which her parents' marital relationship became 'flat, like a spent chord' as the innovative, engaged social worker her mother had been 'deteriorated into the over-medicated, depressed housekeeper, and unpaid PA/editor/secretary servicing her father's burgeoning career',[45] while 'competing with me for my father's attention'.[46] The writers were confused by the energy devoted to maintaining the public face of these marriages as successful.

The girls represented potential that the marital relationship had lost; some of the possibilities that had been suppressed. Perhaps the daughters carried the unfulfilled expectations and displaced hopes of both parents.

Consciousness raising through women's writing

Facility in writing and reading was the explicit basis of educational selection. Like the women in *Truth, Dare or Promise*[47] these girls were all precocious and voracious readers in Primary school, finding in books both an escape and a promise of a wider world beyond the confines of family. The women from this background developed a distinctive voice specific to this generation of feminists.[48] It underpinned the 'vigorous insertion of personal lives into the political domain',[49] and was 'the distinguishing hallmark of that first 'post-war' generation ... '.[50]

Much Second Wave feminist writing was therapeutic but it identified society as needing the therapy. Painful experiences were not personally humiliating but signposts to the institutions that needed changing and how change should occur. The realisation that private suffering is not a purely personal matter, but is located in social institutions and power structures, set women free by circumventing the finger-pointing of personal failure.

There was a flowering of women's biographical and autobiographical writing as this generation sought to deal publicly with the personal contradictions with which they were surrounded. Oakley defends the use of 'the evolving genre of life-writing' arguing that, as vehicles for exhibiting an age, 'biography and autobiography ... help us to understand processes of social change through the medium of individuals' lives'.[51] This approach has produced some remarkably collective biographies, notably in 'education feminism'.[52]

A slightly younger generation, however, affected by post-modern theorising, eventually questioned the value and veracity of autobiography accounts. Post-structuralism destabilised the conception of fixed identity in favour of multiple fluid 'selves', reconstructed in ever shifting 'secondary revisions' of memory.[53] While raising awareness of difference and seeking greater inclusivity, the dissolution of fixed identities nevertheless fragmented the possibilities of coherent political action.[54]

Oakley has been one of the most effective British critics of this development.[55] She seeks to develop a feminist methodology which can support effective advocacy for policy change and therefore material lives. She laments that post-modern feminism has dissolved coherent categories of analysis just at a time when the neoconservative financialisation of the state demands the strict discipline of the accountant. She strives to amalgamate the qualitative and quantitative approaches in 'a methodology of material use'.[56] She writes that 'the arguments of post-modern feminists have especially weakened the political uses of gender'.[57]

The modest scope of this essay seeks to avoid post-structuralism's excessive attention to its own process, while acknowledging the pitfalls of universalising the experiences of a particular selective cohort. It aims to identify the ways 'that individual lives have developed from common roots and values, both culturally and educationally',[58] from a particular set of opportunities made possible through the policies of a modernist state at a specific time, and argues that this grounded the British Second Wave in a predominantly social democratic politics.

A characteristic of Second Wave Feminism is a new tone of self-disclosure and a confidence that personal revelations would be 'recognisable to others'; the point was not 'salaciously to exhibit a purely private history'.[59] For Second Wave feminists, the point of writing like this was to identify the ways in which the apparently personal is structured by relationships of social and political power, especially within intimate familial relationships. It provides a powerful antidote to the relentless demands for women to cast their lives within the wrappings of positive thinking.[60] Puncturing the etiquette of the public-private divide would legitimate the personal in the political and identify the political in the personal.

Oakley writes:

> women now more than ever cannot afford to disregard the task of understanding themselves. 'Revision … is for women more than a chapter in cultural history: it is an act of survival' [… it …] is more than a dilatory self-interested pastime … because it is women who find themselves most discomforted by the gap between who they are and what they are supposed to be.[61]

These acts of re-vision were conducted largely through the written word. Drawing links through the published, written word between the personal and the political was a form of Consciousness Raising. In Britain, perhaps, it was its most important form. The examples cited here suggest that this writing spread feminism and a sense of feminist community well beyond the circles of London-based, left-wing activist circles and did so in a way, for the most part, untouched by the abrasive ideological contests lamented by metropolitan activists.[62]

The grammar school education these feminists received shaped their equalitarian politics. But their feminism was rather preoccupied with the urgent need to escape the fate of the mother, while retaining the values of affiliation. I encountered a deep unease about the mother. By developing an identification with all women they maintained their emotional attachment to the mother without endorsing her limitations. All wrote of the restrictions and evasions in their families' lives but were also unwilling to forgo motherhood themselves. Their writings describe, in painful detail, what had been previously invisible or fictionalised. The three writers would repeatedly return to these themes.[63]

There is a sense of an obligation to disclose which would break through the evasions which had held their mothers in thrall. They shared a belief that truth telling about private lives would set them free. Honesty was imperative to break down the public-private divide that had placed the real lives of women beyond analysis and was essential if the personal was to be understood as structured by relationships of unequal power. This penetration into the heart of family relationships may be the reason why Second Wave feminists were frequently seen as hostile to the family despite their actual preoccupation with maternalist values.

Harnessing the state to address women's issues

I expected to find in the works of Second Wave Feminists that the advent of new post-war educational provision would establish unprecedented opportunities for girls. But I read that, as the women attempted to realise these expectations, they encountered restrictions which precipitated their feminist re-analysis of social and political power.[64]

Unlike some other Second Wave feminist writers, such as non-state school educated Shelia Rowbotham, Australian Lynne Segal, Canadian Barbara Taylor and New Zealand born Juliet Mitchell,[65] none of the women in my study were inclined to either psychoanalysis or Marxism; they were, rather, the daughters of Keynes and Beveridge. They aspired to a State which supported their creative work in both production and reproduction. Strongly equalitarian in impulse and affiliation, their lives were profoundly affected by the welfare state and they were the first generation to enjoy its full fruits. This is not to say that they were uncritical of its shortcomings. They presumed that remedies lay in redistributing the resources of the family and the state. Compared to other Anglo countries British feminists set up few independent institutions; they sought rather to seek adjustments within the comprehensive provisions of the British Welfare State.[66] Oakley, for example advocated making NHS health services more amenable to women, rather than setting up alternative, independent services.[67] Analysis presumed the existence of an activist state and solutions were conceived within its parameters. This was not made explicit but implicitly assumed. The state had transformed their prospects from that of their mothers, as they freely admitted.

Mica Nava has noted that the Second Wave Feminists strove to involve men in the movement and assume that gender equality will achieve social transformation of benefit to all.[68] Their vision of liberation of women within the parameters of the welfare state centred on flexible gender roles which would make it possible to share income generation, familial and domestic labour.

Transforming the sex roles was essential to changing the gender division of labour within the family and household labour. They expected not only that all women would share this benefit but also that men would have a vested interest in such change. The solution to household labour was to share it with men rather than to socialise it as socialists promoted, professionalise it as liberal feminists advocated or pass it to an underclass as the global market currently dictates.[69]

In *Housewife*, Oakley argues that housework is the one thing women of all classes have in common and that all will benefit if it is more equitably shared.[70] Oakley assumes that all women share an equal interest in doing so. She also assumes that men will benefit from greater freedom and flexibility in gender roles. In her own marriage Oakley succeeded in sharing all aspects of income generation, housework and childrearing responsibilities.[71]

An adjunct of this approach was the promotion of closer attachment of men to their children through involvement in childbirth[72] and childcare.[73] The erosion of gender stereotyping it was believed would extend these benefits to men and achieve a degree of general social transformation lacking in previous emancipatory or revolutionary change. Non-sexist childrearing was an obligation to achieve a more equitable future.

These scholarship girls inherited the welfare state and did not share their working class parents' sense of being patronised by people who ran welfare agencies;[74] indeed, they would become such workers themselves so benefitting directly from the employment opportunities the expanded services provided. Five of these six subjects became, at least initially, teachers in schools or higher education and the sixth, Cook, an NHS doctor.

The focus of Cook's feminism is an excoriating dissection of the typical personality of the powerful men who generate these intractable tensions. The 'Mr Big' who 'changes the rules, defies democracy, and drives his stretch limo through human rights'.[75] He and the other alpha males with whom he is so tightly bonded are the 'Senior managers in business and industry who pay themselves giant salaries' while 'No one measures or values ... the productivity of learning, of teaching, of caring , of listening'.[76] The puzzle is that 'the family remains the epitome of inequality' yet women remain committed to it.[77]

Cook, while married to the Foreign Secretary, personally observed the narcissistic self-regard of powerful men. Her visceral 'primal' response to her husband's leaving the family reinforced her belief that the distinction between men and women was grounded in biology. Cook speaks of sexual imprinting as 'something primal and biological' and loss of a pair bond as 'extremely painful ... like the pain of a phantom limb'.[78] While this analysis has an essentialist basis different from those of the other writers, the preoccupation with family, maternal and sexual relationships is shared by them all and endorsed by all my interview subjects.

Cook prescribes political safeguards against limitless personal aggrandisement, along with policies respectful of the primacy of co-operation, connection and conservation. 'Powerlessness begets abuse'[79] she writes and believes that feminism 'may be the saving grace of the world',[80] where 'excessive competition' is degrading human and environmental life.

Educational opportunity and selection through the written word

Selection for grammar school was by a mastery of written culture in a competitive examination taken by all at the end of primary education.

Selection, writes Forster was:

> a big event in our lives. Its significance was clearly understood. It settled our future, it pigeon-holed us, at eleven, as clever, quite clever or stupid.[81]

Ten-year-old Forster believed selection was 'the key to the future'.[82] The 'thought of failing the exam 'made me want to die'.[83] Not to pass would 'be the end of the world'.[84] Reading, writing and arithmetic were the keys to success. By-and-large other aptitudes were not tested in the selection process, or developed in the curriculum or the pedagogy. For most children, these schools were the only route to higher education and the possibility of a professional and public life. When eleven-year-old Margaret Cook passed, she exalted that unlike her sister she 'had won a scholarship and lots of opportunities'.[85]

Forster is a strongly self-identified feminist, novelist and literary biographer. She never loses sight of the excruciating personal impacts of class. Forster is vividly aware of the servant class and women's place within it and the unrewarded reality of household labour.[86] She twinned her biography of poet Elizabeth Barrett Browning with a biography of the restrictive, deprived life of Wilson the lady's maid who made Browning's life and productivity possible. In doing so she subtly highlighted the different impacts of dependence on unequal classes of women.[87]

Hidden Lives is a collective biography of the women in Forster's family in which she minutely details the vulnerabilities of being female and working class.[88] *Significant*

Sisters defends First Wave feminist pioneers who articulated a version of feminism respectful of female experience and maternalist values.[89] Forster laments the imposition of childbearing when it is not supported but salutes those who choose to reclaim its significance and status. In *Good Wives?* Forster examines the changing meaning of being a wife and explores the possibilities for greater self-definition of the role.[90] The historical improvement in the situation of the wives from the mid nineteenth century reinforces her optimism about the possibilities for contemporary re-negotiation of marital roles.

The preoccupations of novelist and feminist academic Oakley are similar. She vividly describes the stresses, joys and irreducible connections forged by the body in sex and motherhood. She asks on what terms these relationships could become a source of both nurturing and freedom. Oakley particularly deals openly with the intimate details of her relationships. A long-running affair provokes relentless questioning of her own desires and the legitimate claims of family.[91]

Absence of career identity

The changing dynamics of class and gender culture under the Welfare State is exemplified by two of these scholarship girls' recall of the precise details of material life of home and the school. They treasured their uniform including its 'most important item: bottle-green knickers, which were not optional'.[92] The 'dark, practical and unglamorous … skirts, ties, jumpers, blazers, berets and macs … in the same drab colour with biscuit-coloured blouses and socks'[93] were part of the legacy of rational dress reform associated with First Wave Feminism which deliberately de-sexualised the image of young women while emphasising freedom of physical movement.[94] In the post-1944 context, these elaborate costumes served rather to affirm the status of the grammar girl and set her apart publicly from her sec-mod contemporary by placing her closer to the image of exclusive, upper class private girls' schools such as Cheltenham Ladies College.[95]

The six girls could recall the name of the middle-class retailer designated by their school to supply the many expensive items of uniform. Forster's pleasure in her longed-for uniform, the insignia of opportunity and possible class mobility, would have been nearly obliterated had it been purchased from the Co-op. She was saved such ignominy by her grandparents pride in her 'amazing feat'.[96] She was later taken to the hospital to give her dying grandmother the treat of seeing her 'in the full glory of my High School uniform'.[97]

These uniforms also extended the discipline of the school beyond its gates and separated the school and home environments. All six girls were expected to make their own way to school. For Cook and reader Jenni this included many hours of independent daily travel on public trains and buses. The rules forbad removing any piece of uniform before reaching home where different rules applied. Most mothers required girls to preserve their uniform by removing it at home. 'Changing after school' also marked a transition to home discipline where domestic chores and errands were required but which also allowed some areas of greater independence, or solitude. At home most girls recalled long hours of unsupervised, often out-door, play and the majority had bikes, 'the customary reward for passing the scholarship',[98] to extend their independent roaming.

Most of the mothers of these girls had only elementary education. All but one were the first person in their families to go to university. For some, this could be more intimidating than liberating.[99] For all these girls it created difficulty imagining what adult identities could follow education. However much the mothers had enjoyed paid or voluntary work, most had given it up when they married. The ideal of all six subjects was to be able to experience the 'joy', as Forster put it, of having 'the best of both worlds'.[100]

Towards the end of school, Oakley, who won a scholarship place at a direct grant school,[101] later had a breakdown when she could not identify 'Who could she be?'[102] There seemed to be no identity to step into. The dilemma was solved temporarily by staying in education, but re-emerged when she found herself married, and at home, with young children when the issues of adult identity became even more acute.[103] He parents were embarrassed by her failure and for nine years rejected her.[104] She began her journey to feminist sociology with the realisation that her anguish was not a mental health issue but a reflection of the gendered structure of society. Her academic father, a prominent advocate of the Welfare State pointedly ignored the gift of her first book examining this subject.[105]

The girls experienced deep ambivalence about loyalty to the disappointed and subtly despised mother. The slow defeat of their gifted mothers was a source of disrespect, guilt and embarrassment. On the one hand was recognition that the mother's mental and emotional health issues arose from the stagnant smallness of her situation; on the other their own path to a different future remained obscure. Oakley wrote:

> Was I to be a dedicated, if irascible, wife, housewife and mother, like my mother? Was I to be the kind of person who found a valid domain of labour and then relinquished it for the domain of the household? Would I, like her in the years to come search for a glory reflected in the polished table tops and the achievements of my husband?[106]

She recalled 'my father's almost vitriolic attacks on working mothers'[107] while being 'always conscious even as a very young child of how much my father's hopes for the future centred on me'.[108] Later she would connect this with his marginalisation of the faculty of experienced 'difficult women' whose initiatives he appropriated, and who he replaced with a close homo-social coterie of 'brilliant' men.[109]

The need to be different from the mother was pressing, but raised what Oakley called 'who am I?' questions. Forster wrote of her mother 'I could NOT be her'.[110] Her mother's 'early married life' had been a 'sequence of giving things up'.[111] She had 'trapped herself' when she made the 'frightful mistake' of marrying.[112] Forster 'hated what she saw'[113] of marriage yet like the other writers she married close to the time of graduation.

As a child, Forster decided 'I'd escape. To where?':

> I sensed I might do it through High School. I felt that somehow the secret was to stay in the school world and cut myself off from the other world my mother was so unhappy in, the home world.[114]

Cook, Forster and Oakley's feminisms were different, which is one reason why I choose them. However, in their different ways, they were preoccupied with similar issues. Nava has pointed out that this preoccupation with familial relationships was common to early Second Wave feminists.[115] Grammar school opened the door; but the path led in no particular direction. Expectations of success were pressing but how were they to be realised? It is striking that none of the writers or the readers were concerned with their place in a Market.

All wrote of the lack of any sense of an adult identity beyond education. Grammar girls often benefited from the dedication of teachers from the 'bereaved generation' of single women who had taken their degrees before the WW2.[116] But teachers could not offer support for a path beyond school because they had no experience of it. For grammar girls and their teachers, working in education was the default option.[117]

Cook, who became an NHS medical consultant, was the only one who aimed towards an identifiable career. But her work imposed inflexible demands in terms of time and place. For her, the dilemmas and preoccupations with how to live a productive life separate from, but maintaining relationships with, family was especially acute. She described herself as 'a revolutionary deep inside'.[118] As a consultant doctor she had reached the pinnacle of employment success but she describes work 'getting progressively more demanding. My repeated and urgent requests for help were gallantly listened to and then ignored'.[119] When 'I'd reached the end of my tether' she began looking for 'another job that would not stretch me so painfully on the rack'. She hoped:

> my desperate plight would no longer be treated so lightly. With the fluency of extremity I put my case yet again to our director of clinical services ... confident that he would have to respond in some way to my cry for help. He listened and did nothing.[120]

Sex and sexual identity

For the post WW2 generation of girls until the 1970s, when the generation born in the second half of the twentieth century arrived in universities and training colleges, accommodation was mostly in single-sex halls and colleges which reinforced a subtle sense of gender solidarity developed in segregated schools.

The experience of university would, for the most part, be a quite different experience for men and women. The rules surrounding women were stricter and more actively policed; the university would presume authority '*in loco parentis*' assuming control over all aspects of the lives of its students, especially its women students, including their social and sexual activities. Women students would routinely be expelled for breaking parietal curfews, sexual misdemeanours and unmarried pregnancy.[121] At the university I attended (Keele), the first pregnant women was allowed to sit her final degree examinations in 1966, albeit decently segregated in a separate room. The tiny number of women, such as Oakley, who gained the permission of their university authorities to marry[122] had their maintenance grant[123] removed or greatly reduced.

This sexual regime, with its inbuilt double standard, began to relax after about 1968 when lowering the age of majority to eighteen removed the legal obligation of universities to act *in loco parentis* and the proportion and numbers of women students increased.[124] I anticipated that tensions about the sexual revolution and anxieties about sexual safety would be a preoccupation for the women I studied, as they had been for me. But I found only one of my readers 'had' to get married. The three writers had been well aware of the perils of getting 'caught'[125] but after 'lucky' early sexual encounters had managed to penetrate the veil of secrecy to obtain barrier contraception. The three writers enthusiastically managed sex and established early marriages to fellow students with matter-of-fact aplomb.[126]

I was surprised to find in all my subjects less anxiety about the sexual revolution and more about maintaining the positive satisfactions of caring roles, especially familial intimacy.[127] Oakley vividly describes the ecstatic pleasures of extra marital sex but prioritises what Mica Nava has called the 'indissoluble knot of passion for our children'.[128] Oakley writes:

> of all the words in the language, 'family' is for me the most powerful: it excites in me a far greater range and depth of emotional reactions than any other word. It signals both the most loving and the most hating of relationships, both the highest degree of liberation and the basest level of oppression. Some of my best moments have been lived in the family and so have some of my worst.[129]

In their different ways these three writers and three readers grappled with bringing these warring attachments into a liveable peace.

Paid work, family and the welfare state

The Second Wave feminists who are the subject of this study articulated a vision of society which was constrained by their own history. Their feminism, although based on perceptive analyses of their personal circumstances, was based on an unquestioned existence of a comprehensive and pro-active welfare state and on the continuation of 'full' employment at living wages and salaries. The employment opportunities provided by the expanding state sector provided a secure basis for the future. Thus, they shared, with Keynes and Beveridge, the main preoccupations of domestic policy immediately post-WWII as implicit assumptions of their social and political analysis.[130] This was why they looked to the state to correct social ills and argued that familial inequalities could be solved by more equal sharing of caring tasks.

They did not develop an alternative political economy to accompany their liberationist approach to gender roles. This was because of a combination of not foreseeing the need and agreement with some aspects of later developments in economic and social policy. Consequently, they did not provide their readers with an alternative to the movements which have undermined the welfare state and raised the importance of Market ideology to its current prominence.

The flexible familial roles envisaged by the Second Wave were made potentially viable by the ability of the family to survive sharing a single wage.[131] This was greatly assisted because the State underwrote some communal provision for family formation and childbearing through health, housing, and education including free maternity care, universal family allowances, vitamin supplements and school food. The family wage was a long held goal of the Labour Movement and was assumed to be progressive by the progenitors of the welfare state. However, to many women born in the second half of twentieth century, the family wage was seen as unfair because it penalised the single and independent women living outside conventional family structures.

As full employment ceased to be a primary aim of economic policy during the 1970s[132] and lowering inflation and fostering Market took over, the ability to support a family on one income was lost. With it went the possibilities of achieving viable equality through flexible gender roles. With the collapse of employment protection, and the rise of global labour competition, one wage is usually insufficient to support a family. The necessity for at least two wages meant that the solution of flexible work time and shared care ceased to be relevant to any but the most privileged. Even the most privileged and successful workers, such as Cook, suffered from the insoluble conflict between increasingly demanding workplaces and the constant needs of the family. Work intensification means that even those with the flexibility of homework or self-employment are finding it difficult to implement this solution unless they are unusually well paid.

Without an explicit, alternative political economy it proved difficult for Second Wave feminism to mount a defence of the welfare state based in current realities or to articulate a coherent vision of communal welfare or social justice in the face of its systematic undermining. In particular, Second Wave feminists were unable to critique individualistic social and economic models without appearing to compromise their beliefs in personal freedom. As a result, their reactions to attacks on the fundamental implicit assumptions of their feminism lacked clarity. The feminist field was left to those for whom individualism was a fundamental tenet of analysis or who, by parsing feminism in postmodern terms, faced no such dilemmas.

Transition to the present

The 1944 Act provided full state funding of three types of secondary schools; namely, mainly single-sex grammar schools, technical high schools, and secondary moderns.[133] The provisions of the 1944 Act applied for little more than twenty years before the transition to non-selective co-education began. By 1964, Anthony Crosland, the Labour Minister for Education, began to move against selection and when Margaret Thatcher became Education Minister, in 1970, she did not reinstate it,[134] but gave LEAs the power to choose comprehensivisation or the retention of grammar schools.[135] Thus the system of elite, single-sex, state-supported education was specific to this particular generation;[136] the generation that articulated Second Wave Feminism. From the late 1960s, co-educational comprehensives combining grammar, technical and secondary modern educations became increasingly common. At the same time that schools were undergoing transition, university places expanded rapidly. The twenty-three new universities founded in the 1960s offered a rapidly increasing number of places in the 1970s while remaining fee-free to students who continued to receive subsistence grants. In the second half of the twentieth century a far larger number of girls went on to university. Dyhouse notes the important role of the 'new universities', such as Keele and Sussex, that accepted a far higher proportion of women students[137] and the gender ratio began to change significantly. Sixteen per cent of girls born in 1955 went to University after leaving school compared to 28.6% of boys.[138] Therefore, girls born after 1950 were increasingly likely not to have experienced single-sex institutions and much more likely to go to university.

These developments led to many, sometimes subtle, differences between the girls whose education was structured by the 1944 Education Act and the feminists born after 1950 who had somewhat different expectations and whose parents were generally younger and had married after WW2.

The mothers of the girls born after 1950 had lived less gender-segregated lives and were more likely to continue in employment after marriage. Differences from their daughters were less dramatic. In their world, it was much easier to believe that success depended on individual application. Segal has argued that the generation, born after 1950, adapted the feminist narrative to one of 'solitary transcendence' over trauma[139] rather than focus on collective, structural change.[140]

If 'girls could do anything' then personal effort not collective provision was the key to security. This generation was primed to accept the ideology of the Market and unprepared to either critique its limitations or defend the emancipatory achievements of the activist state. With the result that Second Wave Feminism appeared irrelevant in the face of the Thatcher/Blair rollback of the state and eagerly embraced the equal opportunity rhetoric of the international corporations which acquired its resources.

To the generation born after 1950, the culture of women's institutions began to seem anachronistic and an 'odd way to treat people who, thanks to generous student grants, were largely independent of their parents'.[141] This slightly younger cohort was more likely to reject a life 'dominated by petty rules' and the 'air of timidity and self-denigration'[142] associated with sexually segregated institutions which was at odds with the experience of the co-ed environment of comprehensive schools in which sex and sexual identity had to be negotiated on a daily basis.

As this change took hold, Women's Liberation and the Sexual Revolution began to elide. During the 1970s, feminism became more concerned with issues of sexual identity and personal freedom. It rejected what was seen as the repressive institutional legacy of the First Wave but founded few new institutions. By the 1980s, therefore, the Women's Movement did not trust the Welfare State to deliver meaningful solutions and turned to the individual rather than collective solutions to women's issues. Feminism moved from issues concerned with women's dual role to post-modern concerns with representation, which sometimes suggested that subversive gestures of non-conformity could achieve, through personal resistance, a liberation that common action had failed to establish.

The Second Wave writers did not express a specific political ideology. They assumed that solutions lay within the parameter of the Welfare State. Moreover, they did not develop an alternative political analysis and so found themselves increasingly unable to address the withering of the state and the rise in influence of global corporations. They did, however, assert optimism that women could become mistresses of their own destiny. This unwittingly foreshadowed the idea of the self-made woman who 'took responsibility' for her own wellbeing through an act of Will.

The idea of women sloughing off 'victimhood' would later pave the way for introduction of the Market. As the 1980s progressed, the next generation increasingly accepted the rhetoric of individual opportunity supported by open market structures.

Many Third Wave feminists have found no alternative to accepting managerialist models of change but struggle with the implicitly male patterns of effort and performance by which they are appraised and rewarded. For most women, this either denies them the satisfactions of familial life or penalises them for enjoying it.

Conclusion

Oakley claims a greater space for women within marriage, motherhood and the family; Forster claims priority within her home and for her family; Cook perceives divorce an act of betrayal of the family. She demanded ownership of the whole marital home while insisting her ex paid off the mortgage, on the grounds that she had always contributed more money to the marriage!

These writers are all acutely aware that education and sufficient income are the perquisites for such assertion but are optimistic that more women will follow their lead. The readers applauded equal pay and increased opportunity at school and work but did not become activists because they believed that feminists lacked respect for women's caring relationships. Neither group had a sense of how flimsy these gains might prove to be in the face of the withering of the Welfare State and the ubiquitous insecurities of the global marketplace.

None of these women deny the choices of others but rather surprise themselves at the strength and depth of their attachments. These arise, said Forster, from 'some subtle force which is not yet either fully understood or controlled'.[143] Each of these different feminists grappled personally and publicly with acknowledging the impact of this force while also claiming the legitimacy of their need to live a life beyond the restrictions of its scope or acquiescence to the limits of their mother's existence. Each found satisfying personal solutions but none found a comprehensive political prescription.

The Second Wave was weakly institutionalised and created few formal organisations. It is not clear if many women participated in left-wing feminist political activism.[144] Few mass mobilisations in the 1960s and 1970s were specifically feminist. But many women read and thought and talked about their experiences in a variety of new, more open, personal ways. There was a flowering of feminist books, reading groups, bookshops, presses, journals and magazines.[145] Established mainstream publishers and booksellers established extensive women's sections. The collection of the Feminist Library holds over 2,000 published texts from the Second Wave.[146] Independent women's bookshops became key centres for exchanging information and establishing contacts between informal feminist interest groups. The principle form of the Second Wave was the written word. And it changed lives.

Notes

1. Miriam David (2014) *Feminism, Gender and Universities: politics, passion and pedagogies* (Farnham UK: Ashgate), p. 57, in her extensive international study of the values and common roots of Second Wave academic feminism also uses a cohort category which also notes a distinct change in women born before and after 1950.
2. The periodisation of 'waves' of feminism was famously utilised in analyses of feminism by Olive Banks (1985) *The Biographical Dictionary of British Feminism, Volume One 1800–1985* (New York: New York University Press) and (1986) *Becoming a Feminist: the social origins of 'first wave feminism'* (Athens: The University of Georgia University Press). As used here the term Second Wave does not, however, indicate a lack of feminist activity between the wars, but rather that it did not have the character or public profile of a mass movement, or demand a significant political response. See also: Ann Logan (2014) Political Life in the Shadows: the post-suffrage political career of S. Margery Fry (1874–1958), *Women's History Review*, 23(3), pp. 365–380; Jane Martin (2013) Gender, Education and Social Change: a study of feminist policy and practice in London, 1870–1990, *Gender and Education*, 25(1), pp. 56–74.
3. Ann Oakley (1984) *Taking it Like a Woman* (London: Cape), pp. 10–11; Interviews and conversations with readers Paulette, Jenni and Sal, 2014.
4. Banks, *The Biographical Dictionary*.
5. Rosemary Deem (1978) *Women and Schooling* (London: Routledge & Kegan Paul), pp. 90–93; Madeleine Arnot, Miriam David & Gaby Weiner (1999) *Closing the Gender Gap: post war education and social change* (Cambridge UK: Polity Press), pp. vii–viii
6. Arnot, David & Weiner, *Closing the Gender Gap*, pp. 49–82.
7. Dave Hill & Mike Cole (2001) *Schooling and Equality: fact, concept and policy* (London: Kegan & Page); Dennis Marsden (1986) *Politicians, Equality and Comprehensives*, Fabian Tract 411 (London: Ark Paperbacks).

8. Brian Jackson (1971) *What did Lord Butler say in 1944?: a discussion paper on a national pre-school policy* (Cambridge: Priority Area Children).
9. Robin Pedley (1963) *The Comprehensive School* (Harmondsworth UK: Penguin Books), p. 39.
10. Brian Jackson & Dennis Marsden (1962) *Education and the Working Class: some general themes raised by a study of 88 working class children in a northern industrial city* (London: Routledge & Kegan Paul). The contribution of the technical and art colleges to the culture of the 1960s and 1970s in which women's liberation developed has yet to be assessed.
11. Lester Smith (1957) *Education: an introductory survey* (Harmondsworth UK: Penguin Books), p. 108.
12. Alfred Yates, P. M. Grundy & Alfred Pidgeon Douglas (1957) *Admission to Grammar Schools. Third interim report on the allocation of primary school leavers to courses of secondary education ... With statistical appendices by P. M. Grundy* (London: Newnes Educational), p. 23.
13. Margaret Cook (1999) *A Slight and Delicate Creature: the memoirs of Margaret Cook* (London: Weidenfeld & Nicolson), p. 39.
14. Ann Oakley, *Taking it Like a Woman*, pp. 10–11; Interviews and conversations with Jenni and Sal, 2014.
15. Martha Vicinus (1985) *Independent Women: work and community for single women, 1850–1920* (London: Virago), pp. 163–210; June Purvis (1981) Towards a History of Women's Education in Nineteenth Century Britain: a sociological analysis, *Westminster Studies in Education*, 4(1), pp. 45–79; Josephine Kamm (1971) *Indicative Past: a hundred years of the Girl's Public Day School Trust* (London: George Allen & Unwin), pp. 31, 217, 189.
16. Pedley, *The Comprehensive School*, pp. 12, 13.
17. Deborah Thom (1987) Better a Teacher than a Hairdresser? 'A mad passion for equality', or, keeping Molly and Betty down, in Felicity Hunt (Ed.) *Lessons for Life: the schooling of girls and women 1850–1950* (Oxford: Basil Blackwell), pp. 124–145.
18. Miriam David (2003) *Personal and Political: feminisms, sociology and family lives* (Stoke on Trent UK: Trentham Books); (2014) *Feminism, Gender and Universities: politics, passion and pedagogies* (Farnham UK: Ashgate).
19. Madeleine Arnot (2002) *Reproducing Gender: critical essays on educational theory and feminist politics* (London: Routledge Falmer), pp. 90–96; Deem, *Women and Schooling*; Rosemary Deem (1961) State Policy and Ideology on the Education of Women 1944–1980, *British Journal of Sociology of Education*, 2(2), pp. 131–143; Rosemary Deem (Ed.) (1980) *Schooling and Women's Work* (London: Routledge & Kegan Paul); June Purvis (1991) *A History of Women's Education in England* (Milton Keynes: Open University Press).
20. Yates, Grundy & Douglas, *Admission to Grammar Schools*, p. 23.
21. Allan Little & John Westergaard (1964) The Trend of Class Differentials in Educational Opportunity in England and Wales, *The British Journal of Sociology*, 15(4), pp. 301–336, http://jstor.org/stable/588862 Table 1.
22. Thom, 'Better a Teacher than a Hairdresser?', pp. 137–144.
23. Hunt (Ed.) *Lessons for Life*, pp. xiv–xix; Pedley, *The Comprehensive School*, p. 33.
24. Jackson & Marsden, *Education and the Working Class*, pp. 11, 14; Demm, *Women and Schooling*, pp. 90–93.
25. Yates, Grundy & Douglas, *Admission to Grammar Schools*, p. 11; Jackson & Marsden, *Education and the Working Class*, p. 147.
26. Stephanie Spencer (2005) *Gender, Work and Education in Britain in the 1950s* (Basingstoke UK: Palgrave).
27. Hunt, *Lessons for Life*, pp. xiv–xix; Jackson & Marsden, *Education and the Working Class*, p. 11.
28. Little & Westergaard, 'The Trend of Class Differentials', 15(4), p. 310.
29. Ibid. Table 1.
30. Jackson & Marsden, *Education and the Working Class*, pp. 142–149, 159, Appendix Table 29. Celia Briar (1997) *Working for Women? Gendered work and welfare policies in twentieth century Britain* (London: UCL Press), p. 111, asserts that until the early 1960s the grant system incentivised the training college option; however, the evidence for her assertion is

not clear. Reader Jenni who went to university in 1957 claimed that the difference was academic performance as measured by A level passes. This is borne out by figures from Paulette's school where girls going to university in 1963 averaged three A level passes while those going to training college averaged passes in 1.8 subjects.

31. *Hove County Grammar School for Girls: prize giving programme*, 14 December 1961.
32. *Hove County Grammar School for Girls: prize giving programme* 17 December 1963.
    This source shows however that not all high achievers went on to higher education. Twenty girls were awarded academic prizes in their O level year but six did not continue to higher education. In their A level year, fourteen girls from the same cohort won subject prizes, three of whom went straight into employment. Only two of those fourteen won three subject prizes; one became a pathologist the other spent her adult life working for East Sussex County Council before retiring from a middle management position (Paulette personal communication). See also Spencer, *Gender, Work and Education*.
33. Liz Heron (Ed.) (1985) *Truth, Dare or Promise: girls growing up in the fifties* (London: Virago Press); Annette Khun (2002) *Family Secrets: acts of memory and imagination* (London: Verso).
34. Margaret Forster (1995) *Hidden Lives: a family memoir* (London: Viking), p. 175.
35. Carol Dyhouse (2002) Going to University in England Between the Wars: access and funding, *History of Education*, 31(1), p. 6; Carol Dyhouse (2006) *Students: a gendered history* (London: Routledge), p. 12
36. Virginia Nicholson (2008) *Singled Out: how two million women survived without men after the First World War* (London: Penguin Books), pp. 143–146.
37. Margaret Forster (1999) *Precious Lives* (London: Vintage), p. 11.
38. Ibid.
39. This is noted by analysts of other states which had at the time well-developed welfare states such as post WW2 New Zealand. See Helen May (1988) Motherhood in the 1950s: an experience of contradiction, in Sue Middleton (Ed.) *Women and Education in Aotearoa* (Wellington: Allen & Unwin/Port Nicholson Press), pp. 57–71; Sue Middleton (1988) A Short Adventure Between School and Marriage? Contradictions in the education of New Zealand 'Post-war Woman', in Middleton (Ed.) *Women and Education in Aotearoa*, pp. 72–88.
40. Forster, *Hidden Lives*, p. 181.
41. Ibid. p. 175.
42. Ibid. p. 178.
43. Heron, *Truth, Dare or Promise*; also Kuhn, *Family Secrets*.
44. Ann Oakley (2014) *Father and Daughter: patriarchy, gender and social science* (Bristol: Policy Press).
45. Ann Oakley (1996) *Man and Wife: Richard and Kay Titmuss: my parents' early years* (Harmondsworth UK: Harper Collins), p. 299.
46. Ann Oakley (2014) *Father and Daughter*, Kindle edn pos. 1459.
47. Heron (Ed.) *Truth, Dare or Promise*.
48. Lynne Segal (2007) *Making Trouble: life and politics* (London: Profile Books), p. 7.
49. Ibid. p. 8.
50. Ibid.
51. Oakley, *Father and Daughter*, Kindle edn pos. 563.
52. Lynda Stone (1994) *The Education Feminism Reader* (New York: Routledge), pp. 1–13; David (2003) *Personal and Political*; Kathleen Wailer & Sue Middleton (Eds) *Telling Women's Lives: narrative inquiries in the history of education* (Buckingham: Open University Press); Jane Martin (2015) Gender, Education and Social Change: a study of feminist politics and practice in London, 1870–1990, *Gender and Education*, 25(1), pp. 56–74; Sue Middleton (1993) *Educating Feminists: life histories and pedagogy* (New York: Teachers College, Columbia University).
53. Kuhn, *Family Secrets*, p. 4.
54. David, *Feminism, Gender and Universities*, p. 62
55. Ann Oakley (2005) Paradigm Wars: some thoughts on personal and political trajectory, *The Ann Oakley Reader: gender, women, and social science* (Bristol: Policy Press), pp. 245–250.

56. Germaine Greer (2005) Preface, *The Ann Oakley Reader: gender, women, and social science* (Bristol: Policy Press), p. vii.
57. Oakley, *The Ann Oakley Reader*, p. 4.
58. David, *Feminism, Gender and Universities*, p. 53.
59. Oakley, *Taking it Like a Woman*, pp. 2–3.
60. Barbara Ehrenreich (2009) *Smile or Die: how positive thinking fooled America and the world* (London: Granta).
61. Ibid. p. 2.
62. Segal, *Making Trouble*, pp. 7–9.
63. Examples from fiction include Margaret Cook (2015) *A Bit On the Side* (MKRY); Margaret Forster (1989) *Have the Men Had Enough?* (London: Chatto & Windus); (1981) *Marital Rites* (Feltham UK: Hamlyn); (2003) *Dairy of an Ordinary Woman 1914–1995* (London: Chatto & Windus); Ann Oakley (1989) *The Men's Room* (New York: Atheneum); (1990) *Matilda's Mistake* (London: Virago); (1992) *The Secret Lives of Eleanor Jenkinson* (London: Harper Collins).
64. Arnot, David & Weiner, *Closing the Gender Gap*, pp. 51–65, explore the contradictions in the welfare state policy between meritocracy and the maintenance of the family arguing that this 'inadvertently' created a pressure for changed gender relations.
65. Shelia Rowbotham (2000) *Promise of a Dream: remembering the sixties* (London: Allen Lane); Segal, *Making Trouble*; Juliet Mitchell (1984) *Women: the longest revolution: essays on literature and psychoanalysis* (London: Virago); Barbara Taylor (2014) *The Last Asylum: a memoir of madness in our time* (London: Penguin).
66. Arnot, David & Weiner, *Closing the Gender Gap*, p. 63.
67. Ann Oakley (1981) *From Here to Maternity: becoming a mother* (Harmondsworth: Penguin).
68. Mica Nava (1983) From Utopian to Scientific Feminism? Early feminist critiques of the family, in Lynne Segal (Ed.) *What Is To Be Done About The Family: crisis in the eighties* (Harmondsworth UK: Penguin in association with the Socialist Society), pp. 65–105. First published in 1972 this article is reprinted in Mica Nava (1992) *Changing Cultures: feminism, youth and consumerism* (London: Sage).
69. Barbara Ehrenreich & Arlie Russell Hochschild (2004) *Global Woman: nannies, maids, and sex workers in the New Economy* (New York: Metropolitan Books/Henry Holt).
70. Ann Oakley (1974) *Housewife* (London: Penguin).
71. Oakley, *Taking it Like a Woman*.
72. Oakley, *From Here to Maternity*.
73. Histories of masculinities are largely silent on this issue, however Lucy Delap and others have begun studying those parts of the men's movement which were closely aligned with the Second Wave Women's Movement. Delap has found significant evidence of efforts to organise sharing the care of children between parents, through private collective provision and at public and political events. Lucy Delap (2014) Unbecoming Men: the 'new man' in the late twentieth century, *Seventh Annual Lecture: History Department*, King's College London, 29 April.
74. Forster, *Hidden Lives*, pp. 135–140.
75. Margaret Cook (2002) *Lords of Creation: the demented world of men in power* (London: Robson), p. vii
76. Ibid. p. 3.
77. Ibid. p. 305.
78. Ibid. p. 275. Essentialism is unpopular with some academic feminists but has a certain resonance for people puzzled by the persistence of the pink, fairy princess. For the interviewees, especially, the intersection between the biological and the constructed remains one appropriate focus for feminist enquiries and has continued to make good sense to them.
79. Ibid. p. 178.
80. Ibid. p. 22.
81. Forster, *Hidden Lives*, p. 174.
82. Ibid.

83. Ibid. p. 175.
84. Ibid. p. 176
85. Cook, *A Slight and Delicate Creature*, p. 38.
86. Margaret Forster (1990) *Lady's Maid* (London: Chatto & Windus).
87. Margaret Forster (1998) *Elizabeth Barrett Browning* (New York: Doubleday); Forster, *Lady's Maid*.
88. Forster, *Hidden Lives*.
89. Margaret Forster (1984) *Significant Sisters: the grassroots of active feminism: 1839-1939* (London: Secker & Warburg).
90. Margaret Forster (2001) *Good Wives? Mary, Fanny, Jennie and me 1845-2001* (London: Chatto & Windus).
91. Oakley, *Taking it Like a Woman*.
92. Cook, *A Slight and Delicate Creature*, p. 39.
93. Ibid.
94. Carol Dyhouse (1981) *Girls Growing Up in Late Victorian and Edwardian England* (London: Routledge & Kegan Paul).
95. Stephanie Spencer (2007) A Uniform Identity: schoolgirl snapshots and the spoken visual, *History of Education*, 36(2), pp. 227–246.
96. Forster, *Hidden Lives*, p. 179.
97. Ibid. p. 184.
98. Kuhn, *Family Secrets*.
99. Eleanor Updale (2013) St Ann's In Our Time, *The Ship: 2012-2013, St Ann's College Record*, 102, pp. 26–28.
100. Forster, *Significant Sisters*, p. 10.
101. Haberdasher Aske School for Girls in Wikipedia at http://en.wikipedia.org/wiki/Haberdashers%27_Aske%27s_School_for_Girls; Oakley, *Father and Daughter*, Kindle pos. 250.
102. Oakley, *Taking it Like a Woman*, pp. 29–35.
103. Ibid. pp. 68–71.
104. Oakley, *Father and Daughter*, Kindle pos. 456.
105. Ibid. pos. 472.
106. Oakley, *Taking it Like a Woman*, p. 30.
107. Ibid.
108. Ibid. p. 32.
109. Oakley, *Father and Daughter*, Kindle pos. 2902–2960. Cook describes such 'same sex bonding' as 'a peculiar male knack': Cook, *Lords of Creation*, p. 52.
110. Forster, *Hidden lives*, p. 151.
111. Ibid. p. 95.
112. Ibid. p. 151.
113. Forster, *Good Wives?*, p. 3
114. Forster, *Hidden Lives*, p. 151.
115. Mica Nava (2014) 'The Family in Second Wave Feminism', paper presented at the Historicising the Second Wave conference, at the Centre for European and International Studies, University of Portsmouth, 4 July 2014.
116. Nicholson, *Singled Out*, pp. 172–174
117. Jackson & Marsden, pp. 155–160; Appendix 29.
118. Cook, *A Slight and Delicate Creature*, pp. 2, 218.
119. Ibid. p. 218.
120. Ibid. pp. 218–219.
121. Rowbotham, *Promise of a Dream*, pp. 47–50, 62. There were more examples from my own and my interviewee's experience.
122. Oakley, *Taking It Like a Woman*, p. 47.
123. Ibid. p. 74; and interviewees.
124. Dyhouse, *Students*, pp. 95–102; 120–132.
125. Forster, *Precious Lives*, p. 11; pp. 246–249.

126. Forster, *Precious Lives*, p. 251; Oakley, *Taking It Like a Woman*, p. 39; Cook. *A Slight and Delicate Creature*, pp. 101–113.
127. Lynne Segal (1983) 'The Most Important Thing Of All': rethinking the family: an overview, in Segal (Ed.) *What Is To Be Done About The Family*, pp. 9–24.
128. Oakley, *Taking it Like a Woman*; Nava, From Utopian to Scientific Feminism?, in Segal (Ed.) *What Is To Be Done About The Family*, pp. 65–105, p. 72.
129. Oakley, *Taking it Like a Woman*, p. 85.
130. William Beveridge (Sir) (1942) *Social Insurance and Allied Services*, Cmnd 6404, 26 Nov. 1942, London UK, HMSO (the Beveridge Report) stated that there were five evils in society; namely, squalor, ignorance, want, idleness and disease.
131. William H. Beveridge (Sir) (1944) *Full Employment in a Free Society* (London: Allen & Unwin). Beveridge argued that full employment would be reached when the number of vacancies matched the number of unemployed. To this end the economy should be planned so that production and demand is maintained.
132. The date for the UK Labour Party's abandonment of full employment as the main aim of economic policy is usually given as the speech by James Callaghan to the Annual Conference in Blackpool in June 1976. At that time he said that the cause of unemployment was excessive wages and added: 'The Manifesto was right when it said that the first priority of the Labour Government must be a determined attack on inflation.' This contrasts strikingly with the 1950 Labour Party Election Manifesto which states that: 'Labour for its part declares that full employment is the corner-stone of the new society.'
133. The Act gave significant discretion to LEAs, which allowed some variations to this general pattern. For example Islington in north London developed co-ed comprehensive schools from 1944, while Kent has retained many of its grammar schools to the present day. Continuing tax incentives to elite and fully private schools has allowed for some single sex schools to continue. While state support for religious schools introduced by the Blair government has re-introduced a significant number of single sex schools to the public sector.
134. Kamm, *Indicative Past*, pp. 197–199.
135. Deem, *Women and Schooling*, pp. 58–73; 90–93.
136. Kamm, *Indicative Past*, pp. 197–199.
137. Dyhouse, *Students*, pp. 99, 101, 104
138. Deem, *Women and Schooling*, p. 70.
139. Segal, *Making Trouble*, p. 7.
140. Ibid. p. 8. Nevertheless, these later accounts of trauma survivors have led to a variety of initiatives to address violence and intimate abuse which the Third Wave will perhaps translate into political action.
141. Updale, *The Ship: 2012–2013*, p. 26.
142. Ibid. p. 27.
143. Forster, *Significant Sisters*, p. 10.
144. Rowbotham, *Promise of a Dream*.
145. Gail Chester (2014) Rolling Our Own Revisited: the feminist book trade during the 'second wave', paper presented at the Historicizing the Second Wave conference, at the Centre for European and International Studies, University of Portsmouth, 4 July 2014.
146. Ibid.

Acknowledgements

I gratefully acknowledge valuable direction from the editors Sue Bruley and Laurel Forster and the anonymous reviewers of this article; and valuable constructive advice from Dr John Lepper Adjunct Professor, Deakin University; Dr Sue Middleton Emeritus Professor, Waikato University; Professor Linda Hancock of Deakin University, and Professor Pat Thane of King's College. All errors of fact, logic or judgement are mine alone.

Spreading the Word: feminist print cultures and the Women's Liberation Movement

Laurel Forster

ABSTRACT
This article investigates the significance of print cultures to the Women's Liberation Movement. It highlights feminist interventions into a male-dominated publishing industry through women's writing, publishing and political commitment, with shifts towards feminist publishing cultures, both emboldened by the WLM and empowered by separatist networks. The construction and publication of feminist magazines was a significant aspect of feminist print cultures and activism. This article discusses the different publishing hinterlands of three important feminist magazines: *Shrew*, *Spare Rib* and *Womens Voice*. Arguing that whilst their concerns were overlapping, their distinctive approaches represented the diversity of print activism of the WLM.

The significance of the printed word to the Women's Liberation Movement (WLM) of the 1970s can hardly be overstated: Marsha Rowe recalled that, 'suddenly words were possible', and Lynne Segal remembered the output of 1970s feminism as an 'explosion of creative work from women ... fiction, publishing, poster-making'.[1] The second wave of feminism, unlike the present fourth wave with a range of online media at its disposal,[2] was dependent upon the written word: 'We ate literature' recalled Bea Campbell, discussing her consumption of feminist reading.[3] This newly-found empowerment was not only about women's writing, in itself described as 'an act of power' by Sara Maitland,[4] but also achieving access to, and control over, the production and publication of women's writing: creating an autonomous publishing space for women so that, unlike previous generations of writers, the 'Queen' no longer had to 'sound like the King'.[5] Women's affinity to print was unquestionable:[6] long in evidence through tracts, novels, pamphlets, periodicals and more, all concerned to augment, bolster and advance the cause of women in diverse ways. Feminists of the second wave did much to recover and reprint the long history of female writing, demonstrating that the written word was a dominant mode for individual testimony, creative cultural expression, and a vehicle for group campaigning and political dissemination. Earlier feminist writing was both a valued legacy in the second wave and a conduit for new generations of feminists to learn from feminist foremothers. However, at the WLM's resurgence of feminist consciousness and intent in Britain in the late 1960s and 1970s, control over the printed word, and its production, was seized upon as a potential portal to power.

In particular, the 'experience of production' was highly valued as a feminist activity.[7] If print was the means of spreading the word, then engagement with the publishing industries or print cultures demonstrated participation in the cause of women's liberation. This paper argues that engaging with the material conditions and processes of print culture may be understood as inherently part of the feminist struggle. In addition to drawing attention to important pressing social issues, feminist participation in print cultures also concerned the right to participate and construct the very means of communication: the production of the written word. If 1970s feminism is deemed to be 'the real thing: an age of activism',[8] then not only was print and publishing a crucial form of activism with manifold points of intersection and contributions to the women's liberation cause, but production of a feminist magazine, one of the movement's most popular forms of print media, was an achievable way of bringing different political identities and hinterlands, as well as women's diverse skills, to political effect. Consequently, magazine production as activism enabled women to both participate in the movement and explore their own particular feminist politics. Spreading the word through feminist print and publishing cultures of the 1970s became both personal and political.

In the WLM in the UK (and elsewhere), there were deeply meaningful shifts in women's relationship with print cultures and related activism which, like other political activity, involved struggle, argument and difficult decisions. Feminist print cultures, though, were pulled divisively: they had to engage with industry requirements and procedures, i.e., the man's world of publishing, whilst also expressing often radically oppositional and newly emergent articulations of feminism. It was both of the world of print, i.e., the public sphere, and a separatist activity. Involvement in the publishing industries, including printing and bookselling, was seen in itself as an opportunity for feminist commitment and activism. This may be witnessed by the number of feminist publishers and printing organisations that established at this time. This article will outline the scope of the diverse engagement of the WLM and its members with the publishing industry, drawing upon feminist histories of print cultures, personal testimonials and critical writing on magazines. This will lead to three contextualised examples of feminist magazines which emerged out of second wave print cultures: *Shrew* (1969–1974), *Spare Rib* (1972–1993) and *Women's Voice* (1972–1982). These magazines, with overlapping content, and of the same moment and movement, emerged out of different circumstances of production and engagements with feminist print cultures.

A diverse engagement with publishing cultures

The diversity of feminist forays into print, publishing and associated industries is currently receiving detailed interdisciplinary critical attention, crossing boundaries of literature, cultural studies, industry analysis, book history, social movement theory and gender politics. Feminist engagement with publishing history sees women variously as objects, subjects, critics, participants and producers, and so extends to: the role of feminist bookshops and booksellers; the history of feminist book publication; women's intervention across the range of printing and publication skill sets; feminist publishers; and of course feminist print media artefacts. Simone Murray, in her important study, has argued that this interdisciplinarity has affected the study of women's broader relationship to print, noting that feminist publishing history has formerly been ignored because it has fallen between two disciplines:

> too literary in its associations to be annexed to feminist cultural studies; and too tainted with commercialism to fall within the purview of literary criticism.[9]

Trysh Travis has noted a further problem: 'this canon of what we might call a feminist book history concentrates primarily on women readers and authors, not on the workings of the communications circuit that transforms manuscripts into books and brings them to market.' Travis continues: 'The desire to document women's presence in the book trades has meant that attention to gender as a form of power has usually been limited to noting that the trades were male-dominated.'[10] However, in relation to magazine production at least, critics are making important connections between gender politics and print artefacts: 'More than instrumental tools, rituals or resources for mobilization, Greenham women's cultural artefacts and communication practices were the very *means* by which their politics garnered shape and meaning.'[11] Feminist activism, then, may be discerned in the specific detail of female groups and individuals, and their very engagement with and utilisation of print.[12]

1970s feminist publishing is difficult to generalise precisely because of its small scale and diverse nature. As movement rather than organisation,[13] the WLM consisted of local gatherings, collectives and some individuals with high profiles. Feminist print cultures emerged from the 'small group' politics of the UK WLM.[14] Some groups and collectives were formal, some casual, frequently they suffered a shortfalls of funding and adequate premises, yet each operated to its own agenda with variable affiliations to the movement. Each contributed differently to feminist publishing, understanding feminism differently and expressing that specific mode in print. Groups were neither always wholly separatist, nor always entirely in sisterly accord, and they variously reacted against, and yet also relied upon, the mainstream press. Feminist print cultures have always had relationships with other kinds of publishing organisations,[15] and interventions into the male-dominated professions of printing and publishing were neither straightforward nor unproblematic for women. The point of similarity was to bring all manner of women's expression to print, and the feminist activism may be discerned in intention and experimentation, in the giving of time, energy and commitment to a practical claiming of the means of production of women's words. A consistent intention was to build a feminist publishing industry aligned with feminist principles, often resulting in complex negotiations with, or attempted total rejection of, extant publishing practices. Thus the notion of independent publishing emerged: 'In 1970s discussions of feminist publishing, the concept of the women-only forum is expanded into that of a "women's independent communications network."'[16] For some, this developed into separatist formations with the 'political necessity of women controlling all aspects of the publication process' so that the hostile male press could be shunned.[17] Hence, 'the central perception with which feminist publishing originates: that production of the printed word and its interpretation constitute forms of *political* power'.[18] This separatist seizing of publishing power was of central significance: for example, of *Trouble & Strife*, a feminist magazine with separatist underpinnings, Cameron and Scanlon state: 'No man ever contributed to *T&S* as an editor, writer, designer, typesetter or illustrator; the only men it dealt with were those it paid to print and distribute the magazine.'[19]

Furthermore, Trysh Travis has described how the US Women in Print movement (WIP) gained strength as a reaction against the publishing industry's sexism and gender hostility. This separatist feminist organisation assembled women working, or wanting to work, in the publishing industry, intending to provide industry training and create its own network of readers, writers, editors, printers, publishers, distributors and retailers, and construct its own printing industry duly hostile to the male publishing industry.[20] It was hugely supported by the energies of lesbian women also seeking a print culture of their own.[21] The first WIP conference (1976) imparted publishing skills and gender politics with the dual aims of increasing women's skills in the printing world, and of creating a feminist print network to counter the male network, proven untrustworthy and undermining to women publishing in the 1960s.[22] It was not that trade publishers were not taking feminism seriously by the 1970s, but that feminist intentionality was to undermine patriarchal capitalist control of feminist writing,[23] and by 1979 a similar 'Women in Publishing' movement (WiP) had started in London.[24]

Personal testimonials from some women working in the publishing industry at the time reveal complex relationships between their feminism and their publishing work. In Chester and Nielsen's *In Other Words*, one editor asks 'What the Hell is Feminist Editing?' and concludes that it implies careful selection and nurturing of important female texts to which only a specifically feminist publishing house would allocate time and resources.[25] Commitment to feminist writing was strong, with one feminist writer becoming involved in publishing out of sheer 'belief in the worth of the writing',[26] and other women who viewed their writing as their most important work, but used those same skill sets in mainstream publishing to earn a living through, say, copy editing jobs.[27] Gail Chester, whose 'employment in publishing began as a political act--[her] desire to see radical literature of all types more widely available', still after eighteen years felt herself to be 'on the outer fringes of the profession', perhaps because of her politics, class, ethnic origins or because, as she puts it, of 'being an uppity woman'.[28] For other feminist writers and publishers, independence was not so unambiguous: *Outwrite* feminist magazine, intended to voice 'Black and Third World women's struggles', whose founders successfully published with only 'few technical skills (initially)', was dependent upon Greater London Council funding as well as the activism and militancy of a movement.[29] Feminist activism in print and publishing, whilst some strove for separatist status, was also subject to important dialogical relationships with a number of industries and agencies, rarely seen as innocent of associated connections and processes.

Women's liberation and the mainstream and underground presses

The relationship of feminists to the presses is complex and varied, with surprising contexts that sometimes belie straightforward assumptions.[30] And production of a feminist magazine always implied some relationship to other forms of print production, even if total opposition. Overall, the WLM's relationship with the daily press was complex, having been described as 'tangled and uncomfortable'.[31] Juliet Mitchell has discussed how the media divisively set different WLM groups against each other, resulting in a national regulation that 'each group could describe its own politics to the press, etc. but not those of other groups'.[32] Despite the 1970 formation of the Women in Media Group, which aimed to improve the situation of women in journalism, broadcasting and publishing, and the reporting of women's issues, such policies caused hostilities and some felt that this 'left reporters with few options but guesswork, caricature or silence on feminist issues'.[33]

However, it is possible to over-simplify the representation of gender in the press,[34] and critics of second wave feminism have problematised the relationship of the press to second wave feminism. Kaitlynn Mendes, applying critical discourse analysis to articles on feminism from the long 1970s, has studied representations of feminists in US and UK national daily newspapers. Mendes argues that:

> it is difficult to make overall, conclusive remarks on news coverage other than to say it was fragmented and contradictory--newspapers simultaneously portrayed the movement as effective and serious and ineffective through trivialising feminists and their concerns.[35]

This contrasts somewhat with other discussions that claim more negative news coverage; however, Mendes did find the *Daily Mirror* 'consistently constructed the women's movement and feminists as de-legitimate and deviant'.[36] Overall, Mendes argues that:

> there was far more legitimising or supportive coverage than previous scholars have claimed, and that these articles frequently engaged with the movement's members, their goals, and constructed it as unified, good for women, necessary, and liberating.[37]

Mendes' findings lead her to suggest that the US movement 'formed highly organised groups […] whose members understood the journalistic conventions needed for attracting the media', whilst, 'Conversely, the UK movement tended to consist of smaller, more fragmented groups, who either made little or no attempt to attract mainstream media attention, or who actively opposed it'.[38]

However, this unevenness in mainstream representation does not imply that the underground press was more consistently sympathetic or harmoniously attuned to women's rights and/or feminist expression. Elizabeth Nelson describes ways in which 1960s underground magazines failed to take the WLM seriously: *IT* magazine, she suggests, remained 'committed to sexism' and certainly 'did not grapple with the issues raised by women's liberation'.[39] *Friendz*, 'had it both ways on the question of women', but saw women's liberation as a joke; and at least *Oz*, 'did seem to understand the necessity to move beyond tokenism with regard to women and their struggle'.[40] Discussing conflict networks and 1960s political movements, Carol Mueller identifies similar dissatisfaction with the 'low status' women experienced, despite their high levels of education, in the 'submerged networks of civil rights and the New Left'.[41] Marsha Rowe, who worked for *Oz* and *Ink*, recalls the role of women in the underground press: 'The women who worked on its magazines and newspapers served the men and did the office and production work rather than any editorial work.'[42] Rosie Boycott, who worked for *Friendz* and co-ordinated the woman's issue, was more explicit about the attitudes of the underground press men:

> The underground press had an ambivalent attitude towards women. 'You can fuck anytime, but ask a girl to make Ovaltine?' *Oz* editor Richard Neville was quoted as saying. He was almost right. Going to bed, or, as the cliché had it, getting laid on the back copies, was expected. To refuse was both old-fashioned and hypocritical in a culture promoting free love.[43]

Boycott explains the ambivalence of editors of *International Times*, Britain's oldest underground paper, while condemning the Miss World competition:

The editors could sigh complacently because they weren't subjecting their girlfriends to parading in swimsuits round the Albert Hall. But they weren't encouraging them to become editors or reporters either.[44]

Nonetheless, the counter-cultural and anti-establishment stance of 1960s underground presses in Britain and elsewhere was an important precursor to the print media of the UK WLM: it provided a platform for oppositional politics and a training ground for writing and publishing.

Despite the underground press's sexism, its informal structures and compressed way of working permitted those women involved in various magazines, such as Sheila Rowbotham on *Black Dwarf* and Germaine Greer on *Suck*,[45] closer proximity to the printing and publication processes, and an introduction to the industry. They may have railed against the sexism, but women such as Rowbotham, Boycott, Rowe, Greer used those industry skills for the feminist cause, some producing ground-breaking writing and journalism.[46] For Marsha Rowe at *Oz*, the political mismatch between the 'sex-objectifying images' and the ideals of women's liberation caused her to 'feel contradictions exploding inside my head',[47] and led to her jointly establishing *Spare Rib* with Boycott:

> This was prompted by all we had learned on the underground press, which included the notion that self-organizing was possible, as well as familiarity with the mechanics of production and distribution. Rosie had some journalistic experience on *Frendz*, while my editorial experience was limited to research and helping on layout.[48]

The emergence of feminist print cultures

A varied and often problematic relationship existed between women of the WLM, and its emergent publishing cultures, and the existing publishing and press industries. Whether feminists rejected the male press industry totally or saw it as a training ground, at the very least there was suspicion caused by gender-hostility and a desire to claim the printed word for the feminist cause. The development of feminist presses became crucial to the dissemination of feminist communication, even being regarded as instigators of social change.[49] They also performed a crucial role in their work of recovery, unearthing and reprinting feminist texts. Feminist publishing houses, such as Virago and The Woman's Press, were also often more successful in both financial outcome and public recognition than other feminist media production such as feminist film or feminist magazines.[50] Often having to weave a difficult path between political authenticity and commercial viability, they persevered, feeling it was a 'duty' to survive.[51] The relationship of feminist presses to other industry sectors imposed difficulties, such as when Virago (1973) was compelled to print very small hardback copy runs just to achieve journalistic reviews. Murray discusses complex industry engagements, certainly in the case of Virago, where business acumen, regular hierarchical management and an instinct for survival vied with feminist activist ambitions and a desire to run women's publishing differently.[52] Murray describes 'the duality of [Virago's] self-conception: it perceived itself simultaneously both as a commercial publishing house *and* as an intrinsic part of the British women's liberation movement.'[53] Indeed, writers for Virago have described a different publisher-writer relationship.[54] Catherine Riley has argued that Virago intended to change constructions of gender through the content of its literature and by influencing and expanding the literary landscape.[55] The history of financial pressures, takeovers and industry dealings of the feminist presses is evidence of a range of approaches to the commercial interface of this feminist expression and activism.

Important contributions were also made by booksellers to feminist print cultures and the dissemination of the feminist printed word. For instance, in the US, the Feminist Bookstore Network was run by the owner of Old Wives Tales bookstore, Carol Seajay. The *Feminist Bookstore Newsletter* (1976–2000), designed to enhance communication amongst fellow feminist booksellers, was described as the 'industry bible for lesbian and feminist booksellers'.[56] Feminist scholarship has discussed the important contributions made by bookstores to the WLM, seeing these women-centred, and sometimes women-only, spaces as feminist meeting places and political entities in themselves. Kristen Hogan argues that from as early as 1970 onwards in the US, bookstores provided public spaces for feminism:

> Different from the leftist and progressive bookstores of the 1960s, the feminist bookstore created an entirely feminist space that provided a context for the publications on its shelves; this more specific collection allowed for broader attention to women's literature and uniquely emphasised the existence of a body of feminist literature.[57]

Hogan follows Nancy Fraser's argument for feminist bookshops as well as journals and publishing companies, seeing them as Habermasian public spheres, part of a 'feminist subaltern counterpublic' which function both as 'spaces of withdrawal and regroupment' and as 'bases and training grounds for agitational activities directed towards larger publics'.[58] Feminist bookstores then, have been seen as an essential resource, circulating mimeographed and Xeroxed copies of otherwise unavailable texts, republishing out-of-print books and operating as libraries with readers studying 'store copies' in situ. Hogan describes bookstores as being closely associated with lecturers and students on women's studies courses, as places where academic and community feminism continued to influence each other, organising and distributing feminist texts, acting as primers for women's studies courses, and offering places for connections and 'collective power'.[59] Thus, feminist bookshops were involved in education as centres themselves, but also in alignment with formal education courses in women's studies.[60]

In the UK, the well-known, and local-council-funded, Silver Moon bookshop opened in 1984 on the Charing Cross Road, London, founded by Sue Butterworth and Jane Cholmeley; eventually taken over by Foyles in 2001; like its American counterparts becoming a centre for feminist information and resources, selling books and magazines unavailable elsewhere. It fulfilled different kinds of feminist work including promoting feminist authors, publishing, producing its magazine, *Silver Moon Quarterly*, and helping victims of abuse find refuge.[61] Thus its connections and activism extended beyond commercial transactions to the local community, the council and the world of feminist publishing. Regional bookshops also offered opportunities for local activism. Jill Radford, in discussing the Winchester Women's Liberation Group, describes how:

> With women from one of the Southampton women's liberation groups and the Ecology Party, we transformed an SWP bookshop into a community bookshop to enable us to begin to acquire the emerging feminist books. October Books—its name never changed—is still trading as far as I know and remains the one alternative bookshop in the area.[62]

Lucy Delap discussed ways in which feminist bookshops were 'nodal' points in a disparate WLM, combining community and commercial spaces, even suggesting a WLM Bookbus to provide feminist education for rural women.[63] However, the history of the bookselling business is a ruthless tale and inevitable difficulties of the crossover between feminism and competitive commercialism have led to arguments that Silver Moon eventually put Sisterwrite (1978–1986), a neighbouring feminist bookshop with an international reputation, out of business.[64]

The circulation of feminist ideas through print media, including written testimony in the form of personal exposés of sexual inequalities, writing by women of colour and by women who felt marginalised by society, feminist fiction, historical recovery and criticism, discussions in the daily press, feminist presses and women working in publishing, and the very act of selling feminist books and magazines—all became hugely important aspects of the WLM. Even placing a book with a non-feminist publisher could cause discussion and debate. However, whilst some women were becoming well known for their writing,[65] or worked towards a feminist press, others expressed their commitment to the WLM through the more modest writing and publishing of a feminist magazine.

Feminist magazines

The scope of women's involvement in print in the 1960s and 1970s provides a crucial context for understanding the diversity of WLM magazines. Second wave feminism emerged from a complex set of social circumstances and an array of political, counter-cultural, anti-establishment and socialist movements. Reflecting this diversity, many small feminist groups across the UK, as well as Europe,[66] had their individual magazines and newsletters, each proffering specific interpretations of feminist engagement.[67] Similar to the suffragette papers, feminist magazines of this later period had to both inform and entertain existing member-readers, whilst spreading the word of the feminist cause to men as well as women.[68] 1970s feminist magazines adopted and adapted the print media form hijacked decades earlier by multinational corporations peddling oppressive capitalist femininities. Indeed, the female oppression evidenced by domestic magazines, so effectively brought to attention by Betty Friedan in the 1960s,[69] is one of the aspects of women's lives strongly attacked by the WLM magazines. These feminist magazines offer a much broader view of women's lives and occupations including housewives, working women, mothers and single women, and mark a huge range of issues, personal and political, from female sexuality and childrearing to women's refuges and improved rights for night workers.[70] They bring history to bear on current issues, reminding readers of previous feminist campaigns and campaigners; report upon events and activism on national and local stages; provide space for individual expression; air debates, share humorous observations and build a feminist culture. They reveal multiple feminisms based in different strands of philosophical and political thought, belying any sense of a singly-focused second wave of feminism.

In addition to diverse content, feminist magazines are also varied physically, ranging from home-typed newsletters, often Xeroxed and stapled, assembled by small consciousness-raising collectives and intended to circulate information within a single-focus group, to publications that in some ways emulate, in content or appearance, more commercial, even feminine domestic magazines.[71] Some magazines had wider, even national, distribution, and some carried feminist-attuned advertisements to generate income, similar to more commercial offerings.[72] The varied tone and appearance indicates that, whilst some magazines had clear political affiliations, others were purposefully open to ranges of opinion. All had in common the pursuit of women's liberation and were instrumental in spreading a diverse set of messages about feminism and gender inequalities.

Membership of a magazine-producing feminist group meant involvement in an all-female enterprise where women could exercise full editorial control over the content, impossible in other in other media productions.[73] A crucial mode of expression of second wave feminism, feminist magazines offered a voice not just to professional writers, feminist historians and academics, but significantly gave access to the printed word and opportunity for sharing experiences to women who were accustomed to having no voice. The processes of collectively producing, writing and publishing was a feminist commitment, and as much activism as other forms of consciousness-raising,[74] offering a route to consciousness-raising through participation, expression and discussion, as well as political identification with the greater movement. As Cameron and Scanlon state: 'The magazine was an important part of our political and intellectual lives; it also made a unique contribution to the life of feminism in Britain.'[75]

Shrew

Shrew (1969–1974) was the unaligned output of a wide range of different women's groups from within the London Women's Liberation Workshop. It was produced by each group in turn, taking on responsibility for the theme of the whole magazine, its contents, layout, illustrations and design. Initially there were only four groups but, as the number of groups grew, a rotating editorship became more difficult;[76] and by 1971 groups had expanded to forty-four plus four special interest groups. With a circulation around 5,000, it was produced several times a year and only available through feminist bookshops such as Silver Moon, therefore circulating within those feminist public spheres already created by bookshop spaces, it appealed to an already-converted audience. Most issues have an alternative, but far from amateurish feel, including hand-drawn and handwritten sections, with items squeezed together on some pages. Individual testimonials lend a personal tone, alongside broader feminist rationale. As each collective had free rein over the magazine they produced, the look and content varies enormously. Some issues focus upon general themes under widespread feminist scrutiny, such as the family, women and work or the plight of women night cleaners.[77] Different workshop groups with particular interests, however, had opportunity to reflect their own feminist direction and priorities within their issue: there was *Psychology Shrew* produced by the Psychology Group of the Women's Liberation Workshop, providing perspectives on therapies from psychotherapists, individual patients and groups; and *Goodbye Dolly*, the children's book issue assembled by the Women's Liberation Literature Collective and the Leeds Group.[78] In the production of this magazine as a mode of feminist expression, some groups took the opportunity to express a distinctive feminism as part of a diverse movement. Each women's liberation group had their own circle of members and operated to their own agendas; they were united by overlapping concerns of gender inequalities and women's rights, but many had their own distinctive approaches, political affiliations and interactions with the WLM.

One particularly focussed issue is *'Goddess' Shrew* (Spring 1977) produced by the Matriarchy Study Group (several of whose members were also involved in the Alternative Socialism group), which was concerned with feminist theology and studying ancient religion and culture. This issue is devoted to explaining Goddess theology, with each article and illustration elucidating a different aspect of Goddess philosophy and beliefs. The issue opens with the introduction, 'Beyond Patriarchy', by exploring and explaining the basis of the Matriarchy Study Group collective, providing an account of their belief in control of the spirit and the influence that this could have on women's oppression of the moment. Explaining that the group came together 'Because several of us already had observed evidence for a previous universal Goddess religion' and seeing this issue as work-in-progress, the main aim is to share their work:

> 1. We want to share with other women our growing confidence that women have not always been 'inferior', subject and oppressed by men in their families and in society. There was a time, universally, it seems, from the beginning of the human race until from 5,000–2,000 B.C. where everyone took for granted matriarchy values and society was organised on the basis of woman-led culture. The Goddess was worshipped not only in terms of fertility and survival but as a way of life in which the feminine, and female, were considered pre-eminent. Great civilisations were built in these cultures.[79]

Articles range from joining a matriarchy study group, to women's spirituality and sexuality, and they embrace ancient Egypt and fertility control, the Bible, priestesses, the moon, stone circles, tress and energy lines. The issue also contains poetry and suggestions for further reading, all illustrated with black, white and shaded line drawings of characters, objects and symbols. It is interesting, detailed and diverse.

This issue of *Shrew* was an important first publication for the Goddess activist and feminist theologian 'Asphodel' (Pauline Long 1921–2005),[80] whose feminist spirituality is seen in the contexts of Marxism, feminism and women's sexuality.[81] One article on Women's Sexuality, signed by 'Pauline', explains that 'Return to knowledge of the Goddess has meant for women, confidence in their own sexuality as part of the world of nature, of intellectual endeavour, of progress to better forms of society', and extends the discussion to 'the Women's Movement today'.[82] Goddess *Shrew*, Daniel Cohen observes, alongside a painting exhibition, 'marked the beginning of the Goddess movement in the British Isles'.[83] Monica Sjöö, now well known for her oil painting 'God Giving Birth' (1968) based on her own birth experiences and her belief in the Great Mother, wrote an article for the issue. Her project to understand ancient 'Womencultures, which link the subconscious to the Cosmic Mother, made expansive connections between:

> the Shaman's rebirth in the cave (the womb of the Mother), the Dead, the Earth's serpentine magnetic force ruled over by the phases of the Moon, the ancient Stone circles and underground chambers, divination, prophecy and oracular sleep.[84]

As a feminist magazine of the second wave, this issue of *Shrew* engages with a specific feminism and represents the belief systems of a particular group. The impetus behind the magazine's production comes from a small collective, and consistently reflects that particular group's convictions, interests, politics and worldview. The flexibility of the magazine format enables a varied and lively presentation of the Matriarchy Study Group, part of the wider WLM, but with its particularised framework for understanding women's oppression. In this way, *Shrew* gave different London area collectives a platform from which to explain their brand of feminist politics, explore their own rationale, engage in consciousness-raising, situate their intersection within the WLM, and perhaps to garner interest and new members.

Shrew offered an opportunity for independent self-representation through print and publication: publication was its activism. Importantly, this enabled a means of working independently from the established media, with its own channels of communication, and intending to 'give as many women as possible the experience of producing a journal'.[85] Consequently, and unlike mainstream, commercial magazines, the production of *Shrew* can truly be seen as a collective effort, reflected in the multiple and varied voices within the different editions. Such variety and scope in expressions of different feminist themes were all accommodated under the umbrella of women's liberation at the time.

Helen Graham has suggested that *Shrew* could use its position as an 'external' publication (as opposed to the London Women's Workshop Newsletter which addressed women already identified with Women's Liberation politics), as a 'communicator' and offer a space for the exploration of identities.[86] Reflecting upon ways in which identity exploration in *Shrew* might have shaped the way women thought about doing politics, Graham identifies the problem of both recognising difference and of joining in the activist political agendas of others:

> The writers in *Shrew* are grappling with these problematics: recognising difference without solidifying it as difference and creating a politics not based on activist identities, but still evoking a 'we' that can reach out to 'anyone else'.[87]

Graham suggests that *Shrew* members, finding it reductive to make women a 'cause', saw communication 'as an end in itself', where involvement in the production of *Shrew* could be seen as 'action' both in the material production of the physical magazine and in the more esoteric, and politically important, assimilation of ideas and raising of consciousness.[88] In drawing attention to prioritising the experience of production, Graham identifies the links between communication and activism, where the 'process is all'.[89] *Shrew* was the forum for women to work through their identification with the movement and to participate in print activism in the very production of the magazine.

Spare Rib

Similarly to *Shrew*, *Spare Rib* (1972–1993) sought to bring the unequal position of women in British society to attention, also focusing upon female identity and female liberation, women and work, campaigns for working women, and debates about the family, raising the consciousness of British women during the second wave of feminism. However, in contrast to *Shrew*, *Spare Rib* emerged out of quite different publishing circumstances. *Spare Rib*, with print runs of 20,000, perhaps 100,000 readers at its peak,[90] and national availability through WH Smith newsagent chain, has become the best-known feminist magazine of the second wave, always produced with the intention of reaching a national audience. Although *Spare Rib* has been criticised for not reaching out to women of all ethnicities and classes, especially in the first few years,[91] in fact it is remembered as the magazine that over its lifetime most prominently represented the WLM. Its digitisation by the British Library (2014) will undoubtedly lead to further scholarship on this important magazine. Such was its impact that recent fourth wave online publications, ezines, feminist web pages and blogs have flattered the original by trying to emulate its sparky, humorous and insightful style, with the short-lived *Feminist Times* (2013–2014) discussing resurrecting 'old Spare Rib' by trying to use the same name.[92]

Spare Rib's presentation demonstrates it emerged from women with more professional understanding of publishing than many feminist magazines. Rosie Boycott and Marsha Rowe, with their experience from *Friendz, Ink* and *Oz*, gathered a group of women to set up *Spare Rib*.[93] The magazine emulates many of the characteristics of more conventional women's magazines, but does so with feminist intent and an openness not possible in a more commercially-oriented publication. The opening editorial letter, for instance, positions the magazine as open to commentary from the readership and, indeed, many personal testimonials were included. In some ways *Spare Rib* covers similar terrain to other, more commercial, women's magazines, but approaches beauty, fashion, cookery and DIY handicrafts from a feminist-consciousness perspective, chiming with anti-capitalist feminism, and the anti-consumerist ethos of a 1970s lifestyle. *Spare Rib*'s early foray into the world of commercial advertising, in order to support the magazine financially, was highly selective.[94] Joanne Hollows has discussed the complex relationship of feminist magazines to commercial advertising, suggesting that *Spare Rib*, influenced by the counter-culture, 'imagined "consuming differently"'.[95] Further difficulties arose in combining professional publishing skills, industry know-how and professional contacts with feminist commitment. Disagreements arose over a sufficiently feminist tone, and arguments ensued between Boycott and Rowe about their different approaches to journalism and feminism, with Boycott giving more time to journalistic gatherings and press parties, and Rowe to feminist groups and conferences.[96]

Nonetheless, the combination of professional journalistic skills, an understanding of the publishing world, alongside the practical know-how of running a successful magazine, enabled a magazine with wide appeal and high-level content to be produced from the very first edition. *Spare Rib*, through its inclusive style, is a fine exemplar of the breadth of approaches to feminism available to women in the early 1970s. Traditional women's interests, especially in early issues, are presented in a way that demonstrates freedom from the masculinised world of manufacture and instead offers a counter-politics of female artisanal protest and subversion of commercialism with domestic crafts and DIY projects.[97] This folk feminism represents an adaptation of domestic skills and crafts, such as the 'hippy love of embroidery', into a personal and political commentary on enforced domesticity and femininity.[98] *Spare Rib* also had a 'News Section' which emulated the newspaper-style column layout and reported the work of local groups and the progress of national feminist campaigns. There were regular consciousness-raising features concerning body and mind, and there were more politically-oriented articles that explore and explain feminist issues of national concern. Alongside this is a more liberal-feminist strand, seeking to educate the reader about feminist histories and feminist perspective on ranges of topics like the workplace and the media. This breadth of content and approaches to feminism undoubtedly accounts for the early and sustained success of *Spare Rib*, maintained even after changes in its running and outlook.[99]

Spare Rib's position allowed it to lend support to later magazines, such as *Trouble and Strife* (1983–2002), a radical feminist magazine, and the narrowly focussed *Mukti* (1983–1987), targeted at British Asian women. Its broad appeal meant it could also include ordinary women and professional writers, including those committed to other politics, such as socialism in the case of Sheila Rowbotham, and those who regularly wrote for established political magazines, including Beatrix Campbell who wrote for the influential *Marxism Today* (1957–1991).[100] *Spare Rib*, then, offered a broad church of views: it was not as focussed as *Red Rag* (c.1973–1980), a more theoretically-oriented Marxist feminist magazine, but nor was it a commercialised glossy like *Cosmopolitan* (1972–ongoing), picking and choosing its way through female sexual liberation and feminist issues.

Womens Voice

Womens Voice (1972–1982), was one of the feminist magazines that emerged out of the socialist movement in Britain, from International Socialists (IS) and then the Socialist Workers Party (SWP).[101] It flourished 1974–78, and summoned a thousand people in 1978 to a rally,[102] yet had a mixed reception: seen by some as a financial burden on the party and by others as important for women socialists. Emerging from an established political movement and party organisation implies a different set of publishing processes and facilities, such as access to established publishers, typesetters etc., from the outset. It also implies accountability, and *Womens Voice* had an uncomfortable relationship with its parent organisation. Tony Cliff, SWP leader, had never really wanted the magazine, but was nervous about losing women activists.[103] As the political commitment of *Womens Voice* grew closer to the newer feminist politics and priorities of the WLM, and attempted a more independent remit, the SWP became concerned that rather than bringing women into the SWP, *Womens Voice* was leading women out to the WLM.[104] The history of the magazine's varied format indicates its uncertain position within the wider political group: it had an early precursor in 1970 as a newsletter by women members of the International Socialists who were 'surprised by the number of IS women that had found their way to the first Women's Liberation Conference, in February of that year', and five bulletins were produced over two years. In 1972, the originally titled *Womans Voice* adopted a women's magazine style and changed its title slightly to the now familiar *Womens Voice*. It established its own approach to feminist issues, taking its lead from the WLM, but offering a distinctively socialist perspective. Additionally, it established Womens Voice Groups, intent upon feminist grassroots activism. The format changed to a newspaper in 1974, but reverted to a magazine in 1977, starting at edition number one, and adopting a glossy appearance a year later.[105] Whilst *Womens Voice* was financially supported and subsidised by the SWP, it was always contentious, as with women's relationship to socialism,[106] and complaints developed about the financial burden of the magazine on SWP branches and the growing autonomy of the Womens Voice Groups.[107] The groups were disbanded by the SWP leadership and *Womens Voice* ceased publication in 1982.

Womens Voice was politically resistant in tone from the outset, with many articles exposing social injustices against women. It particularly actively highlighted and supported working class and working women through articles about working and living conditions. An article about 'The Importance of Equal Pay' bemoans the lack of interest from the unions over this issue and categorically states that 'WOMAN'S VOICE [sic] thinks equal pay *is* very important'; moreover it calls on the unions to 'take women's interests seriously', with the strong implication that the TUC themselves were not giving women equal status.[108] This was an anti-Tory and pro-working-class values magazine for women who felt marginalised by British society, the class system and even by male-dominated left-wing organisations, with a broad appeal to women of colour and women working solely within the home, as well as hospital workers, cleaners, factory and shop workers. It was anti-Tory and pro-working-class values. Furthermore, it was aware of women's working-class history, reprinting an article on the London 'Match Girls' strike of 1888, and other female working-class activism from *Socialist Worker*,[109] and an article on the working class relevance of first wave feminists: 'Sylvia Pankhurst and the East End Suffragettes', encouraging its readers to continue the struggle against poverty.[110] It was alive to sexism in the workplace, exploring the myth of the glamorous secretary and the reality of the regimented typing pool,[111] and aware of the 'fairy story' told of women's lives in glossy magazines.[112] *Womens Voice* had a more urgently political and left-wing feel than early *Spare Rib*, yet later similar outrage at women's place in society is expressed in both magazines. Despite early differences in tone, in a similar way to *Shrew* and *Spare Rib*, *Womens Voice* highlighted issues important to women such as abortion; persistently discussing the matter, exploring and explaining the legal position, exposing those who opposed giving full rights to women such as the proposed Corrie Bill and other attempts to reverse the 1967 Abortion Reform Act. It publicised individual causes and encouraged readers to write in with their personal stories, campaigns and journeys.

Womens Voice covered important social issues such as the Nestlé dried milk scandal and the sale of council houses, but also differed from other socialist magazines, and overlapped with *Spare Rib*, in that it tried to appeal to a wider female readership by including mainstream women's magazines' content with their focus on sex, diets and marriage. Concomitantly, it deliberately approached many of the same issues as other feminist publications, giving space to the impact of rape, contraception options, lesbianism, abortion, the problems with the Miss World competition. The magazine, also like *Spare Rib*, demonstrated direct engagement with feminist culture, for instance interviewing Marge Piercy after the publication of her feminist novels, as well as offering feminist-oriented interpretation of issues covered in the regular press, such as detailed coverage of the Northern Ireland troubles.

Like *Shrew* and *Spare Rib*, *Womens Voice* paid attention to Women's Liberation activism, but was less circumspect than *Shrew*. It encouraged activism and discussed how to establish Women's Voice groups locally to encourage participation in politics and political resistance, such as establishing women's refuges. Information and skills were also imparted to readers through workshops on varied matters including printing posters and establishing rape crisis centres.

As well as evident engagement with feminist issues, *Womens Voice* firmly held to its socialist roots. It acknowledged its place within the world of publication by encouraging writing and publication within its readership, outlined how to write for the magazine and how to write industrial bulletins. *Womens Voice* encouraged women to tell their own stories, in their own words, and often these were augmented with images and commentary. Chris Atton has discussed how, in less centralist party-led forums, readers are encouraged to tell what they know.[113] This mode was important in how *Womens Voice* established an identity: associated with the SWP, but also distinctly feminist-centred. The idea of 'native reporting' gave readers a sense of reliable witnesses telling their stories.[114] One double-page spread contains an image of the letter written by Margaret Llywarch, wife of John Llywarch, a building worker, alongside a photograph of their family.

Additionally an article expresses outrage at the treatment of building site strikers, charged with intimidation whilst picketing, in the 'Shrewsbury 24' case.[115] This example of a male worker's story and the impact upon his family, told from the woman's perspective, combines a reader's letter with professional journalistic commentary to illustrate a wider set of working class and trade union issues. A complex position of feminist interpretation, socialist politics and trade union argument may be discerned here.

Later in the 1970s, an article by Lindsey German, 'Womens Voice: the way forward' makes clear both the relationship to the Socialist Workers Party and the difficulties inherent in that relationship. It describes how *Womens Voice* was launched in its present form in January 1977 by a group of women in the SWP, and how large numbers of women were becoming involved in political activism in the mid-seventies as a result of failure of laws to bring equality and welfare cuts:

> The experience of working in these campaigns showed us that women *were* interested in SWP politics, particularly on issues that affect women directly. *Womens Voice was launched as a way of introducing our political ideas to more women and drawing more women into political activity with us.*[116]

The article continues explaining that magazine sales, Womens Voice meetings and Womens Voice Groups all grew rapidly. The argument was won within the SWP that:

> special forms of organisation are necessary to involve working class women, that we need *Womens Voice* to reach out specifically to women, and that we must deal with problems that affect us as women, as well as issues affecting the working class.[117]

However, problems arose, German continued, when women who were not members of the SWP became involved with *Womens Voice* magazine and groups, raising questions about the magazine's relationship with the Party. Some, it seemed, wanted to break with the SWP and build an 'active socialist feminist organisation'.[118] Others wanted alignment with the SWP enabling work towards unification of all sectors of the working class, believing that 'socialism can only be achieved by the working class *itself*', and that remaining within the Party facilitated greater commitment to working towards socialist aims. An agreed statement was constructed to be 'adopted as our programme and should be on every *Womens Voice* card and in every issue of *Womens Voice*':

> *Womens Voice* is an organisation that fights for Women's Liberation and Socialism. We fight for: equal pay, free abortion and contraception, maternity leave and child care provision, the right to work, against any form of discrimination of grounds of sex, sexual orientation or race. Womens Liberation is only possible through women organising and fighting for themselves. Womens Liberation can only be achieved by linking its struggles to those of the working class and overthrowing the capitalist system. *Womens Voice* supports the aims of the Socialist Workers Party. It is organisationally independent but based on the politics of the SWP. [sic][119]

Slight variations of this statement appear on the inside back cover of each issue of the magazine. Whilst the statement clarified its affiliation to the SWP, it was the independent organisational aspects of the magazine, and the participation of non-Party member women, that were seen as particularly challenging to the existing SWP committee. Tony Cliff saw women's oppression only as part of the 'wider relations of class exploitation',[120] and despite attempts to locate the magazine's outlook within the SWP's aims of liberation from capitalism, the feminist influence over the content and tone was ultimately seen as too removed from the Party.[121] Alignment to existing socialist politics made it impossible for this feminist magazine, with its WLM leanings, to continue as an independent feminist production. Any advantages of party association in the production of the magazine were surely outweighed by the control exerted from that same quarter; something avoided by the determined political separatism of other WLM magazines.

Conclusion

Shrew, *Spare Rib* and *Womens Voice*, all part of the same social movement, emerged from different publishing hinterlands. Feminist magazines were a significant portion of WLM print culture: educating and encouraging women in their fight for equality, circulating the meaning of second-wave feminism, raising consciousness and supporting activism. They brought new feminist ideas and female-centred modes of expression and resistance to their readerships, enabling women to experience activism, resonated with the WLM whilst developing their own politics. Feminist magazines took their place in wider print cultures too: borrowing styles from mainstream magazine formats and skills from the publishing industries, mimicking the satirical tones of the underground presses supporting other feminist magazines, and responding to mainstream press items. All whilst embracing new, less formal, modes of printed expression.

These three magazines, with similar ambitions and content, demonstrate three different approaches to the writing, construction and publication context of a WLM feminist magazine. Despite their overlapping causes, they each had a different set of engagements with the publishing industry, the WLM, their contributors, and with feminism. This resulted in quite different interventions and contributions to the movement. *Shrew* was defined by the very act of its assembly, purposefully drawing different groups, voices and perspectives together to create, construct and publish a feminist magazine. *Spare Rib* emerged out of counter-cultural publication know-how, and deployed those skills for a marginalised group, also inviting other women to write, but in a more mainstream manner than many other feminist magazines. *Womens Voice* grew from within an existing, theoretically sympathetic, political base, and showed women how to understand their position in society from a socialist perspective; what was less well defined, and accounted for, was the role of women within the socialist organisation.

Feminist magazines were a means of teaching women to express themselves through publication and journalistic skills, permitting engagement in feminist activism and contributing to the movement through the very act of producing a magazine. By claiming this access to print cultures, as well as increased and enlarged involvement in all aspects of the print industry from typesetting to bookselling, women of all backgrounds and talents demonstrated the importance of print media and print cultures to the Women's Liberation Movement.

Notes

1. Lynne Segal (2007) *Making Trouble: life and politics* (London: Serpent's Tail). Retrospective correspondence interview with Marsha Rowe, co-founder of *Spare Rib*: both quotations p. 109.
2. This includes online magazines such as *the F-word* (www.thefword.org.uk); websites that invite contribution such as *The Everyday Sexism Project* (everydaysexism.com); the Internet presence of feminist organisations such as the Fawcett Society and Southall Black Sisters;

Twitter feeds and much more all contribute to an ongoing discussion of twenty-first-century feminism. Nonetheless, a fourth wave of feminism is contested: with some arguing that any fourth wave must be more than an online presence; and others arguing that there are increased opportunities for intersectionality, global campaigning and activism.

3. Beatrix Campbell interviewed by Margaretta Jolly (2010) British Library C1420/01 Track 3.
4. Sara Maitland, quoted in Segal, *Making Trouble*, p. 110.
5. Sandra M. Gilbert & Susan Gubar (1979) Infection in the Sentence: the woman writer and the anxiety of authorship, in Robyn R. Warhol & Diane Price Herndl (Eds) (1997) *Feminisms: an anthology of literary theory and criticism*, 2nd edn (New Brunswick, NJ: Rutgers University Press), pp. 21–32, 22.
6. Trysh Travis (2008) The Women in Print Movement: history and implications, *Book History*, 11, pp. 275–300.
7. Helen Graham (2003) 'New' 1970: 'I', 'we' and 'anyone else', in Helen Graham, Ali Neilson & Emma Robertson (Eds) *The Feminist Seventies* (York: Raw Nerve Books), pp. 159–172, p. 164.
8. Jackie Stacey (2003) *The Feminist Seventies*, preface.
9. Simone Murray (2004) *Mixed Media: feminist presses and publishing politics* (London: Pluto), p. 18. Murray also notes that this history was not chronicled by male historians: pp. 10–13.
10. Trysh Travis 'The Women in Print Movement', p. 276.
11. Ann Feigenbaum (2013) Written in the Mud, *Feminist Media Studies*, 13(1), pp. 1–13, p. 2. My emphasis.
12. Also see Barbara Green (2012) Complaints of Everyday Life: feminist periodical culture and correspondence columns in *The Woman Worker*, *Women Folk* and *The Freewoman*, *Modernism/modernity*, 19(3), pp. 461–485.
13. For a discussion of the Australian WLM see Susan Magarey (2014) Women's Liberation was a Movement, Not an Organisation, *Australian Feminist Studies*, 29(8)2, pp. 378–390.
14. Juliet Mitchell (1971) *Woman's Estate* (Harmondsworth: Penguin), pp. 59–60.
15. For a discussion of earlier feminists' engagement with print, see Simone Murray (2000) 'Deeds and Words': The Woman's Press and the politics of print, *Women: a cultural review*, 11(3), pp. 197–222.
16. Murray, *Mixed Media*, p. 41. Murray quotes June Arnold (1976) Feminist Presses and Feminist Politics' Quest, *A Feminist Quarterly*, 3(1), pp. 18–26; Charlotte Bunch (1977) Feminist Publishing an Antiquated Form? Notes for a talk at the Old Wives Tales Bookstore, *Heresies*, 3, pp. 24–26.
17. Murray, *Mixed Media*, p. 41.
18. Ibid. p. 27 (original emphasis).
19. Debbie Cameron & Joan Scanlon (Eds) (2010) *The Trouble & Strife Reader* (London: Bloomsbury Academic), Introduction, p. 8.
20. Travis, 'The Women in Print Movement'.
21. Kate Adams (1998) Built out of Books, *Journal of Homosexuality*, 34(3-4), pp. 113–141.
22. For example, Esmé Langley's difficulties printing the first editions of *Arena Three*, an early lesbian magazine, resulted in a home-produced Roneoed version: see Laurel Forster (2015) *Magazine Movements: women's culture, feminisms and media form* (London: Bloomsbury), p. 92.
23. Travis 'The Women in Print Movement', pp. 281–282.
24. See, http://www.womeninpublishing.org.uk/about-us/ (accessed 8 Aug. 2015). At the time of writing it still holds monthly meetings.
25. Marsaili Cameron (1987) What the Hell is Feminist Editing?, in Gail Chester & Sigrid Nielsen (Eds) *In Other Words: writing as a feminist* (London: Hutchinson), pp. 119–125.
26. Joy Pitman (1987) Why There's A Light-Box Where My Typewriter Should Be––being a feminist writer, in Chester & Nielsen, *In Other Words*, pp. 104–108.
27. Ellen Galford (1987) 'Working in the Word Factory', in Chester & Nielsen (Eds) *In Other Words*, pp. 89–92.

28. Gail Chester (1996) Book Publishing: a gentleperson's profession?, in Sarah Richardson, Merylyn Cherry, Sammy Palfrey & Gail Chester (Eds) *Writing on the Line: 20th century working-class women writers* (London: Working Press). pp. 141–148.
29. Shaila Shah (1987) Producing a Feminist Magazine, in Chester & Nielsen (Eds) *In Other Words*, pp. 93–99.
30. For instance, Adrian Bingham (2004) *Gender, Modernity and the Popular Press in Inter-War Britain* (Oxford: Clarendon), notes that whilst many inter-war papers vilified feminists and feminism, others had a 'coherent feminist perspective' (109), and that there was a more varied relationship to feminism than has been suggested (246).
31. Anna Coote & Beatrix Campbell (1982) *Sweet Freedom: the struggle for women's liberation* (Oxford: Blackwell), p. 204; and Ch 7 for a discussion of the relationship between women and the media.
32. Mitchell, *Woman's Estate*, p. 44.
33. David Bouchier (1984) *The Feminist Challenge: the movement for women's liberation in Britain and the USA* (New York: Schocken Books), p. 99.
34. Bingham, *Gender, Modernity and the Popular Press*, p. 248.
35. Kaitlynn Mendes (2011) Reporting the Women's Movement, *Feminist Media Studies*, 11(4), pp. 483–498, p. 488.
36. Ibid.
37. Ibid. p. 493.
38. Ibid. p. 488.
39. Elizabeth Nelson (1989) *The British Counter-Culture 1966–73: a study of the underground press* (Basingstoke: Macmillan), pp. 138–139.
40. Nelson, *British Counter-Culture*, p. 139.
41. Carol Mueller (1994) Conflict Networks and the Origin of Women's Liberation, in Vincent Ruggiero & Nicola Montagna (Eds) (2008) *Social Movements: a reader* (Abingdon: Routledge), pp. 226–234, pp. 230–231.
42. Marsha Rowe (Ed) (1982) *Spare Rib Reader* (Harmondsworth: Penguin), Introduction, p. 15.
43. Rosie Boycott (1984) *A Nice Girl Like Me* (London: Chatto & Windus), p. 56.
44. Ibid. pp. 56–57.
45. Lynne Segal (2013) Feminist Impacts and Transformations, in Lawrence Black, Hugh Pemberton & Pat Thane (Eds) *Reassessing 1970s Britain* (Manchester: Manchester University Press), pp. 149–166.
46. Also see Scanlan & Cameron (Eds) *The Trouble & Strife Reader*, p. 4, who make a similar comment about the contributors to *Trouble and Strife*.
47. Rowe (Ed.) *Spare Rib Reader*, pp. 15, 13.
48. Ibid. p. 16.
49. Murray, *Mixed Media*, p. 213.
50. Ibid. p. 19.
51. Ibid. p. 39.
52. Ibid. pp. 32–33.
53. Ibid. p. 32 (emphasis in original).
54. Attested by Mary Chamberlain at a Southampton University History seminar, Feminism In 1970s Britain: Society, Culture And Literature (12 February 2014), whose book, Mary Chamberlain (1973) *Fenwomen: a portrait of women in an English village* (London: Virago) was the first Virago publication.
55. Catherine Riley (2014) 'The Message is in the Book': what Virago's sale in 1995 means for feminist publishing, *Women: a cultural review*, 25(3), pp. 235–255, p. 240.
56. Marie J. Kuda (2000) 'Feminist Bookstore Closes' in *Windy City Times*, http://www.windycitymediagroup.com/lgbt/Feminist-Bookstore-News-closes/28678.html. See also Travis, 'The Women in Print Movement', pp. 288–291.
57. Kristen Hogan (2008) Women's Studies in Feminist Bookstores: 'All the Women's Studies women would come in', *Signs*, 33(3), pp. 595–621, p. 595.

58. Nancy Fraser (1992) Rethinking the Public Sphere: a contribution to the critique of actually existing democracy, in Craig Calhoun (Ed.) *Habermas and the Public Sphere* (Cambridge, MA: MIT Press), pp.109–142, p. 124.
59. Hogan, 'Women's Studies', pp. 606–607.
60. Ibid. p. 596.
61. Maureen Paton, 'Eclipse of Silver Moon', *Guardian*, 23 Oct. 2001.
62. Jill Radford (1994) History of Women's Liberation Movements in Britain, in Gabrielle Griffin, Marianne Hester, Shirin Rai & Sasha Roseneil (Eds) *Stirring It: challenges for feminism* (London: Taylor & Francis), pp. 43–50. Also see http://www.octoberbooks.org/
63. Lucy Delap (2015) 'Bookshops and Women's Liberation c1975–2001', seminar paper given at Institute of Historical Research, University of London, School of Advanced Study, Senate House, 16 April 2015.
64. Ibid.
65. Sheila Rowbotham (2013) Introduction: beyond the fragments in Sheila Rowbotham, Lynne Segal & Hilary Wainwright, *Beyond the Fragments: feminism and the making of socialism*, third edition (Pontypool: Merlin Press), pp. 9–18.
66. For a range of women's issues recorded in feminist magazines, see the use made of such testimony and letters in Sheila Rowbotham (1989) *The Past is Before Us: feminism in action since the 1960s* (London: Pandora).
67. See The Feminist Library, London for a range of WLM magazines: http://feministlibrary.co.uk/
68. Maria DiCenzo with Lucy Delap & Leila Ryan (2011) *Feminist Media History: suffrage, periodicals and the public sphere* (Basingstoke: Macmillan).
69. Betty Friedan (2001 [1963]) *The Feminine Mystique* (New York: Norton), Ch. 2.
70. For a range of women's issues recorded in feminist magazines, see the use made of such testimony and letters in Rowbotham, *The Past is Before Us*.
71. Laurel Forster (2010) Printing Liberation: the women's movement and magazines in the 1970s, in Laurel Forster & Sue Harper (Eds) *British Culture and Society in the 1970s: the lost decade* (Newcastle: Cambridge Scholars), pp. 93–106.
72. Joanne Hollows (2013) *Spare Rib*, Second-Wave Feminism and the Politics of Consumption, *Feminist Media Studies*, 13(2), pp. 268–287.
73. Jilly Boyce Kay (2015) Speaking Bitterness: second-wave feminism, television talk, and the case of *No Man's Land* (1973), *Feminist Media Histories*, 1(2), pp. 64–89, 82–83.
74. Linda Gordon (2013) Socialist Feminism: the legacy of the 'second wave', *New Labour Forum*, 22(3), pp. 20–28, p. 24.
75. Cameron & Scanlon (Eds) *The Trouble & Strife Reader*, p. 3.
76. Bouchier, *The Feminist Challenge*, p. 100.
77. See respectively *Shrew*, May 1971 3(4); *Shrew* 4(5); *Shrew*, Dec. 1971 3(9).
78. See respectively *Shrew*, Apr. 1972 4(2); *Shrew*, Oct. 1973 5(4).
79. *Shrew*, Spring 1977, p. 2.
80. Daniel Cohen (2002) Feminist Theology, Men and the Goddess: reminiscences and opinions, *Feminist Theology: the journal of the Britain and Ireland school of feminist theology*, 11, pp. 27–34.
81. Deborah Knowles (2002) Asphodel Long: contexts and paradigms, *Feminist Theology*, 11, pp. 35–45.
82. *Shrew*, Spring 1977, p. 14.
83. Daniel Cohen, 'Feminist Theology, Men and the Goddess', pp. 27–34.
84. *Shrew*, Spring 1977, pp. 5–6.
85. David Bouchier, *The Feminist Challenge*, p. 100.
86. Graham, '"New" 1970', p. 159.
87. Ibid. p. 163.
88. Ibid. pp. 164–165.
89. Ibid. p. 167.
90. Janice Winship (1987) *Inside Feminist Magazines* (London: Pandora), p. 123; Cameron & Scanlon *The Trouble and Strife Reader*, p. 4.

91. Winship, *Inside Feminist Magazines.*
92. Forster, *Magazine Movements*, Ch. 8
93. Palaver, May 4 2010. http://afonsoduarte.tumblr.com/post/538575214/interview-with-marsha-rowe.
94. Joanne Hollows (2013) Spare Rib, Second-Wave Feminism and the Politics of Consumption, *Feminist Media Studies*, 13(2), pp. 268–287.
95. Ibid. pp. 273, 279.
96. Boycott, *A Nice Girl Like Me*, Ch. 8.
97. This resonates strongly with a current fourth wave of craftivism REF. Also see Rozsika Parker (1984) *The Subversive Stitch: embroidery and the making of the feminine* (London: The Women's Press).
98. Parker, *The Subversive Stitch*, pp. 205–210.
99. See Winship, *Inside Women's Magazines*, Ch. 8, for further analysis of these changes.
100. *Marxism Today* carried a debate about the relationship of 1970s feminism to socialism. See Tricia Davis and Catherine Hall (1980) The Forward Face of Feminism, *Marxism Today* (Oct. 1980), pp. 14–16
101. Tony Cliff (2000) *A World to Win: life of a revolutionary* (London: Bookmarks). Ian Birchall (2011) *Tony Cliff: a Marxist for his time* (London: Bookmarks).
102. For an overview of this magazine see: David Renton (26 September 2013), https://livesrunning.wordpress.com/2013/09/26/womens-voice-a-retrospective/ (accessed 1 Nov. 2014).
103. Ian Burchill, *Tony Cliff*, p. 466
104. Sue Bruley (2014) Jam Tomorrow? Socialist women and women's liberation, 1968–82: an oral history approach, in Evan Smith & Matthew Worley (Eds) *Against the Grain: the British far left since 1956* (Manchester: Manchester University Press), pp. 155–172, p. 165.
105. *Womens Voice* (Jan. 1980), p. 28 (back page)
106. The difficulties of this relationship are discussed by Sheila Rowbotham (2013 [1979]) The Women's Movement and Organising for Socialism, in Rowbotham, Segal & Wainwright, *Beyond the Fragments*, pp. 125–240.
107. Bruley, 'Jam Tomorrow?', p. 165.
108. *Womens Voice* (Nov./Dec. 1972), pp. 7–8.
109. *Womens Voice* (Jan./Feb. 1973), p. 7.
110. *Womens Voice*, (July/Aug. 1973), pp. 10–11. Also see 'Review: the Rights of Women by Mary Wollstonecraft', *Womens Voice* (May/June 1973), p. 14.
111. 'Goodbye to Costly Dolly Birds', *Womens Voice* (May/June 1973), pp. 6–7.
112. 'Behind the Glossy Pages', *Womens Voice* (Jan./Feb. 1973), p. 10.
113. Chris Atton (2002) *Alternative Media* (London: Sage), p. 104.
114. Ibid. p. 112.
115. *Womens Voice* (Jan./Feb. 1973), pp. 8–9.
116. Lindsey German (Nov. 1979), '*Womens Voice*: The Way Forward', p. 16 (emphasis in original).
117. Ibid.
118. Ibid.
119. Ibid.
120. Burchill, *Tony Cliff*, p. 467.
121. Lindsey German went on to be editor of *Socialist Review* (1978–2005; 2007–ongoing), from 1984 to 2004.

Fighting for Recovery: foremothers and feminism in the 1970s

Janet Floyd

ABSTRACT
This article argues that the feminist recovery of 'a history of our own' during the 1970s proved difficult in ways not fully addressed in generalising narratives (celebratory or regretful) of feminist historical work. The recovery of a nineteenth-century 'pioneer woman', Mary Hallock Foote, demonstrates the competing interests in play—feminist and anti-feminist, popular and scholarly, public and familial, national and local—as well as the problematic positions of that these cross-cutting debates. The question of recovery, use and even ownership, of Foote and her history retains its ability to spark argument almost fifty years later.

This article is concerned with the feminist recovery of foremothers in the US during the 1970s, and the setting within which that work was undertaken. The process of recovering figures from the past and attributing meaning to them is of course fundamental to traditions in historical research and writing. It is always an intellectually and ideologically charged project, not infrequently freighted with personal meaning as well. However, the recovery by second-wave feminists of a history 'of our own' has always been acknowledged—and was recognised from the start—to be deeply significant for the feminist movement itself. In the US it was a project looking to affirm the centrality of women to national culture through rediscovering women of national influence and inserting them within key historical narratives. Just as important was the possibility of finding and developing a back-story—bright or baleful—to inform and historicise contemporary feminists' understanding of their own experience, thought and aspiration. This was work that could power changes in consciousness as well as inspiring activism. Indeed, the writing of history generally was experienced by some feminists as a strand of activism: Judith Bennett describes the 'clarity of that 1970s ideal of a seamless union of history and feminism' in a 'heady mixture of activism and writing'.[1]

The work of feminist recovery in the US at this time has been narrated in a number of ways: as an arc of triumph at the outset of second-wave historiography, as interrupted or problematised by other feminist projects, and, especially, as undercut by the growing awareness on the part of dominant groups in US feminism of the significance of difference, particularly in terms of 'race' but also in relation to class.[2] Here I want to reflect on this history from another perspective: through the recovery—or recoveries—of a particular white middle-class American woman. My aim is to show how difficult and complicated this recovery work proved to be, even at its most blithely Anglo-American in focus, its most untroubled by difference, its most evidently mainstream.

By the mid-1970s, the work of 'making the invisible woman visible'—the invisible white woman that is—had reached a high point in academe, whether such activity involved bringing historical figures' roles in public life and the professions back into mainstream history, or proposing root and branch change in the categories that structured conventional historical research (for example to include the quotidian life of the domestic space). These activities operated in parallel with one another, in some cases oblivious of their differences, in others deeply engaged in debate. But, of course, the project of recovery of foremothers was scarcely confined to universities. Patrice McDermott has described 'a chasm' opening up between feminist scholarship and a broader feminist community of activists outside the academy.[3] This may have been the case with respect to activism, but recovery was an activity shared across feminists within and outside the academy. Many amateur and local historians shared their scholarly sisters' commitment to recuperating women from the past, and indeed their ideological diversity. In the introduction of a volume of pioneer reminiscence published in 1976 by the Women's Press, for example, the editors wrote of their excitement in finding 'heroines we could call our own—magnificent women of whom we'd never before heard a word' and the sense that theirs 'was not the first generation to be humiliated by women's traditional role … to dare to question'.[4] The tone and method of volumes like this were somewhat different, sometimes very different, to that of academic works, but the projects were similar. Meanwhile, beyond the feminist field, recoveries of women—historical types and figures that had long been culturally resonant—were being investigated across the American mainstream. It is this complex terrain of recovery, in which projects collided with one another within and beyond the movement, that I want to open up here through looking at the fate of a single figure.

In using 'fighting for recovery' in my title, I want to suggest the energy and force with which those involved strove to make their different understandings of historical figures stick, and indeed to claim these figures for their own. There is also, as I hope to show, a quality of compression in the interpretative space available to those working to recover their subjects, a sense that for all the vitality of the investigative urge, there was a check on the outcomes available.

The figure whose recovery I want to trace here is that of Mary Hallock Foote, a white middle-class writer and illustrator of some reputation in the late nineteenth century who, on her marriage in 1876, migrated to California, Colorado and Idaho. Her recovery in the 1970s does not, however, begin within the feminist project, but rather with a novelist for whom feminism was deeply problematic and a novel that struggled with questions prompted by the recovery of female figures. This was Wallace Stegner's *Angle of Repose*, published in 1971 to some acclaim: it won the Pulitzer prize.[5] Stegner, a western American writer, cultural historian of the west and conservationist recently retired from teaching at Stanford, had been granted unrestricted access, by Foote's descendants, to her unpublished letters and memoirs. His novel included transcriptions of Foote's letters, sometimes at great length, as well as quotations from her (at the time) unpublished reminiscences. Stegner did not attribute these quotations to Foote because he had made an agreement with one of Foote's grandchildren to change the names of the key figures in order to maintain the family's privacy. The family had been pleased that a well-known writer wanted to recover their grandmother's experiences in a novel, but they did not wish to become the object of public attention. Accordingly, Stegner changed Foote's name to Susan Burling Ward, along with the names of other central figures.

Subsequently, however, when *Angle of Repose* appeared, some members of the family were surprised and irritated by how much of Foote's own writing was reproduced in the novel, writing that readers of the novel would naturally assume to be of Stegner's invention. So, for example, Stegner had been praised in reviews for his sense of place, yet his perceptions had derived—in some cases had actually been lifted—from Foote's writing. Foote's granddaughter wrote: 'I resent the fact that he got the Pulitzer Prize for his sense of place, when most of the things that established the sense of place are direct quotes of what my grandmother wrote.'[6] Much of the recovery of women during this period, after all, feminist or otherwise, was undertaken by, or under the auspices of, family members. This gave descendants a measure of control, if not complete editorial power. Foote's direct descendants had not been prompted to recover their grandmother for their own purposes of family definition, but nor had they anticipated this apparent loss of ownership of her life and work.

The difficult and apparently already sensitive question of recovery as appropriative was not the only problem, however. What proved much more contentious for the family (and subsequently others) was Stegner's claim that, given that he had decided to write a novel and agreed to change the names of the central characters, he had gained the right to manipulate the material to which he had access. Actually, it had not been Stegner's original intention to write a novel based on Foote's experiences. Faced with her papers he considered whether to write a biography before turning to fiction, on the grounds that there was not enough material of interest for a full volume. And having decided to generate a fiction from Foote's papers, Stegner struggled with the task: 'The novel got very complex on me before it was done. It gave me trouble: I had too many papers, recorded reality tied my hands ... '[7] Foote's life and recovered writing, in other words, proved insufficient to the themes he wanted to use her life to explore. As a result (and this was the move that was to cause most outrage) Stegner decided to 'warp' Foote's life—to use his term—and to insert a sexual intrigue within a narrative that otherwise followed Foote's life quite closely. Actually, he added an unconsummated affair between Foote and one of her husband's employees: an absorbing distraction that results in the drowning of her little daughter as well as the ruin of her relationship with her husband.[8]

Finally, appropriation and fictional warping aside, *Angle of Repose* drew attention to elements in Foote's correspondence that had not been known or acknowledged by the family (who had not studied the papers themselves). First, finding in the letters indications of the emotionally charged relationship between Foote and her friend Helena Gilder, Stegner raised the issue of whether theirs was a sexual relationship. Second, reading hints in Foote's letters as to her husband's problems with drinking, Stegner gave Arthur Foote's alcoholic binges a determining role in the plot. Put in simple terms, he portrays a prudish coldness in his Foote figure that plays a part in driving her husband to the bouts of drinking binges that, in turn, cause her to look elsewhere for emotional fulfilment.

As we shall see, an argument ensued over what might be made—what should and what 'needed' to be made—of a particular woman's life. Yet Stegner, even as he struggled with the novel, had himself clearly become highly sensitive to the significance in terms of gender of these problems of appropriation, distortion and exposure, to the point of attempting to address them in a second sketchily-written plot. Here a retired academic,

Lyman Ward, becomes absorbed in his grandmother's papers and forms a narrative of her life; a position closely comparable, of course, to Stegner's. Lyman Ward assumes his grandmother to be easily recovered by reference to broadly held beliefs about genteel Victorian women; but we witness him finding her breaking free from his assumptions about what he believes her to have been capable of knowing, feeling and doing. In sum, Stegner's 'trouble' with recovery, that Foote was in some sense insufficient, is projected onto his surrogate's developing relationship with a female ancestor that becomes flooded with meaning.

This plot shows—rather presciently—two protagonists fighting over the recovery of Foote and, particularly interesting for the current discussion, one of them is a feminist. On one side, Stegner has his surrogate, Lyman Ward, a wounded and very vulnerable figure, engaged in recovery of a grandmother he loved and knew well; a woman over whom he has some measure of ownership (as Stegner had been given the right by Foote's family to use her papers). On the other, Stegner plots a situation in which the recovery of this Foote figure cannot be committed to print by the exhausted and disabled Ward. Instead Stegner produces the figure of a young feminist, Shelly, a 'card carrying member of this liberated generation', who questions Ward's pained vision of his grandmother's life.[9] Shelly may have none of Ward's historical understanding, but Stegner undoubtedly gives her a direct and urgent interest in understanding and interpreting a foremother.

Further, Shelly is particularly attentive to Susan Burling Ward's sexual life. She offers her own views on it, while giving the horrified Ward (who has been abandoned by his wife in favour of another man) chapter and verse on her own sexual adventures and counter-cultural aspirations for male-female relationships. Ward finds himself tortured by questions around women's sexual autonomy and the lack of sexual fulfilment in marriage: why does 'Susan Burling Ward' desire her husband's employee and not her husband, and, above all, why has his own wife, apparently content, left him for a new sexual partner? Why does Shelly set such store by sexual freedom? Thus Stegner's address, in *Angle of Repose*, to the problems around recovery is not only positioned within an argument about feminist recovery, it is also closely linked with questions of women's autonomy (epitomised in sexual autonomy) germane to the feminist movement. As Deborah Paes de Barross points out, it was in imagining Foote's sexual life, her sexual repression and then her passion for a man who was not her husband, that Stegner was most evidently inventive: 'Stegner—who changes so few facts about Foote's life—dramatically changes those facts that have to do with Foote's sexuality.'[10] *Angle of Repose*, far from being an untroubled, somewhat inaccurate recuperation of a forgotten woman, is a novel striated with anxious questions about the recovery of women by men. Stegner makes his hostility to feminism clear, but he seems also to come close to suggesting that the recovery of foremothers may be best handled by women. The questions of sexual autonomy and sexuality at the heart of the work of recovery are left unresolved.

Angle of Repose makes an interesting and perhaps surprising entrance for the recovered figure of Mary Hallock Foote: appearing in mainstream fiction, multiply entangled with the feminist project of the period, and the subject of immediate argument on the part of Foote's family. What did the feminist recovery of Foote look like by comparison?

In 1975, as the vanguard of feminist history saw a turn to the 'celebration of an at least semi-autonomous separate cultural realm' for women 'with distinctive values and institutions', Foote was mobilised, albeit briefly, in one of the most significant essays in the feminist historical field of the late twentieth century: Caroll Smith-Rosenberg's 'The

Female World of Love and Ritual: relations between women in nineteenth-century America'.[11] This time Foote's writing proved more than sufficient to Smith-Rosenberg's argument about the past and, implicitly, the past's links with the present. Smith-Rosenberg had found a route out of the conventional cultural practice of portraying nineteenth-century women as repressed and profoundly limited in a patriarchal society. She drew instead a picture of a richly emotional intimacy enjoyed between women within and across their homes: 'a secure, empathetic world' in which 'women could share sorrows, anxieties, and joys, confident that the other had experienced similar emotions'.[12] Of Smith-Rosenberg's two key examples of 'intense, loving' and life-long friendships between women, one was the relationship between Mary Hallock Foote and Helena Gilder to which Stegner had drawn attention in *Angle of Repose*. Smith-Rosenberg's analysis rested, of course, on the same correspondence to which Stegner had gained access through Foote's descendants and that had subsequently been lodged in the Green Library at Stanford.

Three issues come to the fore when one considers Smith-Rosenberg's work in the light of what had come before in Stegner's recovery of Foote: the use of the letters, the reflection on method, and the representation of the life. Where Stegner had reproduced (and in some cases altered) lengthy sections of the letters in *Angle of Repose* in order to trace the contours—and the limitations—of the genteel Victorianism, Smith-Rosenberg, by contrast, uses much briefer sections to emphasise the high emotional pitch of Foote's and Gilder's relationship. Those elements of the letters that dealt with other issues (shared cultural capital, life experiences outside the home, the sense of alienation from friends) were not allowed to complicate the argument. This is a far more tightly controlled recovery of Foote. Smith-Rosenberg, doubtless sensitive to the powerful importance given at the time to women's association, creates a nineteenth-century emotional hothouse of same-sex friendship. She erases Foote's lengthy discussions of her other relationships.

Yet Smith-Rosenberg showed a surprising uncertainty about the process of recovery. Like Stegner, she reproduced the following passage from one of Foote's letters:

> I wanted so to put my arms round my girl of all the girls in the world and tell her … I love her as wives do love their husbands, as friends who have taken each other for life—and believe in her as I believe in my God … If I didn't love you do you suppose I'd care about anything or have ridiculous notions and panics and behave like an old fool who ought to know better. I'm going to hang on to your skirts … You can't get away from [my] love.[13]

Stegner's wounded surrogate, Lyman Ward, comments that reading 'that one makes me feel like a Peeping Tom'. Stegner's anxiety about recovery is expressed through his narrator's reference to the limited perspectives and compromising nature of male intrusion: his embarrassment. Smith-Rosenberg's was a different point of departure, clearly, but also an equivocal one. While making the point that 'Molly and Helena were lovers—emotionally if not physically', she immediately situates herself at 'a distance of a hundred years and from a post-Freudian cultural perspective', averring that 'It is clearly difficult … to decipher the complexities of Molly and Helena's relationship'.[14] Foote's writing was too distant, too different, and too difficult to read quite confidently: a surprisingly hesitant approach.

Finally, focused on the private letters they found so compelling, Stegner and Smith-Rosenberg both tend to seal their subjects within the private sphere. Both remove

Foote's (and Gilder's) public career and ambitions from the discussion. Neither acknowledges Gilder's role in launching and sustaining Foote's career. ('Helena' is glossed in a footnote as 'a New York friend' in Smith-Rosenberg's article.)[15] Nor did the 'female world of love and ritual' engage the complex interplay of private and working lives played out in Foote's and others' homes with any more enthusiasm than Stegner in his representation of an emotionally strangled Victorian household. Thus the questions about women's intimate lives that Foote raised for these two ideologically opposed workers in the field of recovery drove them to contain her within the domestic space. For all that leaving home in some form had always been seminal to the feminist project, it was Foote's life behind closed doors that proved compelling to those who had recovered her thus far.[16] There is some irony here given that Foote had left home as a young women to pursue a career, had been highly successful, married late and periodically supported her family with her work. Stegner diminishes Foote's career. Smith-Rosenberg erases it.

Nothing can detract from the magisterial significance of Smith-Rosenberg's article. The idea of a 'female world' was not only powerful ideologically and responsive to important strands of contemporary feminism, it also generated a wealth of subsequent scholarly recovery. What I want to note here, however, is that Smith-Rosenberg keeps a tight hold, as it were, on what Foote's writing is required to express and explore. There are limits on this recovery.

Meanwhile, another recovery of Foote had taken place, though not this time to feminist or even women's history, but rather to the scholarship of the American west. In 1972, Rodman W. Paul published an edition of Mary Hallock Foote's unpublished autobiographical writing, in *Reminiscences of a Victorian Gentlewoman in the Far-West*. For Paul, a highly distinguished historian of mining in the American West, Foote was engaging as the writer of an account of a series of settings and as the wife of an engineer with an interesting career, yet limited by her background, class and gender.[17] No objection was raised to this commentary on Foote or, for that matter, to Paul's decision to splice together two separate autobiographical texts, one written for publication and one for her family. Working, on the other hand, with Foote's descendants, in particular her grand-nephew, Paul shared the family's view that Stegner's portrait in *Angle of Repose* was ill-judged. He referred, with a disapproval no less pointed for being measured in its expression, to the 'sheer invention—at times *unrestrained* invention' [my italics] of *Angle of Repose*, gesturing to a lack of scruple in Stegner's 'inferences derived from … nothing more than a novelist's sense of what would complete his development of chapter and plot'.[18] Paul was not specific about what was invention or inference. The implication of Paul's note, however, was that Stegner had behaved badly. Certainly Stegner later recalled that Paul had been 'mad at me'.[19]

Paul's intervention raises a question, however. The history of the American west had been a popular field for feminist historians from the start, not only because western history was unquestionably of national importance, but also because the figure they recovered (or perhaps more accurately revisited with different aims), that is, the unfettered and economically active pioneer woman, seemed to have acted out, before the fact, key second-wave feminist solutions to the frustrations of middle-class suburban domesticity.[20] The west had always and could still, in the 1970s, be imagined as a *tabula rasa*: a new, empty space in which to reinvent behaviour and social relations. Now it could form a setting for women to begin afresh. Why, then, did Foote not appear in this field of recovery?

The figure of Elinore Pruitt Stewart, like Foote a published writer, offers an interesting example of a pioneer who proved easy to recover: a popular figure for feminist historians and an instructive indication of the reasons for Foote's neglect during most of the 1970s. Pruitt Stewart, a widowed, or possibly divorced, migrant to Wyoming before World War One, wrote up her experiences of ranching and homesteading in terms recalling the popular tradition of emigrant writing as well as the literary tradition of James Fenimore Cooper. Her *Letters of a Woman Homesteader* was published in the *Atlantic Monthly* in 1913, and then by Houghton Mifflin in 1914, catching, inadvertently or otherwise, the same tide of patriotic interest in the frontier as *O Pioneers*! It was reprinted in the early 1960s in the Bison Books imprint of the University of Nebraska Press, a press with a proud tradition of printing and reprinting the memoirs of ordinary emigrants, male and female. This edition appeared with a brief introduction by the western writer Jessamyn West. West's introduction lauded the traditional virtues of this 'homesteader with her enormous vitality, humor and tenderness': 'We marvel at her capacity for work. We admire her openness to the world and its inhabitants ... '[21] Here, then, was an example of a recovered female figure ripe for mobilisation on feminism's behalf, and writing that delivered the 'reflection' on 'current concerns about women and women's roles', that feminist historians were looking for, and a means 'to understand the historical roots of issues that especially touch women today'.[22]

Unsurprisingly, Pruitt Stewart's book was taken up by two feminists in Montana, Beth Ferris and Annick Smith, who wrote and produced a film, *Heartland*, with a company they set up for the purpose: Wilderness Women. In the film, we watch Pruitt Stewart achieving some of 1970s feminism's ideal positions: leaving home, earning wages for housework, finding common ground with women and marrying in order to file a claim rather than in the spirit of romance (or indeed desire). But if the film was explicitly feminist in intention and in content, still *Heartland* was shown at the White House and bought by the State Department 'to be shown in embassies abroad'. Whether or not it was inflected with feminism, it represented a history that conformed to mainstream values. Pruitt Stewart's descendants raised no objections to the alterations to the events of her life made by the makers of the film.[23] In short, it was possible for feminists to recover pioneer women as rebellious feminists (or proto-feminists) without much altering their conventional appearance.

The celebrated national figure of the pioneer woman had a dark opposite, and no less familiar or usable a figure: a woman on the 'frontier' with no interest in radical change, no sense of the west as a *tabula rasa*, no desire to let go of the conventions of class and gender. This alternative figure was just as useful to feminists of the 1970s, especially those at the radical end of feminist history, where Anglo-European women were shown internalising and reproducing patriarchal oppression as well as failing to see the space for self-development in the west. John Faragher and Christine Stansell, for example, publishing 'Women and their Families on the Overland Trail to California and Oregon, 1842–67' in *Feminist Studies* in 1975, began their article with an extract from a poem published the year before by the radical feminist poet Adrienne Rich, 'From an Old House in America', which recalled the patriarchal identification of land as 'virgin', and the migration enforced on women by their husbands:

> I am not a wheat field
> nor the virgin forest
> I never chose this place
> yet I am of it now

Faragher and Stansell's subsequent discussion expresses regret tinged with exasperation with their ancestors:

> The vicissitudes of the trail opened new possibilities for extended work roles for women, and in the cooperative work of the family there existed a basis for a vigorous struggle for female-male equality. But most women did not see the experience that way.[24]

These feminist historians approached their subjects' private writing expecting to act as cheerleaders for their recovered predecessors, but ended up making rueful excuses for these blinkered, perhaps wilfully blinkered, foremothers. Just as the makers of *Heartland* were able to harness their feminism to a national mythology of pioneer womanhood, so Faragher and Stansell could read the familiar figure of the reluctant pioneer in feminist terms.

In essence, both Stegner and Paul, in recovering Mary Hallock Foote to the history of the American west, produced her in the form of this type of unhappy figure. However, what Stegner chose to add, his material about Foote's extra-marital sexual relationship and the discussion of it, was what marked his departure from these well-recognised western subjects. Pioneer women, as they were recovered over the twentieth century and through the 1970s into the 1980s were usually married, sometimes single and, in my reading, invariably heterosexual. Feminist historians of the American west discussed issues of equality in marriage, economic independence and access to contraception. They steered clear of the world of desire and sexual pleasure. It was in dwelling on both that Stegner provoked a row which drew Foote into the arena of feminist debate.[25]

It was Stegner's mode of recovering Foote by 'warping' her life that prompted the first public argument about the gender politics of *Angle of Repose*. It was not a discussion conducted on feminist terms but it was formed around a feminist argument. It appeared in the middle pages of the *San Francisco Chronicle* in September 1976 (the occasion was the opening performances of Andrew Imbrie's opera of *Angle of Repose*). An in-house columnist, Blake Green, had interviewed Stegner about how he had dealt with his subject and then telephoned Foote's granddaughters, Janet Micoleau (who had been responsible for granting Stegner access to Foote's papers) and Marian Conway. The resulting article raised questions about how a woman, her life and her work could be treated and what aspects of her life might be said to be off limits; questions, indeed, that Stegner had raised in his novel and that Foote's family had subsequently picked up.

Green tackled the issue in terms of gendered inequality, reading Stegner's use of Foote as the exploitation of a woman by a man, and she imagined the case as one in which Stegner had exerted sexual power over Foote. It is possible that she was responding to feminist debates about sexual harassment and rape that feminism was forcing Americans to engage in the mid-1970s.[26] What she used, though, was the language of sexual exploitation: Stegner had taken 'liberties' with Foote, she wrote, and 'the liberties themselves might not have been so bad had he not sometimes remained quite true to her'; he had 'lived with her' but he 'did not find her interesting enough' for a biography ('she was not quite that important').[27] The range of reference here seems to move between a sense of traditional conventions of male-female relations violated ('taking liberties', 'being true'), and more contemporary doubts about sexual experience outside marriage ('living' together). One senses that Green welcomes the opportunity afforded by a squabble about a historical novel to find a way of exploring questions of male power.

Green quotes Foote's granddaughter in the article, and she seems to use a comparable expressive range. For Marian Conway, though, this was not a feminist issue or a discussion shaped by feminist discourses circulating at the time. She uses terms recalling patriarchal discourses of women's lack of agency, seduction and the attending threat of loss of a woman's value, expressing the disturbing sense that Foote had been damaged by Stegner; that he 'did their grandmother wrong'; 'She can't defend herself and all her contemporaries are dead.' For Foote's family, *any* detail of a woman's sexual life, even the sexual life of a woman born in 1847 who had been dead some forty years, ran the risk of making her (and those close to her) the object of commentary, as well as damaging her descendants' narrative of their ancestor's life. To go on to add new fictional material (as Stegner had done) about sex and sexuality was difficult, if not impossible, to justify.

For the first five years after the first recovery of Foote, then, her relationship with feminism had been indirect (as the object of debate about feminism in Stegner's novel), partial (in brief quotation in Smith-Rosenberg) and partly coded (in Green's article); otherwise, to her family and to Rodman Paul, she appeared wholly uncoupled from feminist argument. Nor had Foote been recovered as a western woman by feminist historians, even in the wake of Stegner's, Smith-Rosenberg's and Paul's recovery work. It was only eight years after the publication of *Angle of Repose* that Foote appeared at the centre of an explicitly feminist debate.

The views of Foote's granddaughters publicised by Blake Green's article had been picked up in the academic setting of the University of Idaho, where Richard Etulain, a friend of Stegner and himself something of a promoter of Foote's work, was working alongside Mary Ellen Williams Walsh, an associate professor in western American literature. In late 1978 Etulain invited Walsh to speak on the female figures in *Angle of Repose* at the 1979 annual conference of the Western Literature Association. Walsh, having made contact with Foote's family, delivered a conference paper that named as 'theft' the use of Foote by Stegner, accusing him of besmirching Foote's reputation:

> Finally scholars are beginning to learn exactly how little hesitation Stegner felt about warping Mary Hallock Foote's personality and the events of her life to his fictional needs ... Stegner has warped Foote into monstrous shapes—an Eve who destroyed her husband's western Eden, a lesbian, an adulteress, a filicide.[28]

Clearly the tone of this is very different to what had come before. It recalled the forthright anger and energy of 1960s and early 1970s feminism's aggressive attack on the status quo, and also evoked the defensive stance produced by the mainstream backlash against liberal feminism at the end of the decade. Notwithstanding the separate and differently chronologised energies and triumphs of Black, Chicana and Native feminist activism, the 'mood of the American movement' as David Bouchier puts it, 'was one of disillusionment and demoralisation'.[29] The very title of Walsh's conference paper, 'Succubi and Other Monsters: the women in *Angle of Repose*', in referencing the succubus, a sexually aggressive demon incarnated as a woman, spoke to the rise of misogyny directed at feminists in mid- to late 1970s popular culture.[30] By all accounts, the paper received a hostile reception amongst her audience of twenty to twenty-five people, unsurprisingly so given that Stegner had become a canonical figure in contemporary western American literature and someone personally known to key people at the conference.[31]

Walsh's positioning of herself as somehow defending Foote's family and their memory of Foote was disingenuous. While some family members had argued that Stegner's was not fair use and that he had exploited Foote's obscurity as a figure, others' objection was precisely that Foote was being incorporated into a feminist debate. Evelyn Gardiner (a third granddaughter), disgusted that Foote had been 'taken up by the feminists', complained that she had become a focus of feminist interest: 'and boy, every once in a while, I run into some lesbian feminist who wants to make her out as this downtrodden woman who supported a drunken husband.'[32]

Walsh's subsequent essay, published in 1981 in a collection of essays from the conference, was by all accounts a toned down and much-edited version of her paper. The issue that Foote's obscurity had allowed Stegner to use her as he wished was still important, as was the way in which Foote had been made literally invisible in a novel that quoted her verbatim but then gave her the false name of Susan Burling Ward. Walsh's scholarship showed that around 10% of *Angle of Repose* had indeed been lifted from Foote's own writing.

Most striking in Walsh's intervention, though, was the fury she expresses that Stegner had extrapolated a sexual life from Foote's papers, starting with her same-sex attachment to Gilder, moving through sexual reserve in marriage and finishing with a literally destructive desire:

> Stegner chose to make Susan Burling Ward an adulteress, to make her responsible for the death of a child, to show her estranged from her son for ten years, and to create a terrible rift between her and her husband because of her adultery and her responsibility for the child's death. None of these negative events occurred in Mary Hallock Foote's life.[33]

Walsh had by now been joined in her discussion of what Stegner had 'made' Foote do by her subsequent co-editor, Barbara Cragg, who used the language of penetration and unrestrained lust to describe what Stegner had done:

> Stegner struck a rich vein in Foote's memorabilia and he mined it thoroughly. Having delved into her life, work, and intimate correspondence, he fashioned a novel based less in creative imagination than in thinly disguised fact ... Stegner did not hesitate to distort the Foote family and their friends to satisfy the fictional needs of his book.[34]

In Cragg's argument, what Stegner had done was something like a rape.

Two reactions to Walsh's argument are significant here, I think. The first and most obvious one is the angry—one is tempted to say almost hysterical—reaction of Stegner and his supporters. Walsh's work was that of a nonentity ('Does she need four names before she'll believe she exists?'); as a spiteful attack on an individual ('an *ad hominem* attack on a writer of great integrity and dignity'); 'It is a nasty piece of character assassination'; 'Some of the charges grew out of misunderstanding and miscommunication; some out of spite and, no doubt, jealousy'.[35] Stegner himself seemed to go out of his way to describe what he had done in sexually charged terms in which he subordinated Foote to his creative and intellectual life, as, for example, in:

Molly Foote is raw material for Susan Burling Ward... As far as I'm concerned the Mary Hallock Foote stuff had the same function as raw material, broken rocks out of which I could make any kind of wall I wanted to.

He insisted, too, that he and Rodman Paul deserved praise for recovering Foote at all: 'Between us we've more or less revived Molly Foote... She was dead as a doornail before we began working on those papers.'[36]

Above all, though, the ripostes of Stegner and his supporters identified Walsh's attack as feminist and dismissed it accordingly as 'angry denunciations by feminists'; 'She has taken all the family's objections at face value, become their spear-carrier, and set out to slay the male dragon'.[37] It was as if the discussion of feminism in *Angle of Repose* had not existed, and therefore no argument mobilising feminism could possibly engage appropriately with the novel. Subsequently, in writing about *Angle of Repose*, the argument between Stegner and 'the feminists', represented invariably and relentlessly by the single figure of Mary Ellen Williams Walsh, was revisited and summarily demolished again and again, referred to repeatedly in interviews, rehashed by journalists, its minutiae rehearsed in biographies of Stegner and work on Foote.

If this first response gives some flavour of the unrestrained, highly personalised attack that a young feminist critic could expect if she engaged a well-known, well-established novelist in argument at the end of the 1970s (even if he had raised the feminist significance of recovery himself), what I find more surprising is the feminist response to Walsh. She seems to have attracted little support from academic colleagues. Simone Murray has argued that feminism was disappearing down the 'congenial bolt-hole in the academy' by the end of the 1970s, yet the bolthole available to Walsh scarcely operated to offer her safety or congeniality.[38]

Perhaps we can catch a sense of a more febrile atmosphere in academe with respect to feminism than Murray's comment suggests. In the rather unlikely source of a detective novel published in 1981, *Death in a Tenured Position*, the feminist literary scholar Carolyn Heilbrun (writing under the pseudonym of Amanda Cross) conveys something of that setting. The plot is propelled forward by a vindictively staged encounter between the newly appointed and anti-feminist woman professor of literature and a radical activist, divorced from an oppressive husband and angry. Indeed, the novel visits the point made earlier about the increasing divide between feminist scholarship and feminist activism. It is resolved with the professor's suicide and the disappearance of the latter character from the plot. The novel's point of view is provided by a feminist professor at Columbia, bored both with lecturing 'unceasingly' on 'George Eliot's purposeless heroines' and with acting as a token woman on university committees; and viewing the 'changes of the seventies' with irony shading into impatience. Feminism in academe has apparently achieved little, while danger lies in wait if 'one defined oneself too sharply'.[39] This was certainly what Walsh had done.

A more recent comment made by Linda Karell may also be suggestive. She takes Walsh to task thus:

Walsh is at pains to eradicate the possibility of lesbianism in the text... If Lyman is ill at ease with his grandmother's potential for a lesbian attachment, Walsh is more so, actively working to reel Susan, and Foote through her, back into contained heterosexuality.[40]

The 'pains' 'actively' taken by Walsh actually consist of a single endnote of five lines in her essay, where she refers to Stegner's 'advance' of 'the lesbian theme in *Angle of Repose*', referring the reader to Carroll Smith-Rosenberg's essay exploring intimate relationships between women in a period before same-sex love was codified.[41] Still, there is resonance in Karell's larger point that Walsh particularly dislikes the representation of the sexual life of Foote. David Bouchier, writing about the blocked progress of the Equal Rights Amendment (still not ratified across the states) at the end of the 1970s, argues that even liberal feminists in the US were happy to 'de-emphasize issues like lesbianism ... which could damage' feminism's 'prospects in the conservative heartlands'.[42] Clearly some feminists at least were keen to dodge the explosive potential of discussions of sex and sexuality. Walsh's motives were, I think, less politic. She wanted to recover, as did many feminists, the familiar pioneer woman that had defined the American project of Anglo-European expansion, albeit given the feminist identity I have already described earlier. Conveniently, this national icon did not stray from heterosexual marriage.

What, then, is to be learned about the feminist recovery of the past during the 1970s from this series of troubled recoveries of Foote? Reading the excited accounts of busy activity in the work of feminist historians of the 1970s, one has the sense that they shared the assumption that recovery offered a fertile arena for feminism. Separated from, though far from unrelated to, the vicissitudes of activism's battlefields, feminist historians, professional and amateur, planned their restorative recoveries. In an important feminist article written in the mid-1970s, Dawn Lander describes the impulse to recover female writers as finding 'my own feelings ... duplicated in the experiences of historic and contemporary women'. Lander described her experience in the following terms:

> Ten years after I left Arizona, I began my graduate studies in American literature, and, not surprisingly, my interest focused upon literature of the wilderness. Repeatedly, however, I could find no place for myself and for my pleasure in the wilderness in the traditionally recorded images of women on the frontier ...[43]

In the 1970s, feminist recovery was suffused with this desire to find 'duplicated feelings' in settings that feminists could re-envisage. Walsh was looking to populate an American west that was not a 'playground of masculine adventure', Smith-Rosenberg a counter-cultural world of intimacy between women in stuffy Victorian America.[44] A defence from present alienation could be constructed from forebears: pioneer women could become feminist pioneers or indeed bands of sisters.

The politics of recovery proved far more fraught than such statements suggest, however. The case here drives home the point that feminist recovery did not necessarily operate in a supportive environment, but could find itself in an extraordinarily hostile one. It was subject to the play of cross cutting recovery projects and the interventions of figures whose attitudes to feminism were as much in flux as the movement itself. It suggests how many players there might be with different interests in resurrecting a woman, and the sense of ownership that accompanied recovery on the part of all concerned. Walsh ended her paper with a rallying cry for the recovery of Foote, but on her own terms:

> It is true that *Angle of Repose* has reawakened interest in Mary Hallock Foote and her work. It is unfortunate that many readers have accepted the novel as a valid interpretation of her life.

It is doubly unfortunate that few readers have recognised how much of her work Stegner used to build his book. Her life is fascinating in its own right.[45]

Walsh, like the other figures I have discussed here, believed that Mary Hallock Foote deserved to be recovered, but only in a 'valid' form. Yet that meant containing Foote's meaning, and selecting what was 'fascinating'. Finding 'duplicated' feelings required a forceful effort. In the end, then, Foote's re-appearance in the 1970s, steeped in debate about feminism, offered feminism little satisfaction. It was a limited, anxious, reproachful affair.

Notes

1. Judith M. Bennett (2006) *History Matters: patriarchy and the challenge of feminism* (Philadelphia: University of Pennsylvania Press), p. 7. Gerda Lerner gives a comparable account in: Women among the Professors of History: the story of a process of transformation, in Eileen Boris & Nupur Chaudhuri (Eds) (1999) *Voices of Women Historians: the personal, the political and the professional* (Bloomington: Indiana University Press), pp. 1–11, p. 1. See also, for a discussion of the implications of feminist scholarship for the personal life, Peter Novick (1988) *That Noble Dream: the 'objectivity question' and the American historical profession* (New York: Cambridge University Press), p. 499.
2. Useful accounts of the shape of debate among feminist historians include: Bennett, *History Matters*, pp. 1–20; Barbara Melosh (1990) Recovery and Revision: women's history and West Virginia, *West Virginia History*, 49, pp. 3–6; Pamela S. Nadell & Kate Haulman (Eds) (2013) *Making Women's Histories* (New York: New York University Press), esp. essays by Gerda Lerner and Kathy Peiss; Linda Nicholson (1997) Introduction, *The Second Wave: a reader in feminist theory* (New York: Routledge), pp. 1–5. In a massive field, the following contemporary analyses give a flavour of the separate and distinctive strains in the field of feminist history: Ann D. Gordon, Mari Jo Buhle & Nancy Schorm Dye (1976) The Problem of Women's History, in Berenice A. Carroll (Ed.) *Liberating Women's History* (Urbana: University of Illinois Press), pp. 75–92; Mary Hartman & Lois W. Banner (1974) Preface, *Clio's Consciousness Raised: new perspectives on the history of women* (New York: Harper & Row), pp. vii–xii.
3. Patrice McDermott (1994) *Politics and Scholarship: feminist academic journals and the production of knowledge* (Urbana: University of Illinois Press), p. 85.
4. Linda Rasmussen, Lorna Rasmussen, Candace Savage & Anne Wheeler (1976) *A Harvest Yet to Reap: a history of prairie women* (Toronto: Women's Press), p. 9.
5. Wallace Stegner (1971) *Angle of Repose* (New York: Doubleday).
6. Quoted in Philip L. Fradkin (2008) *Angle of Unrest, Wallace Stegner and the American West* (New York: Knopf), p. 263.
7. Quoted in Jackson J. Benson (2001) *Down by the Lemonade Springs: essays on Wallace Stegner* (Reno: University of Nevada Press), p. 145.
8. The concept of warping appears in the novel's epigraph, but Stegner used it again in a 1971 letter to Janet Micoleau, quoted in Fradkin, *Angle of Unrest*, p. 253.
9. Stegner, *Angle of Repose*, p. 163.
10. Deborah Paes de Barross (2004) *Fast Cars and Bad Girls: nomadic subjects and women's road stories* (New York: Peter Lang), p. 44.
11. Carroll Smith-Rosenberg (1975) The Female World of Love and Ritual: relations between women in nineteenth-century America, *Signs* 1(1), pp. 1–29. The significance of this work is discussed in McDermott, *Politics and Scholarship*, pp. 142–146; Melosh, *Recovery and Revision*; Novick, *That Noble Dream*, pp. 500–502.
12. Smith-Rosenberg, 'The Female World of Love and Ritual', p. 14.
13. Stegner, *Angle of Repose*, pp. 57–58; Smith-Rosenberg, 'The Female world of Love and Ritual', pp. 7–8.
14. Smith-Rosenberg, 'The Female World of Love and Ritual', p. 3.
15. Ibid. p. 5, fn. 12.

16. The emphasis on leaving home in second-wave feminism is wonderfully well explored in Lesley Johnson (1996) As Housewives We Are Worms, *Cultural Studies*, 10(3), pp. 449–463.
17. Rodman W. Paul (1972) *A Victorian Gentlewoman in the Far West: the reminiscences of Mary Hallock Foote* (San Marino: Huntington Library).
18. Asking 'was Mary Hallock Foote really a "westerner"?' Paul answers 'In a few respects, yes; in greater part, no … Nothing about Mary Hallock Foote suggested the quiet courage and stoic endurance popularly attributed to the western wife of pioneer days' (pp. 3–4).
19. The field of feminist recovery, during the 1970s, of Anglo-European emigrants to the American west, is a rich one of which the following are much-cited examples: John Faragher (1979) *Women and Men on the Overland Trail* (New Haven: Yale University); Julie Roy Jeffrey (1979) *The Frontier Woman: the Trans-Mississippi, 1840–1880* (New York: Hill & Wang); Joan M. Jensen & Darlis Miller (1980) The Gentle Tamers Revisited: new approaches to the history of women in the American West, *Pacific Historical Quarterly*, 49(2), pp. 173–213; Glenda Riley (1977) Images of the Frontierswoman: Iowa as a case study, *Western History Quarterly*, 3, pp. 189–202; Lillian Schissel (1977) Women's Diaries on the Western Frontier, *American Studies*, 18, pp. 87–100.
20. Interview with Stegner quoted in James R. Hepworth (1998) *Three Interviews with Wallace Stegner* (Albuquerque: University of New Mexico Press), p. 68.
21. Jessamyn West (1961) Foreword, *Letters of a Woman Homesteader* (Lincoln: University of Nebraska Press), p. vii.
22. Hartman & Banner, *Clio's Consciousness Raised*, p. xi.
23. *Heartland*, dir. Richard Pearce (Wilderness Films, 1971). Fred Ferretti, '"Heartland": a triumph of true grit', *New York Times*, 22 Nov. 1981, http://www.nytimes.com/1981/11/22/movies/heartland-a-triumph-of-true-grit.html (accessed 15 Feb. 2015).
24. John Faragher & Christine Stansell (1975) Women and their Families on the Overland Trail to California and Oregon, 1842–1867, *Feminist Studies*, 2(2/3), pp. 150–166. p.151.
25. The fullest exposition of this dispute appears in Fradkin, *Angle of Unrest*, though, for a version less sympathetic to Stegner, see Susan Salter Reynolds (2003) Tangle of Repose, *Los Angeles Times*, 23 March 2003, http://articles.latimes.com/2003/mar/23/magazine/tm-stegner12 (accessed 15 Feb. 2015). The argument has been thoughtfully revisited in terms of literary critical debate in Linda K. Karell (2002) *Writing Together Writing Apart* (Lincoln: University of Nebraska Press), pp. 153–180.
26. I am thinking here, for example, of the publication of Susan Brownmiller's *Against Our Will* in 1975, the NOW Task Force on Battered women in 1976, and the beginning of the Take Back the Night Marches across university campuses during this period.
27. Blake Green, 'The Genteel Western Lady behind this Season's New Opera', *San Francisco Chronicle*, 8 Sep. 1976, p. 18.
28. Quoted in Reynolds, *Tangle of Repose*.
29. David Bouchier (1984) *The Feminist Challenge: the movement for women's liberation in Britain and the USA* (New York: Schocken Books), p. 139; For a range of interesting discussions of mainstream's feminism's fading profile, see Bouchier, *The Feminist Challenge*, pp. 124–139, 160–175; Mary D. Garrard (1994) Feminist Politics: Networks and Organizations, in Norma Broude & Mary D. Garrard (Eds) *The Power of Feminist Art: the American movement* (New York: H. N. Abrams), pp. 88–103; Becky Thompson (2010) Multi-Racial Feminism: recasting the chronology of second wave feminism, in Nancy A. Hewitt (Ed) *No Permanent Waves: recasting histories of US feminism* (New Brunswick: Rutgers University Press), pp. 39–50.
30. Natalie Angier (1999) *Woman: an intimate geography* (London: Virago), p. x.
31. The talk is described in Fradkin, *Angle of Unrest*, pp. 257–258.
32. Fradkin, *Angle of Unrest*, p. 260.
33. Mary Ellen Williams Walsh (1982) Angle of Repose and the Writings of Mary Hallock Foote, in Anthony Arthur (Ed) *Critical Essays on Wallace Stegner* (Boston: GK Hall), pp. 184–209, pp. 205–206.
34. Barbara Cragg (1980) Mary Hallock Foote's Images of the Old West, *Landscape*, 24, pp. 42–47, p. 42.

35. Stegner quoted in Page Stegner (Ed) (2007) *Selected Letters of Wallace Stegner* (Emeryville, CA: Shoemaker & Hoard), p. 96; Anthony Arthur quoted in Fradkin, *Angle of Unrest,* p. 260; Jackson J. Benson (1996) *Wallace Stegner: his life and work* (Lincoln: University of Nebraska Press), p. 355; Stegner in Benson, *Down by Lemonade Springs: essays on Wallace Stegner* (Reno and Las Vegas: University of Nevada Press), 2001, p. 140.
36. Interview with Stegner quoted in Wallace Stegner & Richard W. Etulain, *Wallace Stegner: conversations on history and literature* (Salt Lake City: University of Utah Press, 1983), p. 85; interview with Stegner quoted in James R. Hepworth (1998) *Three Interviews with Wallace Stegner* (Albuquerque, University of New Mexico Press), p. 68.
37. Benson, *Down by Lemonade Springs,* pp. xx–xxi.
38. Simone Murray (2004) *Mixed Media: feminist presses and publishing politics* (London: Pluto Press), p. 47.
39. Amanda Cross [pseud] (1981) *Death in a Tenured Position* (New York: Random House), pp. 56, 54, 65.
40. Linda Karell (2002) *Writing Together, Writing Apart* (Lincoln: University of Nebraska Press), p. 176.
41. Walsh, *Angle of Repose* and the Writings of Mary Hallock Foote, p. 209, fn. 11.
42. Bouchier, *The Feminist Challenge,* p. 124.
43. Dawn Lander (1977) Eve Among the Indians, in Arlyn Diamond & Lee R Edwards (Eds) *The Authority of Experience: essays in feminist criticism* (Amherst: University of Massachusetts Press), pp. 194–211, p. 195.
44. Barbara Cragg, Mary Ellen Williams Walsh & Dennis M. Walsh (Eds) (1988) *The Idaho Stories and Far West Illustrations of Mary Hallock Foote* (Pocatello: Idaho State University Press), p. xvii.
45. Walsh, *Angle of Repose* and the Writings of Mary Hallock Foote, p. 208.

Theorising the Women's Liberation Movement *as* Cultural Heritage

D-M Withers

ABSTRACT
Recent interest in documenting and re-evaluating histories of the UK Women's Liberation Movement has produced varied appraisals of the movement. These have emerged from feminist communities wishing to preserve, organise and collect their histories. Such recovery and dissemination, I argue, is cultural heritage rather than 'history', as heritage offers different tools for re-presentation as well as creating alternative socio-cultural relationships with the legacies of the WLM. This article draws upon my practice as a curator of feminist histories, and argues for the articulation of a politics of transmission, essential for the longevity and sustainability of feminist cultural heritage and histories.

The recent interest in documenting and re-evaluating the histories of the UK Women's Liberation Movement (WLM) has produced a number of significant and multifaceted appraisals of the movement. From academic monographs,[1] TV programmes,[2] academic conferences, oral history dialogues,[3] exhibitions, digital archives, activist events, witness seminars, radio shows, the establishment of networks[4] and film screenings[5] to claims within parts of the left-leaning media that there is a widespread resurgence in contemporary feminist activism, the WLM is often used as touchstone and inspiration for feminist activism across history.[6] Large oral history initiatives such as the *Heart of the Race* project collected by the Black Cultural Archives (2009–2010), and *Sisterhood & After*, housed at the British Library (launched 2013), are complemented by smaller initiatives that have captured the local distinctiveness of the movement(s), as well as examining how women engaged with a range of cultural forms, such as music, screen printing and theatre.[7] Thanks to these varied initiatives there is now an abundance of diverse memory resources circulating both within physical and digital archives that interpret the stories of feminist activisms during the WLM and Black Women's Movement.

What is significant about these publicly orientated projects is that they often make an attempt to foreground the experiences of, and archive materials produced by, women who were active in the movements. This suggests that the impetus to collect and take care of WLM histories does not arise from a specifically academic desire to *historicise* the movement, but to ensure that its different viewpoints are recorded and, increasingly through the use of digital technologies, disseminated. While it may be tempting to see these gathered memory resources within the category of historical evidence alone, I want to examine this material as examples of *feminist cultural heritage*. In doing so, I examine whether different kinds of knowledge and value are expressed if the eventful archives of the WLM are treated *as* heritage, and how this relates to the figuration of political generations, transmission processes and community formations yet to be explicitly articulated within feminism. If the heritage dimension of the material collected is not attended to, will this overlook how history and tradition are invoked and recovered within feminist political communities across different historical times? How do communities of practice (those communities that practice feminist activities, ideas and culture) mobilise traditions in order to sustain feminist political action, ideas and identities? Before exploring these questions in detail, I begin by offering some very schematic distinctions between history and heritage. I then discuss the role of heritage and tradition within the WLM before reflecting on my own curatorial practice. I conclude the article by discussing the transmission of feminism's archive as a practice of organisation, selection and emphasis, foregrounding material from the Black feminist movement in the analysis.

Some brief distinctions between heritage and history

> History involves a series of erasures, emendations and amalgamations […] history splinters and divides what in the original may have presented itself as whole, abstracting here a nugget of descriptive detail, there a memorable scene […] History composites. It integrates what in the original may have been divergent, synthesizes different classes of information […] it creates a consecutive narrative out of fragments, imposing order on chaos, and producing images far clearer than reality could be.[8]

> There is, really, no such thing as heritage.[9]

> Heritage is not given, it is made and so is, unavoidably, an ethical enterprise.[10]

Placing heritage and history side-by-side will inevitably invite comparison between two interpretative practices that often draw upon the same archival source material. In this article I want to tease out the different uses of feminist archives when they are framed as history or heritage. After all, how historians and heritage practitioners utilise the feminist archive, as well as how material is framed for people in everyday life *as* history or heritage, can vary. History, as glossed by Raphael Samuel above, risks a very particular kind of interpretative distortion: *written* by the historian, whose ideal stance is to survey archival evidence and draw from it objective conclusions, history can transform the chaos of life into neat summary, assimilating dis-synchronous details through an act of storytelling. Such narrative representations are, for Hayden White, 'marked by a desire for a kind of order and fullness in an account of reality', a 'completeness and fullness of which we can only imagine, never experience'.[11] While I do hope the reader will forgive what is an ungenerous caricature of the historian's practice, the idea that history is a professional discipline comprised of certain orthodoxies, methodologies and linear modes of transmission, located predominantly in narrative and the written word, remains resilient despite challenges presented by postmodern, post-structuralist and other deconstructive approaches.

Less familiar perhaps to readers of this journal, and indeed the feminist theoretical community in general, are conceptions of heritage. Laurajane Smith argues that there is no such *thing* as heritage, only a complex set of social processes through which objects, buildings, music, storytelling, landscapes, dance and so forth accrue cultural value, and subsequently establish 'a measure of social reverence'.[12] This is echoed in David Harvey's claim that heritage is always made (and therefore always open to contestation) in its iterations across historical time.[13] These writers, and many other contributors to the field, theorise heritage as an active process through which communities make sense of their place and time in the world through a rootedness within selected traditions. Often this conception of tradition, particularly from the nineteenth century onwards, has been narrow in scope, localised within the boundaries of the nation state, or aligned with ethnic identities and other forms of identity tied to a place or location. This conception of heritage corresponds with what Smith calls the 'Authorised Heritage Discourse (AHD)', which 'asserts the legitimacy of expertise', a 'dominant and professional discourse [which] is institutionalized within public policy, heritage statutes, agencies and amenity societies'.[14] Yet, as both Smith and Harvey note, although ideas such as the AHD are normative, they are not the only way to conceptualise heritage.

A crucial argument in this paper is that there can be such a thing as feminist cultural heritage, or, following Smith, a process of ascribing *heritage value* to feminist activities that have occurred across history. This process is often an unofficial, grassroots affair that challenges the tenets of the AHD in the sense that it is rarely officially sanctioned or requires professional validation. I situate this claim in relation to recent critical reflections on feminist histories within which it is possible to detect an emerging consciousness about feminist heritage. Kate Eichorn has argued, for example, that imagining the possibility of feminist tradition emerges from a 'relationship to time and history that has only recently become possible'. It is something that 'one can only experience after one is both certain that they have history (perhaps, only after one begins to feel the weight of such a history and at least some responsibility for its preservation)'.[15] Margaretta Jolly has outlined interpretative practices that 'contribute to our respect for feminism as a maker of community'.[16] Such observations are noteworthy because feminism is often perceived as a political ideology, a social movement or a set of diverse methodological approaches. Feminism is less often thought of in terms of how it creates forms of sociality, cultural practices and (im)material culture that may aspire to something akin to 'tradition'.[17] Generally, people are not rooted within feminism in everyday sociality; it is something that must be discovered, that one must become.[18] This can be extended to the conception of feminist cultural heritage and tradition: it is an idea that must be (re)claimed by scholars, activists, journalists, artist and practitioners; its value must be carved out, demonstrated and argued for. As Eyerman and Jamison have made clear, heritage and tradition, particularly when enshrined in participatory cultural forms such as music, storytelling and dance, can be key parts of political struggle when they are selected and mobilised by communities.[19] Heritage, understood in this unofficial sense and without recourse to, or recuperation by, the AHD, can be a key nexus where identities, values and ideas are negotiated and transmitted. Such acts of negotiation and creativity were also a key part of the WLM in its own time, as we shall see below.

Heritage and tradition within the WLM

Acts of cultural recovery were a key part of activist practices in the WLM. They populated feminist media stories, political meetings, were the subject of conferences and defined the purpose of activist groups. The most enduring example of this remains the fondly remembered Virago Modern Classics series that published books by women writers that had, by the 1970s, 'gone out of print'.[20]

Furthermore, as Jalna Hanmer has reflected, early in the WLM:

> women began to understand how the loss of knowledge of earlier women's struggles and demands is a major way of securing the social and personal subordination of women. These ideas led to women collecting, preserving and making available to other women a map, a guide, for future generations of women so that women who did not share a particular moment in time may have access to it. Early materials were turned out on duplicators, often indistinct or blurred, and circulated to small numbers through women-only publications.[21]

The idea of a 'women's culture', where women's interests, practices, aesthetics and values were foregrounded, gained particular traction among some women's liberation music makers. Consider this excerpt taken from an A4 pamphlet-magazine *Women and Music* (1978) that indicates how strong emotional attachments to *the practice* of rediscovering cultural traditions circulated among certain parts of the women's movement:

> These songs are one way of *partially rediscovering* our *hidden history*. If art is about trying to express the truth as we see it, *making sense and shape out of the chaos and complexity and trying to make us more whole as people in a society that fragments, stereotypes and divides us*, then the best of the tradition can be said to stand alongside women artists. *The creators of these songs were our ancestors*—all those grandmothers and great-great-grandmothers forced into service or the mills and *finding comfort* in the old and new popular songs.[22]

The rediscovery of feminist or female-centred cultural traditions is presented here as a key technique through which fragmented social selves become whole and integrated through alignment with ancestral voices. The significance of culture as a form of social or community 'glue' is discernible here, particularly how songs act as evidence of the existence of women's social and political agency in different historical times. It is a clear and striking articulation of how heritage, understood as a rootedness within selected traditions, was used to furnish identities with strength and meaning, identities that were essentially 'cut off' without the imagining of tradition. Such practices do of course risk romanticising cultural traditions, misrecognising them perhaps as authentic expressions of a bygone women's culture. Such a critique has great validity, but it does not help us understand how heritage was *used* in the WLM and, perhaps, feminist social movements more widely. For the important aspect to note is how the authors of this text are 'finding comfort' in tradition, which underlines again the social function of heritage as a way to root and align identities with historical relations that make activist work coherent, purposeful and meaningful.

A strong foothold for women's liberationists was of course found in the recent history of the suffrage movement. Women's history featured strongly in feminist magazines such as *Spare Rib*, as Krista Cowman explains: the UK-feminist 'newsstand' magazine 'published history from the outset, reflecting the broader desire of second-wave feminism to historicize its activity'.[23] While 'the magazine connected feminist historians to a non-academic readership', the demand for 'attractive copy' meant the 'complex nuances of historical research were not easily conveyed in the small space of a few columns'.[24] This led to the:

> retention of key aspects of the non-feminist narrative (a small number of charismatic leaders; a campaign largely restricted to London) within features whose stated aim was to challenge

> [these narratives] says much about the pervasive nature of mainstream history. With limited resources in the form of available primary material, it was hard to escape existing paradigms.[25]

Such narrative coherencies are not necessarily the product of non-feminist narratives alone. Laura Mayhall has written, for example, about how the militant activist practices of the Women's Social and Political Union (WSPU) came to dominate the cultural memory of the suffrage movement. This was achieved through a myopic 'suffragette spirit', the 'self-conscious creation of a small group of former suffragettes in the 1920s and 1930s' which 'enshrined a narrative of authentic suffrage militancy that has remained surprisingly coherent since'.[26] June Purvis has also argued that the 1970s BBC suffrage drama *Shoulder to Shoulder*, a key contact point with feminist histories for women and young girls in the early 1970s, was strongly influenced by Sylvia Pankhurst's autobiography *The Suffrage Movement: an intimate account of persons and ideals,* and consequently emphasised particular historical narratives.[27]

Cowman's article reminds us of the 'fragility of feminist knowledge and the speed with which critical events could be forgotten'.[28] She explains that, even when diverse accounts of the suffrage movement were published, 'such texts were so marginalized that they could be overlooked even within the context of feminist research'.[29] Even published books can drop out of print and commerce. This helps us to think about the circulation of feminism's archive in very concrete, pragmatic terms, although as Cowman's work instructs us, the existence of a book is not enough for it to be adopted within the context of research and, consequently, knowledge. To be operational the artefact must be accessed, used and placed within circuits of reference and association. It must be transmitted as a singularity rather than subsumed into dominant narratives that are, as we have seen, remarkably resilient.

The digitised twenty-first century is of course a markedly different context for accessing, archiving and publishing historical information, and is characterised by a far more familiar everyday relationship to 'the archive'.[30] This does not mean, however, that feminist knowledge, and feminism's archives, is any less marginal or fragile.[31] Those wishing to seek out the heritages of the WLM will benefit from the significant amount of memory resources collected in feminist archives and libraries in the sense that there is simply a greater volume of material available in 2015 compared with 1967 or even 1989 (to select some arbitrary dates). Yet the diversity of these archives, the singular artefacts they contain, must be continually re-affirmed and transmitted if they are to achieve consistency and value. How we interact with and re-present archival resources are always active processes that engender relationships with, and points of access to, the transmitted material. As we shall see below, the modes of presentation available within a heritage context, when appropriated by grassroots activists seeking to open up different kinds of relationships with and knowledge about feminist archives, offers a different kind of transmission trajectory to the composite historical narrative—the kind that has gained concentration via repetition and familiarity, as outlined by Cowman, Mayhall and Purvis.

Heritage and re-presentation

In an exhibition the range of historical information, the materiality and diversity of individual artefacts can be foregrounded to audiences. Curators do of course *select* which material is put on display and which is not, but they can also help visitors turn toward a diversity of artefacts and materials in particular ways. Such an approach was key to my own curatorial work presenting what I perceived, and experienced to be, the marginalised cultural histories of the WLM. By 'cultural histories' I refer to the cultural production of women's movements (writing, theatre, music, imagery and so forth), but also, as Gail Lewis described in relation to her participation in the Black Women's Movement:

> not just that. I mean something about a kind of, our culture of being, how we related to each other, were we just there really to always do organising and politics or should we also being doing something about providing a space in which we can kind of meet together with like minded people in more recreational sociality, that was important because this was also part of consciousness raising in a way.[32]

Across two Heritage Lottery Funded exhibitions, *Sistershow Revisited: feminism in Bristol, 1973–1975* (2010) and *Music & Liberation* (2012) and the creation of an non-funded online digital archive, the *Women's Liberation Music Archive* (2010–ongoing), my aim was to create spaces where audiences could encounter archive materials that presented the diversity and multiplicity of WLM activism, particularly in relation to music, theatre and the feminist 'world-making' activities attached to such practices. As a curator I had no professional training. I gained rudimentary curatorial skills from working as a volunteer in a people's history museum, and my impetus to construct exhibitions emerged from an enabling do-it-yourself/punk context that I was immersed in. Everything else about curating I learnt through critical observation and books—no one authorised me to act. Although utilising a form normatively associated with authoritative heritage practices, these two exhibitions were grassroots, activist projects as much as they were heritage ones. Indeed, these works highlight the key role that heritage performs within contemporary feminist activism.

The exhibitions were attempts to render certain aspects of feminist histories known, but also create points of identification for visitors with those histories. My aim was to create a context where people could forge relationships with these materials, perhaps 'using' them as supports for their identities and wider sense of being in the world as a feminist. The exhibition form was, I felt, an ideal container for enabling such modes of engagement and identification, a 'politicised practice of opening up relationality'.[33] My curatorial practice was further influenced by the work of Frank Ankersmit, specifically the idea of creating a context where 'historical experience' could emerge outside the flat confines of historical representation.[34] A historical experience is defined by Ankersmit as one that engenders a mundane sense of temporal collapse, so, quite literally the sense that material from Other historical times intrude into and co-exist in the now. For Ankersmit, historical experiences become possible through proximity with and exposure to everyday ephemera such as scrawled notebooks, receipts, invoices or letters. Such items formed a significant part of the material displayed in *Sistershow Revisited* and *Music & Liberation*. Ephemera can emit historical sensations, appearing as 'indestructible, uncannily close, and-despite [their] closeness and [their] durability—[they are] utterly impossible to conserve in "representations"'.[35] A crucial part of identifying with the materials on display was then about creating a context where visitors could, if they were open to it, form sensory relationships with the artefacts. This was achieved through the artefact's mundane intrusion into, and co-existent mingling within, the historical scene visitors and artefacts co-occupied in the exhibition. One simple display tactic in this regard was to place artefacts confrontationally within the exhibition space, rarely behind glass or barrier, often to enable visitors' movement around it, allowing them to look at the displayed object from different angles. I also included photocopies of key documents within exhibitions that visitors could pick up, read and perhaps 'steal' if they felt impelled to, as well as other opportunities to interact with what was displayed, such as turning pages of publications, pressing play on tape decks and selecting oral histories to listen to or watch on digital playback devices. These subtle, low-financed techniques were deployed to involve the visitor in what was happening within the exhibition, a rare opportunity to feel literally close to the displayed artefacts (see Figures 1–4).

I was keen to accentuate within my own curatorial practice the way exhibitions *can* foreground diverse voices, artefacts and perspectives. Such a technique differs from the historian's compressed narrative that is premised within a dynamic that raises one voice—the historian's—above others—the artefacts. I wanted to create a public transmission context where the rough multiplicity of feminist archive materials could be exposed to visitors as an initial point of contact. I was keen to empower visitors with a range of historical evidence so they could authorise their own interpretations of events. To assume that my role as mediator and curator was not without bias or intention, or that I did not represent the material in any way and point visitors towards this or that interpretation, would of course be a remarkably un-reflexive claim. I understand my influence was there as curator, as *carer for* those artefacts. Nevertheless I wanted to ensure that my own authorial voice was minimised. I perceived my role within the exhibitions as *selector* and *arranger* of the artefacts, and I will go on to discuss this practice of selection in more detail later in this article. My aim was to enable visitors' access to different voices and perspectives, utilising the multi-medial forum of exhibitions that offer a platform for text, images, film, video, ephemera, objects and audio (including music and oral histories) to *co-exist* in their singularity. This method seemed to allow the greatest degree of self-representation for the material displayed, a self-representation I deemed necessary because the political activities of the WLM and '70s feminism' have been caught within peculiar cycles of identification and denigration within the academic feminist project, as Clare Hemmings' work has pointedly shown.[36] Iris van der Tuin and I have both discussed how such dynamics have undermined the feminist archive as a site of epistemic value; we have both been shaped by the ambivalence of whether or not there is anything worth knowing about feminist histories. Yet, equally, we have both been energised through our engagements with the archive.[37] Popular culture has also been fairly unforgiving to the WLM. From the backlash dynamics outlined by Susan Faludi to postfeminist masquerades that nurture the 'spectral dimensions'[38] of feminism which call into question its relevance as a political practice and form of identification.

This was another reason to engender identification and recognition of the diverse forms of feminist activism from the WLM within the exhibitions: to challenge generic representations and claims about a social movement that was incredibly diverse strategically, culturally and politically. Within *Music & Liberation* I deliberately eschewed chronological organisation in my arrangement of the materials. This was, in part, hostility to imposing a straight, linear unfolding idea of historical time onto the artefacts. I did not want to temporalise the materials as belonging to 'the 1970s' or '1980s' because, quite literally, in their uncannily close manifestations, their material existence endures in the twenty-first century, and the ideas, sounds, images and energies of the historical actions are re-enacted through the exhibition, releasing their temporal-historical differences.[39] Removing affective biases attached to blanket temporalisation, which produces a kind of knowledge about historical phenomena that is not knowledge but performs itself as such,[40] also informed the refusal to impose a pre-given temporal framework. I instead chose to use themes, such as 'Professional or Amateur', 'Distribution' or 'What Makes Music Feminist?' in order to highlight key themes and strategies deployed by feminist music makers, while posing questions about their activities to aid interpretation.

While I have little empirical evidence about whether or not I was successful in realising my theoretical aims in *Music & Liberation* and *Sistershow Revisited*, this discussion should make it clear how I sought to appropriate the exhibition form in order to activate the transmission of feminism's marginal cultural histories. As a curator my aim was to make selections from existing archival material and emphasise them in an interpretative context that enabled a range of multiple voices and materials to co-exist: the exhibition. Understood in this way, the exhibition, as a mode of transmission, transmits materials from the feminist archive differently to the written historical narrative that, by the necessity of its technical form, compresses multiple perspectives and foregrounds the authorial voice of the historian. My appropriation of heritage techniques to transmit the artefacts from the feminist archive at a particular historical time was in this sense strategic; it aimed to engender a context where identification, sensation and valuation could occur in relation to a collection of archive materials that remained invisible and dis-identified within early twenty-first-century feminism. In the final section of this paper I will further elaborate on how the practice of selection can be a useful way to understand subsequent practices that transmit feminism's rich archives.

Figure 1. Exhibition attendee reads from magazine on display.

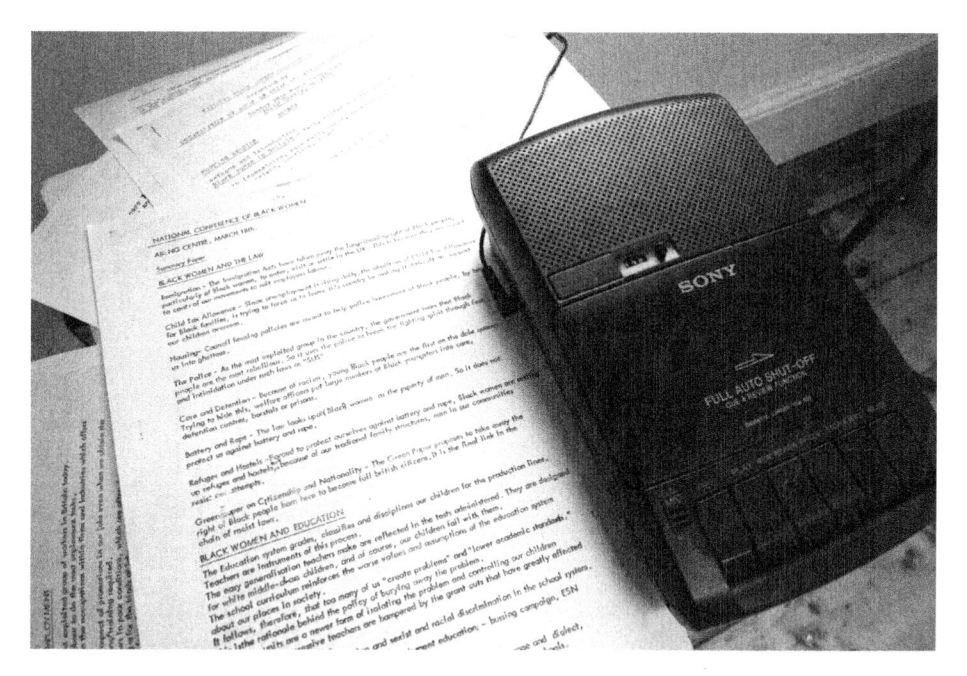

Figure 2. Photocopies from Black Cultural Archives with audio cassette player;

Heritage: organisation, selection and emphasis

How then can the cultural heritage of the WLM and Black Women's Movement be mobilised through practices that organise the material (through making an archive or by

Figure 3. drum, shoes and socks from the York Street Band.

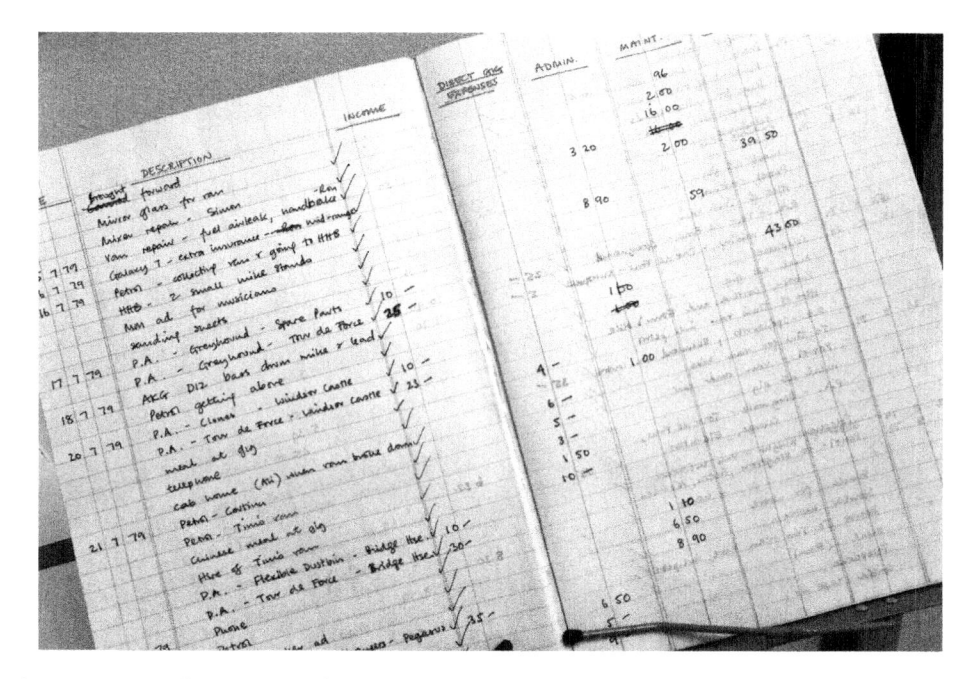

Figure 4. Jam Today Income and Expenditure Book (displayed on a music stand).
Source: All images Figures 1–4 are from Music & Liberation at the Butetown History & Arts Centre, Cardiff, September 2012. Copyright Eva Megias.

cataloguing an existing collection in more detail), selection (isolating particular items from a collection for the purposes of interpretation) and emphasis (foregrounding certain items over others in order to accentuate 'what is, importantly, already there')?[41] In what follows I outline transmission as an active practice of artificial selection. These observations draw on the work of Bernard Stiegler who argues that the 'human' is supported by external (artificial) prosthesis, mnemotechnical forms—and in our case the material stored in feminist archives—that compose our consciousness and wider orientation in the world. Stiegler's work makes clear that 'we' are the product of what we inherit, even as we can change that inheritance through our actions.[42] There is no human, in other words, outside whatever mnemotechnical context conditions it. While Stiegler's work consistently highlights the vulnerability of 'the human' in an era where consciousness is subject to sophisticated forms of control and manipulation by the marketing forces of globalised capital,[43] I am re-purposing his insight by focusing on the role artificial selection can perform in the transmission of feminist archives.

My suggestion is that new practices, theoretical and tangible, need to be developed in order to transmit feminism's archives and understand what is politically at stake in those transmission processes. This is important if we want understandings of the WLM to be produced through access to a diverse range of artefacts and perspectives which emerged from within the movement rather than, say, a single authorial voice, be it the professional historian or a well-known participant. Transmission here is understood as a practice that everyone can potentially participate in. Not everyone, of course, has the cultural power or resources to transmit information with duration, amplitude or influence. For example, we may share our knowledge of feminist archives with a small group of friends, but that act of transmission may only reverberate within a fairly closed circle. If the same materials are displayed as part of an exhibition at a well-respected gallery, the extensiveness of the transmission will be increased, perhaps even solidified, due to lingering values of taste and distinction which structure the cultural field.[44] Transmission can therefore be thought of as a practice of scale and depth that ultimately everyone has responsibility for, because all human life is composed by its inheritances: we are transmitting all the time anyway, whether we consciously know it or not. Why not, then, render transmission a more deliberate process through acts of artificial selection?

My understanding of transmission is as a form of activism that can *potentially* activate feminist archives. A politics of transmission can help address the extent that legacies are encountered and become part of a 'common' feminist cultural heritage. As Claire Colebrook explains, drawing on Stiegler's philosophy, 'the greater the difference of the archive the more complex the encounters among individuals with the past and each other'.[45] What would it mean if Black feminist activist traditions present in grassroots publications such as *FOWAAD! Mukti* and *Outwrite* were widely and consistently transmitted in the foreground, rather than pushed to the periphery? What if these materials were repeatedly used as sources for documentaries, clip art, in lessons, essays, articles, books and exhibitions? These publications do of course exist in collections within feminist archives, but they are not necessarily organised *as coherent tradition* outside of what has been ascribed to them by Black feminist and heritage communities.[46] This is not to denigrate the work of those in organisations such as the Black Cultural Archives who have contributed significant interventions in this area. Projects such as the Heart of the Race oral history project, conducted in 2009, are an invaluable record of these activist histories, the collection of these histories was an immense endeavour. My point is that the transmission of this material needs to be actively practiced across all feminist communities so that a wide range of scholars, activists, broadcasters and curators cite and utilise this material so it accrues not only heritage, but, crucially, epistemic value. As Yula Burin and Ego Ahaiwe Sowinski recently noted, 'as far as we are aware, there is not a black British feminist herstory and/or archive association, and this is urgently needed'.[47] As such, these memory resources can, like much feminist heritage, be fragmented and elliptical, which makes them harder to transmit. Such dislocation is not necessarily conscious or deliberate. It is part of a complex process where value is ascribed and resources allocated, a process that is however entangled within institutional and structural forms of racism and misogyny that shape what is perceived as valuable (culturally, economically, epistemically).

Consider the following example from my experience of my volunteer work as trustee of the Feminist Archive South, Bristol, which should underline the current haphazard organisation of the Black feminist tradition within feminist archives. In our collection of audiocassette tapes there is a single copy of Wilmette Brown, author of *Black Women and the Peace Movement*, delivering a lecture at St Werbughs community centre, Bristol, in 1984. The recording was migrated to a 24 bit/ 96 kHz digital WAV file in 2014 and is now available for consultation in the archive.[48] It is hard to specify when the tape was last played prior to that transfer, or how many people have heard it. To organise this rare recording—to connect it with wider Black feminist traditions—it needs to be discoverable through archival practices such as metadata, categorisation and tagging. If this does not happen, despite being housed in a feminist archive (think also of all those items that are *not* in the feminist archive) the item is subsumed into an undifferentiated mass of information that is only found by accident (as indeed I did, as I was looking through a box that had been called up from store—I was not deliberately looking for the tape). Its existence as a memory resource needs to be promoted via community knowledge; it needs to be consulted and emphasised. As we noted at the start of this article, heritage is an ethical struggle, a process of attributing value to artefacts. Such practices therefore need to be attentive to the marginalisation and truncation of transmitted voices across historical time, due to structural factors, lack of finance and appropriate technological infrastructure, and redress them through acts of transmission. To change the historical record, in other words, you must transmit the historical record.

Let me now use an analogy from sound recording to help us understand transmission as a practice of artificial selection and emphasis. Let us imagine that I have made a selection from feminist archives and each artefact is inserted into a 18-channel recording (see Figure 5). On playback, some of the channels are pulled up (emphasised) so they can be heard louder than others. This is an act of transmission that changes our degree of exposure to parts of the feminist archive. Because culture (even feminist culture) is organised on the premise of uneven transmission (some parts of the archive move across historical time more easily than others and are granted extended legitimacy and intelligibility), some channels need to be emphasised in the mix.[49] When the mix is played back (operationalised, performed, transmitted), following selections from the transmitter, the information trajectory may experience greater evenness, balance and accountability to a wider range of historical circumstances and actors.[50] Through such transmission practices, if widely socialised, previously under-emphasised parts of the archive may spread, condense and achieve stability. We will notice if this process is effective when things change, for example when texts from the British Black Women's Movement form a consistent part of syllabuses.[51] The change may also be, is likely to be, less tangible, more akin to a change in values.

Altering the concentration of the transmission through an act of emphasis may be understood as applying obfuscation to the historical record. Yet, as I have stated,

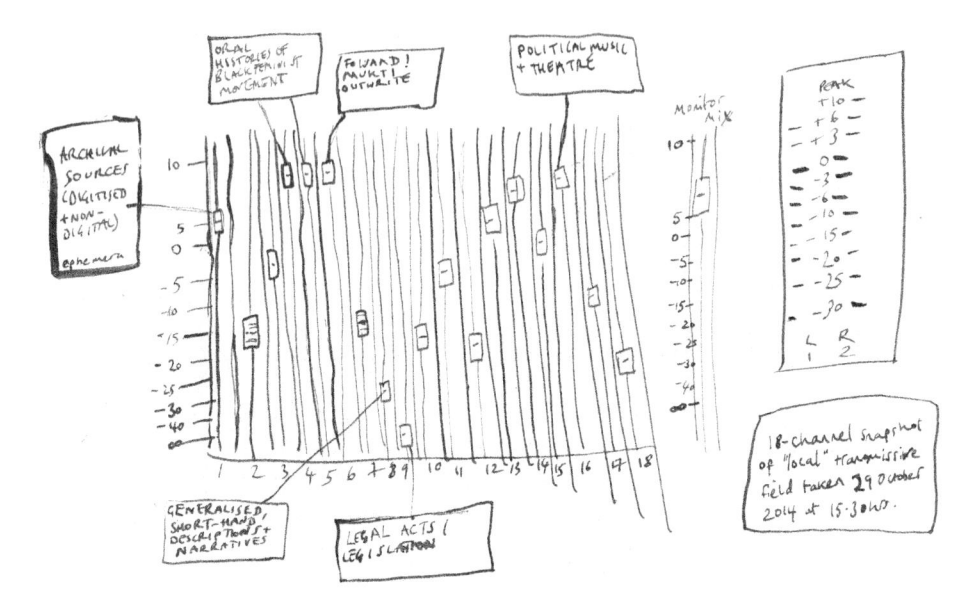

Figure 5. 18-Channel Snapshot of the Transmissive Field, drawing by the author.

transmission is a historically uneven process, meaning that certain cultural forms acquire greater concentration and stability according to factors such as ethnicity, geo-political location, gender, financial endorsement and state or civic interests that place them higher in 'the mix'. This means that the *actual amplitude* may well be balanced, or aspires to balance in *the long term*. Furthermore, as culture changes through the distribution of historical information, the mix can change; the mix is always necessarily contingent and adaptive. Each transmission is 'mixed' local to a situation, in accordance to the needs of the dominant transmission context. The example used in this article is the relative lack of access to the heritage of Black British women's movements, a situation accentuated by the inherited legacies of imperialism and white supremacy that shaped the tenor of politics of the WLM, and its aftermaths. Through transmission the balance of distributed historical information is always modified. Substantial change occurs when the emphasised parts of the mix achieve concentration, distribution and accrue acknowledged value, but this is never achieved once and for all.[52] Transmission is always necessarily a site of struggle and contestation, be it on a personal or more macro political level; the mix has to be continually played and (re) adjusted. Transmission is a process; it can be studied, yes, but foremost it is *practised*.

Transmitting the feminist archive

This article has explored how historical and heritage practices, although woven from the same archive material, can transmit that archive very differently. If the time has now come to historicise the WLM, as this special issue declares, we must also remember that there are other ways to interpret and transmit feminist archives. Moreover, these other interpretative practices exceed the writing of history as the only means to transmit historical records. As discussed above, throughout my curatorial work in *Sistershow Revisited* and *Music & Liberation* my aim was to appropriate the exhibition form in order to foreground contents of the feminist archive. It was a process whereby I organised, selected and emphasised feminist archive material relating the cultural histories of the WLM. I wanted exhibition visitors to encounter the different voices, energies, perspectives and material forms I had discovered through archival research. I wanted to construct encounters where identifications with the material displayed could potentially emerge. I was trying to engender among visitors a sense of (their) feminist heritage that may make them feel 'more whole as [feminist] people in a society that fragments, stereotypes and divides us'.[53]

My use of exhibition was also strategic because I felt it offered a wider platform for the expression of archival material. Sensitive to the way that common narrative tropes have come to compress recent feminist history, I was charmed by the way archival artefacts could carry their own stories within them. Artefacts, in this sense, invite interpretation because they appear as discontinuous or fragmented. They are, as Marina Warner suggests, open wounds.[54] They cannot be digested or processed easily. It is my contention that those invested in the transmission of feminism's archive—be they historians or heritage practitioners—need to devise strategies to ensure the complexities of the material are attended to. The transmission of history, in other words, is not always a healing or 'smoothing over' process, particularly when large, historically enacted wounds (i.e., systemic inequalities) remain open. Honouring those wounds may require elaborating alternative transmission models as I do in the final part of the essay. Although it may have seemed like a speculative and theoretical exercise, it aims to imagine the possibility where such interpretive practices—that is the ability to organise, select and emphasise the feminist archive—are widely socialised throughout society. Within such a context transmitting one's history or heritage is not the purview of professionals or specialists, but a more fundamental part of how identities and communities, composed of selected inheritances, are constructed at a grassroots, everyday level. With such thoughts in mind, we can note that the archives of the WLM and the Black Women's Movement offer us many resources, challenges and lessons to explore these possibilities.[55]

Notes

1. See for example Sarah Browne (2014) *The Women's Liberation Movement in Scotland, c.1968–c.1979* (Manchester: Manchester University Press).
2. The BBC series made by Vanessa Engle (2007) *Angry Wimmin*, http://www.bbc.co.uk/programmes/b008431p/episodes/guide and (2010) *Women* http://www.bbc.co.uk/programmes/b00rgphp, last accessed 2 October 2014.
3. 'In Conversation with the Women's Liberation Movement: intergenerational histories of second wave feminism' event, held at the British Library 12 October 2013: http://historyfeminism.wordpress.com/conference-2013/, last accessed 2 October 2014.
4. For example the Feminist Libraries and Archives network is currently active (http://feministlibrariesandarchives.wordpress.com/), while the activist work of the Feminist Activist Forum (2007–2009) was inspired by the history of the WLM, and desired to make connections with the activisms of feminists at different points in history. You can access the FAF website on the way back machine http://web.archive.org/web/20080217212745/http://www.feministactivistforum.org.uk/index.htm. Please note this is a text-only capture of the website (i.e., not a verbatim representation of the site), last accessed 4 October 2014.
5. *Rapunzel, Let Down Your Hair* (1978) and *In Our Own Time* (1981) were shown at the *Translation/Transmission* women's film season (2014): translationtransmission.wordpress.com; Mary Kelly presented a screening of the *Nightcleaners* (1975) at Birkbeck on 29 November 2013, https://www.eventbrite.co.uk/e/mary-kelly-presents-nightcleaners-part-1-tickets-8757675443.
6. Many of these events focus on a comparison of feminism then and now, or where 'we' were then, and where we are now. See for example the excellent discussion held at the LSE in January 2014 with Yasmin Alibhai-Brown, Natalie Bennett, Camille Kumar, Finn Mackay, Pragna Patel and Professor Lynne Segal. Documented online: http://www.lse.ac.uk/newsAndMedia/videoAndAudio/channels/publicLecturesAndEvents/player.aspx?id=2195, last accessed 2 October 2014.
7. See for example the Bolton Women's Liberation Oral History project, http://www.bolton-womens-liberation.org/; Sistershow Revisited, http://sistershowrevisited.wordpress.com; Unfinished Histories, http://www.unfinishedhistories.com, Music & Liberation, http://music-and-liberation.tumblr.com and the Women's Liberation Music Archive, http://womensliberationmusicarchive.co.uk, among others.
8. Raphael Samuel (2012 [1996]) *Theatres of Memory* (London: Verso), p. xxiii.
9. Laurajane Smith (2006) *The Uses of Heritage* (London: Routledge), p. 11.
10. David C. Harvey (2001) Heritage Pasts and Heritage Presents: temporality, meaning and the scope of heritage studies, *International Journal of Heritage Studies*, 7(4), pp. 319–338, p. 336.
11. Hayden White, The Value of Narrativity in the Representation of Reality, *Critical Enquiry*, 7(1), pp. 5–27, pp. 20–24, quoted in Victoria Browne (2014) *Feminism, Time and Non-Linear History* (Basingstoke: Palgrave), pp. 75–76.
12. Geoffrey Cubitt (2007) *History and Memory* (Manchester: Manchester University Press), p. 181.
13. Harvey, Heritage Pasts and Heritage Presents: temporality, meaning and the scope of heritage studies.

14. Laurajane Smith (2011) The 'Doing' of Heritage: heritage as performance, in Jenny Kidd & Anthony Jackson (Eds) *Performing Heritage: research, practice and innovation in museum theatre and live interpretation* (Manchester: Manchester University Press), pp. 69–82, p. 71.
15. Kate Eichorn (2013) *The Archival Turn in Feminism: outrage in order* (Philadelphia: Temple University Press), p. 54, author's italics.
16. Margaretta Jolly (2008) *In Love and Struggle: letters in contemporary feminism* (New York: Columbia University), p. 20.
17. Of course there are exceptions, such as Sasha Roseneil (2000) *Common Women: uncommon practices* (London: Continuum).
18. Carly Guest (2013) *Young Women's Narratives of Becoming Feminist: a multi-method study* (PhD thesis, Birkbeck); Sian Norris (2011) *The Lightbulb Moment: the stories of why we are feminists* (Bristol: Crooked Rib); Alex Brew's (2008) *Feminist Outings* played on the idea that one must come out as a feminist, reflecting also upon the ambiguous connotations of feminism and lesbian sexuality. See her website archived on the way back machine: http://www.webarchive.org.uk/wayback/archive/20100602065646/http://www.alexbrew.co.uk/gallery_150871.html (accessed 9 Oct. 2014).
19. Ron Eyerman & Andrew Jamison (1998) *Music and Social Movements: mobilizing traditions in the twentieth century* (Cambridge: Cambridge University Press).
20. Rachel Cooke, 'Taking Women Off the Shelf', 2 April 2008, *Guardian*, http://www.theguardian.com/books/2008/apr/06/fiction.features1 (accessed 28 Oct. 2014).
21. Jalna Hamner (2014) Transcript of Speech Given at the Feminist, Libraries and Archives session at the Feminism in London conference, Saturday 25 Oct. 2014.
22. Our Own Music, *Women and Music Newsletter* (1978), p. 1. Author's italics.
23. Krista Cowman (2010) 'Carrying a Long Tradition': second-wave presentations of first-wave feminism in Spare Rib c. 1972–80, *European Journal of Women's Studies*, 17(3), pp. 193–210, p. 198.
24. Ibid. p. 202.
25. Ibid. author's italics.
26. Laura Mayhall (2005) Creating the 'Suffrage Spirit': British feminism and the historical imagination, in Burton Antoinette (Ed.) *Archive Stories: facts, fictions and writings of history* (Durham: Duke University Press), pp. 232–251.
27. June Purvis, 'The March of the Women', *History Today* (Nov. 2014), p. 5.
28. Cowman, 'Carrying a Long Tradition', p. 203.
29. Ibid. p. 204.
30. Jussi Parikka (Ed.) *Digital Memory and the Archive: Wolfgang Ernst* (Minnesota: University of Minnesota Press).
31. Wendy Chun (2011) The Enduring Ephemeral, or, The Future Is a Memory, in Erik Huhtamo & Jussi Parikka (Eds) *Media Archaeology: approaches, applications and implications* (Berkeley: University of California Press), pp. 184–207.
32. Gail Lewis (2011) Interviewed by Rachel Cohen as part of Sisterhood & After. http://cadensa.bl.uk/uhtbin/cgisirsi/?ps=dftkoGSvHL/WORKS-FILE/97220073/9. Transcribed by the author from the audio file.
33. Amelia Jones (2012) *Seeing Differently: visual identification and the visual arts* (London: Routledge), p. 193. This process of identification and dis-identification Amelia Jones names 'queer feminist durationality' (p. 193).
34. Frank Ankersmit (2005) *Sublime Historical Experience* (Stanford: Stanford University Press), p. 369.
35. Eelco Runia (2006) Spots of Time, *History and Theory*, 45(3), pp. 305–316, p. 316.
36. Clare Hemmings (2011) *Why Stories Matter: the political grammar of feminist theory* (Durham: Duke University Press).
37. D-M Withers (2015) *Feminism, Digital Culture and the Politics of Transmission: theory, practice and cultural heritage* (London: Rowman Littlefield); Iris Van der Tuin (2014) *Generational Feminism* (New York: Lexington).
38. Rebecca Munford and Melanie Waters (2014) *Feminism and Popular Culture: investigating the postfeminist mystique* (London: IB Tauris), p. 22.

39. Rebecca Schneider (2011) *Performing Remains: art and war in times of theatrical reenactment* (London: Routledge).
40. Hemmings, *Why Stories Matter*.
41. Ibid. p. 180; Withers, *Feminism*.
42. Bernard Stiegler (1998) *Technics and Time, 1: the fault of Epimetheus*, trans. Richard Beardsworth & George Collins (Stanford: Stanford University Press, 1998), p. 207.
43. Bernard Stiegler (2014) *Symbolic Misery: vol. 1, the hyperindustrial epoch*, trans. Barnaby Norman (Basingstoke: Polity), p. 12.
44. Pierre Bourdieu (1986) *Distinction* (London: Routledge).
45. Claire Colebrook (2015) *Impossible and Unprincipled: on Bernard Stiegler*, available online: https://www.academia.edu/13208007/Impossible_and_Unprincipled_On_Bernard_Stiegler.
46. See also Heidi Mirza, 'Black British Feminism: then and now', *Media Diversified*, 23 March 2014, http://mediadiversified.org/2014/03/23/black-british-feminism-then-and-now/ (accessed 23 Oct. 2014).
47. Yula Burin & Ego Ahaiwe Sowinski (2014) Sister to Sister: developing a black feminist archival consciousness, *Feminist Review*, 108, pp. 112–119.
48. To explore the FAS catalogue go to http://oac.lib.bris.ac.uk/DServe/
49. While it is impossible to reduce the extent of feminist cultural heritage to sonic forms alone, I have used sound as an example here because it neatly communicates my analogy which I can represent through a visual graphic. Sound is also profoundly relational, not only felt as vibrations but also potentially absorbed by the body.
50. A transmissive circuit could be three people reading/listening to the Wilmette Brown tape and discussing it, but it can also be a website hosting that same recording, making it available to a potentially very large transmission circuit. Within such contexts 'transmission […] is the essence of education. What is education in this sense? Education is *the relation between diverse generations,* and contact is its mode of transmission': Bernard Stiegler & Irit Rogoff (2010) Transindividuation, *e-flux*, 14, http://www.e-flux.com/journal/transindividuation/ (accessed 26 Jan. 2015).
51. Gail Lewis, 'Black Feminist Texts', *Sisterhood and After* (2013), http://www.bl.uk/learning/histcitizen/sisterhood/view.html#id=143433&id2=143140 (accessed 25 March 2015).
52. Régis Debray (2004) *Transmitting Culture*, trans. Eric Rauth (New York: Columbia University Press).
53. Our Own Music, *Women and Music Newsletter*, p. 1.
54. Marina Warner (2014) Unhealing Time, in *Table of Contents: memory and presence* (London: Siobhan Davies Dance), pp. 6–15, pp. 10–12.
55. This article is dedicated to Shannon Woodcock.

Index

18-Channel Snapshot of the Transmissive Field 160
1944 Education Act 95–97; free secondary education 95; provisions 106; removal of financial barriers 96
1970s: divide between feminist scholarship and feminist activism 144; individual rather than collective solutions 107; Miss World competition protest 15; Sexual Revolution 107
1970s art practices 9–12; activism against trade unions 11; blanking out or removing perpetrators of patriarchy 21–22; decolonising the female 19; emotions 12; female bodies 21; female body hair 18; feminine and humanist camp 10; Feminist Art Program at California Institute of the Arts 10; focusing on points of tension 12; *Framing Feminism: art and the women's movement 1970–1985* 14; male bodies 20–21; male dominance 12–13; politically feminist, anti-essentialist and theory-based camp 9–10; rejection of Modernism 13; reproductive and sexual inequalities 18; US *versus* UK feminist art history approaches 9–10; weak feminine touch 14; WLM influence 14–17; women's domesticity 11–12; women's representations of men 13
1970s feminist publishing: experience of production 115; feminist engagement with publishing cultures 115–117; separatist seizing of publishing power 116
1970s recovery of foremothers 134–135; containing within domestic space 139; descendant control 136; fighting for 135; finding duplicated feelings 145; letters and representation of the life 138–139; Mary Hallock Foote 135–139; misogyny against feminists 142–143; pioneer womanhood 140–141; Smith-Rosenberg's 'The Female World of Love and Ritual: relations between women in nineteenth-century America' 137–138; valid form 145–146; western history 139
1980s feminist print-making 7–8

absence of career identities 102–104
academies: exclusion of women 19
activism: divide between feminist scholarship and feminist activism 144; establishing the movement 31; marginalized low-income women's groups 78–85; NAC denial of stay-at-home motherhood as a legitimate option 87; sympathizers comparison 95; trade unions 11; WFH and NAC tensions 86
adult education lecturers 31
AHD (Authorized Heritage Discourse) 151
all purpose local WLM groups 36
all-women exhibitions: 1970s/1980s 13
Alpert, Jane: open letter to Weather Underground women 67–68
Althusser: cultural representations of power and difference 9
anger: 1970s/1980s art practices 12; aggressive attack on the status quo 142
Angle of Repose 135–136; fictional warping 136; gender politics 141–142; lesbian theme 145; loss of ownership of Foote's life and work 136; sexuality 137
anti-imperialist feminism 61; antiracism 64; armed resistance 65; Boston-area women's liberationists 61–62; frustrations with racial injustice 64; Harvard's war research 62–63; influences 65; Jane Alpert open letter to Weather Underground women 67–68; racism, sexism, and imperialism connection 69–70; socialist feminists division 63; urgency for release of political prisoners 65; Weather Underground response to Jane Alpert's letter 69; Women's School 66–67
anti-nuclear protests at Greenham Common 15–16
APEX (Association of Professional, Executive, Clerical and Computer Staff): Grunwick strike 53
appropriation 1
archives: balancing transmission 161; organizing 159–160; re-presenting in exhibition form 153–156; selection and emphasis 160–161;

INDEX

transmission 161–162; transmission of the historical record 160
art: exclusion of women in history 19; women's' positions compared to male artists 7–8
artefacts: balancing transmission 161; organization 159–160; selection and emphasis 160–161; transmission 161–162; transmitting historical records 160
art practices of 1970s 9–12; activism against trade unions 11; emotions 12; feminine and humanist camp 10; Feminist Art Program at California Institute of the Arts 10; focusing on points of tension 12; male dominance 12–13; politically feminist, anti-essentialist and theory-based camp 9–10; rejection of Modernism 13; US *versus* UK feminist art history approaches 9–10; WLM influence 14–17; women's domesticity 11–12; women's representations of men 13
art practices of 1980s: blanking out or removing perpetrators of patriarchy 21–22; decolonising the female 19; emotions 12; female bodies 18, 21; *Framing Feminism: art and the women's movement 1970–1985* 14; male bodies 20–21; male dominance 12–13; rejection of Modernism 13; reproductive and sexual inequalities 18; weak feminine touch 14; WLM influence 14–17; women's representations of men 13
Asian women workers strike 53–55
Asphodel 123
Association of Professional, Executive, Clerical and Computer Staff (APEX) 53
authoritarian fathers: escaping 97
Authorized Heritage Discourse (AHD) 151
autobiographical writings 27–28, 98

Badges Women 12
balancing cultural heritage transmission 161
Bambara, Toni Cade: *The Black Woman* 66
Banks, Olive: activists *versus* sympathizers 95
Barron, Jackie 33
Baxandall, Rosalyn: motherhood activists 75
Bennet, Judith: 1970s clarity 134
Bennett, Gay: formation of Bolton women's liberation group 29
Bhopal, Kalwant: empowering interviewers 27
biographical writing 98
Black Dwarf 119
Black Panthers: Party-hosted Revolutionary People's Constitutional Convention 62; women members 2
'The Black Struggle and White Radical Response' class 66
The Black Woman 66
Black Women and the Peace Movement 159
Black Women in White America 60

Black Women's Movement: balancing transmission 161; organizing artefacts 159–160; selection and emphasis 160–161
body hair 18
bohemian feminist circles 38
Boland, Rose: Dagenham equal pay strike 48–49
Bolton WLM: communal lifestyles 38; formation of women's liberation group 29; Fortalice 34–35; local health services manual 31; meetings 29; personal lives and lifestyle changes 38; *Sweetie Pie* educational play 31; WAVAW involvement 36
Bonheur, Rose 19–20
bookstore contributions 120–121
Boston-area women's liberationists 61–62
Bouchier, David: feminists de-emphasizing lesbianism 145
boy children in women's centres and WLM events 39
Boycott, Rosie: *Spare Rib* 125; underground press male attitudes 118–119
Bradford Dykes 32
Bradford WLM: sexual violence campaigns 35; working class women 32
Bravo, Jenn: institutionalization of women's organizations 35
Breines, Winifred: Black Power wedge between white and black women 61
Brighton WLM: communal lifestyles 38; National Abortion Campaign 34; Reclaim the Night marches 36; WEA 31; Women's Aid refuge 34; women's centre 33–34
Bristol WLM: consciousness raising 30; Cristel 36; Introductory sessions 31; meetings 29; National Abortion Campaign 34; national campaigns 36–37; peace movement 37; Women's Centre 33; Women's House Project 34
Brown, Wilmette: *Black Women and the Peace Movement* 159
Browne, Sarah: regional diversity 28
Bruley, Sue: consciousness-raising 16; Grunwick strike 54
Buck, Marilyn: women's liberation groups 64
Butterworth, Sue: Silver Moon bookshop 120

CAG (Cleaners Action Group) 50
California Institute of the Arts Feminist Art Program 10
Cambridge Women's Center 63
campaigns 34–37; all purpose local 36; Bristol national 36–37; hierarchical management structures and cultures 35; institutionalization 35; local 37; National Abortion Campaign (NAC) 34; revolutionary feminism 35; sexual violence 35; violence against women 35–36; Wages for Housework 36; women's aid 34–35; YBA Wife 36–37

166

INDEX

Campbell, Bea: consumption of feminist reading 114
Canadian low-income mothers' activism: marginalized low-income women's groups 78–85; NAC agenda 77–78; NAC and WFH tensions 86; NAC denial of stay-at-home motherhood as a legitimate option 87
career identities absence 102–104
Chapeltown WIRES group 30
Chester, Gail 117
Chicago, Judy: Feminist Art Program at California Institute of the Arts 10
children: boy children in women's centres and WLM events 39; MLU position on daycare 79; welfare rights 82
Cholmeley, Jane: Silver Moon bookshop 120
Clark, Joan: FBWG 81; MLU 80
class: absence of career identities 102–104; balancing class and gender politics 51–53; cross-class alliances between women 45; Dagenham equal pay strike 47–49; dependence on inequalities 101; difference feminism 75; differences 46; feminism relationship 45–46; higher education inequalities 96; Night Cleaners' Campaign 49–51; socialist-feminist histories 46; solidarity 54; Wages for Housework (WFH) 84
Cleaners Action Group (CAG) 50
Cliff, Tony: *Womens Voice* 126
co-educational opportunities 106–107
Cohen, Daniel: Goddess movement 123
Colebrook, Claire: cultural archives 159
collective organization: London Women's Art History Collective 13
collectivity: anti-nuclear protests at Greenham Common 16; shifting focus towards individuals 107
colonialism struggles 64
communal lifestyles 38
communication: UK WLM 30
Comprehensives 95
conferences: social events 38; UK WLM 31
consciousness raising 16–17; establishment of the movement 30–31; post-war writing 98–99; print-making 20
content: feminist magazines 121
Conway, Marian: Stegner's damage of Foote 142
Cook, Rachel: career identity 104; powerful men 101; transportation to grammar schools 102
Cot 12
Coward, Rosalind: 'Underneath We're Angry' 12
Cowman, Krista: *Spare Rib* history of suffrage movement 152
Cristel 36
Crosland, Anthony: non-selective education 106
Cross, Amanda: *Death in a Tenured Position* 144
cross-class alliances between women 45

cultural heritage: balancing transmission 161; history comparison 150–151; oral history initiatives 149; organizing artefacts 159–160; rediscovery 151–153; re-presenting in exhibition form 153–156; selection and emphasis 160–161; transmission 161–162; transmitting historical records 160
culture: production 37–38; representations of power and difference 9

Dagenham equal pay strike 47–49; equality on the political agenda 47–48; gendered perspectives 49; influence on Labour Party 48; media response 48; sexual discrimination 48–49; solidarity between male and female trade unionists 48; trade union histories 48
daily press: WLM relationships 117–118
Dalston women's liberation workshop: Cleaners Action Group (CAG) 50
Dalton, Pen 30
daughters: born after 1950 differences with mothers 106–107; unfulfilled expectations and displaced hopes of parents 98
Davis, Angela: points of tension 12; 'Reflections on the Black Woman's Role in the Community of Slaves' 66
daycare: MLU position 79
Death in a Tenured Position 144
decolonising the female 19
Delap, Lucy: feminist bookshops 121
dependence on class inequalities 101
descendant control: foremother recovery 136
devaluation of women's unwaged domestic and parenting labour 76
development of feminist presses 119–121; bookstore contributions 120; political authenticity and commercial viability conflict 119; relationship to other industry sectors 119
difference feminism 75
differences: cultural representations of 9; mothers 103; race, class, sexuality 46
direct action campaigns 15
Direct Grant schools 95
displaced hopes of parents: daughters carrying 98
distressed mothers: escaping 97
distribution: feminist magazines 121–122
diversity: feminist publishing cultures 116–117; UK WLM 36
divisions: between feminist scholarship and feminist activism 144; household/family labour 100; WLM movement 16
domesticity 11–12; conflicts with workplace demands 105–106; devaluation of women's unwaged domestic and parenting labour 76; family wage 105; pensions for homemakers 78; sharing housework, income generation, and childrearing responsibilities 100

INDEX

double slavery of paid employment 84
Dromey, Jack: Trico equal pay strike 52
dual nature of working-class women's oppression 50
Dulude, Louise: daycare support 87; pensions for homemakers 78

economic independence through wage labour 76
Education Act 1944 95–97; free secondary education 95; provisions 106; removal of financial barriers 96
educational culture from 1945–65; 1944 Act provisions 106; absence of career identities 102–104; adult education lecturers 31; breaking with class culture and gender expectations of families 97–98; conflicts between workplace demands and family needs 105–106; consciousness raising through feminist writing 98–99; daughters carrying unfulfilled expectations and displaced hopes of parents 98; dependence on unequal classes of women 101; Education Act 95–97; family wage 105; feminists born after 1950 106; financial barriers removal 96; gender and class inequalities 96; parental antipathy 97; redistributing family and state resources 100; renegotiation of marital roles 102; sexual revolution 104–105; tensions between daughters and parents 97; transition of non-selective co-education 106; welfare state 106; WLM 15; written competitive exam for grammar school selection 101
Eichron, Kate: heritage 151
emotions: aggressive attack on the status quo 142; art practices in 1970s and 1980s 12
emphasis: transmission of cultural heritage 160–161
empowerment: language of 30
Engels, Friedrich: *The Origin of the Family, Private Property, and the State* 66
equality: Dagenham equal pay strike 47–49; equal rights feminist policies 16
Equal Pay Act 15; Dagenham equal pay strike influence 48
Erlien, Marla: do something dramatic 62; Harvard University occupation 62–63
essentialism: anti-nuclear protests at Greenham Common 16
establishing the movement 29–30; activism 31; adult education lecturers 31; all purpose local groups 36; campaigns 34–37; communication 30; conferences 31; consciousness raising 30–31; cultural production 37–38; diversity and specialty groups 36; Introductory sessions 31; language of empowerment 30; local campaigns 37; modes of organizing 29; municipal feminism 37; peace 37; personal lives and lifestyle changes 38–39; public urban spaces 31; race 36; revolutionary feminists and heterosexual women problems 39; sisterhood 31–32; women only physical spaces 29–30; women's centres 32–34
etching process 17
Evans, Sara: newer histories of US WLM problems 60
exclusion of women: art history and academies 19
exhibitions re-presenting cultural heritage 153–156
experiences: production 115; respecting female experiences and maternalist values 102
Eyerman, Ron: heritage 151

Family Benefits Work Group (FBWG) 81–82
family wage 105
Faragher, John: migration enforced onto women by their husbands 140–141
FBWG (Family Benefits Work Group) 81–82
female bodies: 1980s art practices 21; decolonising 19; hair 18; vaginal imagery 10
The Female Eunuch 18
Female Rejection Drawing 10
female sensibility via central-core visual motifs 10
'The Female World of Love and Ritual: relations between women in nineteenth-century America' 137–138
Feminism in Bristol 1973–5 38
Feminist Art Program at California Institute of the Arts 10
Feminist Bookstore Network in US 120
Feminist Bookstore Newsletter 120
feminist cultural heritage *see* cultural heritage
feminist magazines 121–129; distribution 121–122; diverse content 121; feminist group membership 122; informing and entertaining 121; physical appearances 121; *Red Rag* 126; *Shrew* 122–124; *Spare Rib* 124–126; *Womens Voice* 126–129
Feministo 11–12
feminist presses: bookstore contributions 120–121; political authenticity and commercial viability conflict 119; relationship to other industry sectors 119
feminist readings: consumption 114
feminists born after 1950 106
Ferris, Beth: *Heartland* 140
fictional warping 136
financial barriers: education 96
flexible gender roles 105
flower painting 20
Floyd, Janet: recovery and appropriation 1
Foote, Mary Hallock recovery 135–139; *Angle of Repose* 135–136; containing within domestic

INDEX

space 139; fictional warping in *Angle of Repose* 136; gender politics in *Angle of Repose* 141; granddaughter views 141–142; history of the American west 141; lesbian theme in *Angle of Repose* 145; loss of ownership of her life and work 136; Lyman Ward's recovery 137; Paul's *Reminiscences of a Victorian Gentlewoman in the Far-West* 139; private intimate life 138–139; sexuality 137; Smith-Rosenberg's 'The Female World of Love and Ritual: relations between women in nineteenth-century America' 137–138; Stegner's damage 142; Stegner's warping of her sexual life 143–144; Walsh's defense 143; Walsh's intervention of Stegner's warping of Foote's sexual life 143–144

foremother recovery *see* recovery of foremothers

Forster, Margaret: 1944 Education Act 96–97; authoritarian father 97; different from the mother 103; grammar school selection 101; parental antipathy 97; renegotiating of marital roles 102; uniform 102

Fortalice 34–35

Foucault: discursive formations of historical oppression of women 9–10

Framing Feminism: art and the women's movement 1970-1985 13–14

Fraser, Nancy: devaluation of women's unwaged domestic and parenting labour 76; insurrectionary spirit 12

Friendz 118

'From an Old House in America' 140–141

funding: women's centres 34

gender: absence of career identities 102–104; *Angle of Repose* 141; balancing class and gender politics 51–53; connection with racism and imperialism 69–70; discrimination in workplace 48–49; flexible roles 105; higher education inequalities 96; male dominance of 1970s/1980s art practices 12–13; representation in press 118; sharing housework, income generation, and childrearing responsibilities 100; tertiary education gender inequalities 96; white women liberationists focus 64

German, Lindsey: 'Womens Voice: the way forward' 128

Girls Public Day School Trust 95

global colonialism struggles 64

Gluck, Sherna Berger: US WLM history 60

'Goddess' *Shrew* 123

Goddess theology 123

'God Giving Birth' 123

Goodall, Phil: points of tension 12

Goodbye Dolly 122

Good Wives? 102

Gordon, Linda: devaluation of women's unwaged domestic and parenting labour 76

Graham, Helen: *Shrew* 124

grammar schools 95; breaking with class culture and gender expectations of families 97–98; gender and class differences 96; in loco parentis 104; parental antipathy 97; sexual revolution 104–105; transportation 102; uniforms 102; written competitive exam for grammar school selection 101

Green, Blake: gendered inequality 141–142

Greenham Common anti-nuclear protests 15–16

Greer, Germaine: body hair 18; researching female artists 8; *Suck* 119

Grunwick strike 53–55

Hammer, Alison: Brighton women's centre 34

Hanmer, Jalna: inter agency work 37; rediscovery of heritage 152

Harvard University occupation 62–63

Harvey, David: heritage 151

Harwin, Nicola: Introductory sessions 31

Heartland 140

Heart of the Race project 149

Heilbrun, Carolyn: *Death in a Tenured Position* 144

heritage: history comparison 150–151

Heritage Lottery Fund (HLF) 27

heterosexual women: problems with revolutionary feminists 39; shifting away from heterosexual relationships 38

Hewitt, Nancy: waves in feminist history 2

Hidden from History 15

Hidden Lives 101

hierarchical management structures of womens' centres 35

history: heritage comparison 150–151

HLF (Heritage Lottery Fund) 27

Hobbs, May: Night Cleaners' Campaign 50

Hogan, Kristen: bookstores as public spaces for feminism 120

Hogarth: political satire and print-making 20

Hollows, Joanne: relationships of feminist magazines to commercial advertising 125; routes to feminism 8

Homer, Sheridan: working class women in the movement 32

Horowitz, Liz: political action and history of racism 65–66

Housewife 100

Howard, Judy: peace movement 37

identities: absence of career identities 102–104; balancing class and gender politics 51–53; lesbianism as normal 16; sexual 104–107; working-class 54–55

IMG (International Marxist Group): Cleaners Action Group (CAG) 50

INDEX

imperialism: connection with racism and sexism 69–70; Harvard war research 62–63

individuals: focus on individual not collective solutions 107

industrial disputes: Dagenham equal pay strike 47–49; Grunwick 53–55; Night Cleaners' Campaign 49–51; Trico 51–53

industrial politics: part-time women workers 47; shopfloor movement 47

inequalities: dependence on class inequalities 101; gender 141–142; gender and class in educational institutions 96; wages 47

Ingram, Ruth: sexual violence campaigns 35

in loco parentis 104

In Other Words 117

institutionalization: women's organizations 35

insurrectionary spirit 12

inter agency work 37

International Marxist Group (IMG) 50

International Socialists (IS) 126; local Women's Voice groups 37

International Women's Day 2014 6

intersectionality 2

Introductory sessions of Bristol WLM 31

Irregular Periods 16–17

IS (International Socialists) 126; local Women's Voice groups 37

IT magazine 118

'It was as if she had painted with the brush between her toes…' 7–8

Jaffe, Naomi: organizing whites against racism 64

Jamison, Andrew: heritage 151

Jam Today Income and Expenditure Book 158

Jeffreys, Shelia: revolutionary feminism 35

Jolly, Margaretta: heritage 151; individuals representing a collective 27

Jones, Allen: *Women As Furniture* series 13

Karell, Linda: lesbian theme in *Angle of Repose* 145

Kelly, Mary: *Post-Partum Document* press response 12–13; sexual division of labour 11

Kodar, Freya: pension proposals for homemakers 78

labour: participation 47; sexual division 11

Labour Party 37; Dagenham equal pay strike influence 48; Trico equal pay strike 52

Land, Hilary: women's financial and legal independence 36

language of empowerment 30

LEAs (Local Education Authorities) 95

leaving home for university education: breaking with class culture and gender expectations of families 97–98

Leeds WLM: Labour Party 37; Metropolitan University International Women's Day 2014 6; rape crisis centre 35; revolutionary feminism 35

Lerner, Gerda: *Black Women in White America* 66

lesbianism: normal identity 16; recovery of past 144–145; shifting away from heterosexual relationships 38

letters and representation of the life: recovery of foremothers 138–139

Letters of a Woman Homesteader 140

Lewis, Gaby: formation of Bolton women's liberation group 29

Lews, Gail: Black Women's Movement participation 154

life history approaches 27–28

lifestyle changes 38–39

Llywarch, Margaret: native reporting 127–128

local campaigns 37

Local Education Authorities (LEAs) 95

local health services manual 31

location in art history: 'It was as if she had painted with the brush between her toes…' 7–8

Lockyer, Bridget: consciousness-raising 16–17

London focus 28

London Women's Art History Collective 13

Long, Pauline 123

Lovatt, Rosemary: Brighton women's centre 34

loyalty to disappointed mothers 103

Lyman, Susan: Harvard University occupation 63

MAG (Mothers Action Group) 82–83

magazines 121–129; distribution 121–122; diverse content 121; feminist group membership 122; informing and entertaining 121; physical appearances 121; *Red Rag* 126; *Shrew* 122–124; *Spare Rib* 124–126; *Womens Voice* 126–129

male bodies: 1980s art practices 20–21; blanking out or removing perpetrators of patriarchy 21–22

male dominance: 1970s/1980s art practices 12–13; blanking out or removing perpetrators of patriarchy 21–22

Malos, Ellen: Bristol Women's Centre 33

marginalized low-income women's groups 78–85; Family Benefits Work Group (FBWG) 81–82; Mother-Led Union (MLU) 79–81; Mothers Action Group (MAG) 82–83; Wages for Housework (WFH) 83–85; Welfare Rights Coalition (WRC) 83

martial roles: renegotiating 102

Marxism: influences on artists 11; Wages for Housework (WFH) 83

Massey, Doreen: spatial organization 30

maternalism 75–76; anti-nuclear protests at Greenham Common 16

INDEX

Matiland, Sara: power in print culture 114
Matriarchy Study Group: Goddess theology 123
MAW (Mothers Are Women): conflict with NAC over stay-at-home mothers 87
Mayhall, Laura: rediscovering cultural heritage 153
McKeen, Wendy: welfare rights activist mothers 76
McNeill, Sandra: WAVAW groups 36
media: response to Dagenham equal pay strike 48; response to Mary Kelly's *Post-Partum Document* 12–13; *see also* print culture
Melville, Sam 68
men: female workers comparison 47; powerful 101; sharing housework 100; solidarity action with female workers 48; solidarity action with women workers 53; women's artistic representations of men 1970s/1980s 13
Mendes, Kaitlynn: daily press representations of feminists 118
militant white groups: white feminists links 64
misogyny against feminists 142–143
Mitchell, Juliet: WLM and daily press relationship 117
MLU (Mother-Led Union) 79–81
Modernism: rejection 13
Modern schools 95
monogamy 38
Moseley, Rachel: routes to feminism 8
motherhood: being different from mothers103; devaluation of women's unwaged domestic and parenting labour 76; differences with daughters born after 1950 106–107; loyalty to disappointed mothers 103; marginalized low-income women's groups 78–85; maternalist feminists 75–76; NAC agenda 77–78; NAC and WFH tensions 86; NAC denial of stay-at-home motherhood as a legitimate option 87; pensions for homemakers 78; respecting 102; stay-at-home motherhood 76; welfare rights activists *versus* women's movement 75–76
Mother-Led Union (MLU) 79–81
Mothers Action Group (MAG) 82–83
Mothers Are Women (MAW): conflict with NAC over stay-at-home mothers 87
Mudie, George: feminizing local state 37
Mueller, Carol: low status of women in underground press 118
Mulvey, Laura: sexual division of labour 11; 'You don't' know what is happening, do you, Mr Jones?' 13
municipal feminism 37
Murray, Jen: Brighton women's centre 33
Murray, Simone: divide between feminist scholarship and feminist activism 144; feminist publishing history 115–116; Virago's duality of self-conception 119
Music & Liberation 154–156

NAC (National Abortion Campaign) 15, 34; Canadian movement agenda 77–78; denial of stay-at-home motherhood as a legitimate option 87; WFH tensions 86
national campaigns: Bristol 36–37; National Abortion Campaign 34
national conferences: 1978 collapse 16
national focus 28
National Joint Action Campaign Committee for Women's Equal Rights 15; Dagenham equal pay strike 49
National Organisation of Women (NOW) 2
native reporting 127–128
Nava, Mica: sharing housework, income generation, and childrearing responsibilities 100
Nelson, Elizabeth: underground press relationship 118
newsletters 30
new social movements 1
NHS health services: availability 100
Nielsen: *In Other Words* 117
Night Cleaners' Campaign 49–51
Nightcleaners Part 1 11
non-selective co-education 106–107
Norwich WLM 31; consciousness raising 30; violence against women campaigns 36; WLM formation 31; Women's Centre 33
NOW (National Organisation of Women) 2

Oakley, Ann: adult identity 103; connections from the body in sex and motherhood 102; life-writing genre 98; loyalty to disappointed mothers 103; NHS health services 100; relationship with father 97; sexual revolution 104–105; sharing housework 100
The Obstacle Race: the fortune of women painters and their work 8
Ociepka, Maria: MAG 82
O'Connell, Dorothy: AGM speech 86–87
Off our backs: Jane Alpert open letter to Weather Underground women 67–68; Weather Underground response to Jane Alpert's letter 69
Old Mistresses 19
Old Wives Tales bookstore 120
One in 4 safehouse 35
open relationship 38
oral history initiatives 149
oral testimony 27
organizing artefacts 159–160
The Origin of the Family, Private Property, and the State 66

INDEX

Outwrite 117
OX series of drawings 10
Oz 118

Page, Kate: radical feminism 39
Pankhurst, Sylvia: East End Suffragettes 127; *The Suffrage Movement* 153
parents: antipathy 97; daughters carrying unfulfilled expectations and displaced hopes 98
Parker, Rozsika: flower painting 20; *Framing Feminism: art and the women's movement 1970–1985* 13–14; London Women's Art History Collective 13; Old Mistresses 19; The Subversive Stitch 19
participation in labour-force 47
part-time women workers 47
Pasolli, Lisa: child care movement 77
patriarchy: art practices of 1970s/1980s 12–13; blanking out or removing perpetrators of patriarchy 21–22
Paul, Rodman W.: recovery in the history of the American west 141; *Reminiscences of a Victorian Gentlewoman in the Far-West* 139
peace movements: UK WLM 37
pensions for homemakers 78
personal lifestyles 38–39
physical appearances: feminist magazines 121
Pine, Jacqui: Women's School 66
pioneer womanhood 140–141
'Playful Acts: Gender, Performance and Visibility' 5–6
points of tension focus 12
political identities: balancing class and gender politics 51–53; working-class identities 54–55
political satire: print-making 20
Pollock, Griselda: flower painting 20; *Framing Feminism: art and the women's movement 1970–1985* 13–14; London Women's Art History Collective 13; Old Mistresses 19; US versus British feminist art history approaches 9–10; women's weak feminine touch 14
Porter, Marilyn: personal lives and lifestyle changes 38–39
Post-Partum Document: press response 12–13
post-war feminism: 1944 Act provisions 106; absence of career identities 102–104; breaking with class culture and gender expectations of families 97–98; conflicts between workplace demands and family needs 105–106; consciousness raising through women's writing 98–99; daughters carrying unfulfilled expectations and displaced hopes of parents 98; dependence on unequal classes of women 101; Education Act 95–97; family wage 105; feminists born after 1950 106; gender inequalities in education 96; redistributing family and state resources 100; renegotiation of marital roles 102; sexual revolution 104–105; transition of non-selective co-education 106; welfare state 106; written competitive exam for grammar school selection 101
power: cultural representations of 9; print culture 114; printed word 114; women's artistic representations of men 1970s/1980s 13
powerful men 101
print culture: bookstore contributions 120–121; consumption of feminist reading 114; development of feminist presses 119–121; experience of production 115; feminist engagement with publishing cultures 115–117; feminist magazines 121–129; intentionality to undermine patriarchal capitalist control 117; power 114; separatist seizing of publishing power 116; underground press relationship 118–119; US Women in Print (WIP) movement 117; WLM relationship with daily press 117–118; Women in Media Group 117–118
printed word: power 114
print-making: blanking out or removing perpetrators of patriarchy 21–22; decolonising the female 19; etching process 17; female bodies 21; feminist publishers 8–9; 'It was as if she had painted with the brush between her toes…' 7–8; male bodies 20–21; political satire 20; story of Rose Bonheur 19–20; women's location in art history 7–8
privileged schools for girls 95
'Protecting our Own' report 82
Pruitt Stewart, Elinore 140
Psychology Shrew 122
public demonstrations: National Joint Action Campaign Committee for Equal Rights in London 1969 15
public urban spaces: establishing the movement 31
publishing culture 8–9: bookstore contributions 120–121; development of feminist presses 119–121; experience of production 115; feminist engagement 115–117; feminist magazines 121–129; intentionality to undermine patriarchal capitalist control 117; separatist seizing of publishing power 116; underground press relationship 118–119; US Women in Print (WIP) movement 117; WLM relationship with daily press 117–118; Women in Media Group 117–118
Purvis, June: feminist histories 153

race 2; connection with sexism and imperialism 69–70; differences 46; global colonialism struggles 64; Grunwick strike 54; UK WLM 36; US WLM 60–61; WFH 85

INDEX

racial justice and US WLM: African American history classes at Women's School 66; global colonialism 64; Harvard University occupation 62–63; Jane Alpert open letter to Weather Underground women 67–68; organizing whites against racism 64; racism, sexism, and imperialism connection 69–70; violence relationship to resistance 65; white anti-imperialist feminists links with militant white groups 64; Women's School conflicts with Women's Center 67

Radclyffe Hall 35

Radford, Jill: national and London focus 28; Winchester Women's Liberation Group 120

rape crisis centre in Leeds 35

Reclaim the Night protests 3, 15, 35–36

recovery 1

recovery of foremothers 134–135; containing within domestic space 139; descendant control 136; fighting for 135; finding duplicated feelings 145; letters and representation of the life 138–139; Mary Hallock Foote 135–139; misogyny against feminists 142–143; pioneer womanhood 140–141; Smith-Rosenberg's 'The Female World of Love and Ritual: relations between women in nineteenth-century America' 137–138; valid form 145–146; western history 139

rediscovering cultural heritage 151–153

Red Rag 126

Rees, Jeska: regional diversity 28

'Reflections on the Black Woman's Role in the Community of Slaves' 66

regional diversity in UK WLM 28

rejection of Modernism 13

release of political prisoners 65

Reminiscences of a Victorian Gentlewoman in the Far-West 139

renegotiating of marital roles 102

re-presenting heritage in exhibition form 153–156

reproductive inequalities 18

resistance: violence relationship 65

'Resistance, Repression, Rebellion' class 66

respecting female experiences and maternalist values 102

revisionists: differences over race, class, sexuality 46

revolutionary feminism 35; problems with heterosexual women 39

Revolutionary People's Constitutional Convention (RPCC) 62

Rich, Adrienne: 'From an Old House in America' 140–141

Riley, Catherine: Virago 119

Roseneil, Sasha: anti-nuclear protests at Greenham Common 16; individuals representing a collective 27

routes to feminism 8

Rowbotham, Shelia: *Black Dwarf* 119; *Hidden from History* 15; Night Cleaners' Campaign 50

Rowe, Marsha: power of the printed word 114; *Spare Rib* 125; women's role in underground press 118

RPCC (Revolutionary People's Constitutional Convention): Black Panther Party-hosted 62

Ruskin trades union college conference 15

Ryan, Ginger: 'Resistance, Repression, Rebellion' class 66; Women's School 66

Sahara 35

Samuel, Raphael: history 150

Saunders, Shelia: inter agency work 37

Schapiro, Mariam: Feminist Art Program at California Institute of the Arts 10

scholarship: divide between scholarship and activism 144

scholarship girls: 1944 Act provisions 106; adult identities 103; conflicts between workplace demands and family needs 105–106; family wage 105; feminists born after 1950 106–107; loyalty to disappointed mothers 103; sexual revolution 104–105; transition of non-selective co-education 106–107; transportation to grammar schools 102; uniforms 102; welfare state 106

Seajay, Carol: Feminist Bookstore Network 120

Secondary Modern schools: gender and class inequalities 96

second wave feminism *see* WLM

Segal, Lynne: autobiographical/life history approaches 27–28; creative work explosion 114

selection: grammar school 101–102; transmission of cultural heritage 160–161

separatists: seizing of publishing power 116

Setch, Eve: feminist cultural production 37

Sex Discrimination Act of 1975 15

sexism: art 13; connection with racism, and imperialism 69–70; discrimination 48–49; division of labour 11; inequalities 18

sexual identities 104–107

sexuality: *Angle of Repose* 137; differences 46; vaginal imagery 10

Sexual Revolution 107

sexual violence campaigns 35

sharing housework, income generation, and childrearing responsibilities 100

Sheba 9

Sheridan, Dorothy: monogamy 38

shopfloor movement 47

Shorerocks, Elizabeth: consciousness raising 30

Shoulder to Shoulder 153

INDEX

Shrew 122–124
Shrewsbury 24 case 128
Significant Sisters 101–102
Silver Moon bookshop 120
Silver Moon Quarterly 120
sisterhood 31–32
Sisterhood & After 149
Sistershow 37
Sistershow Revisited: feminism in Bristol, 1973–1975 154–156
'Situating Women's Liberation, Historicizing a Movement' conference 3
Sjöö, Monica 38; 'God Giving Birth' 123
Smith, Annick: *Heartland* 140
Smith, Laruajane: heritage 150–151
Smith-Rosenberg, Caroll: 'The Female World of Love and Ritual: relations between women in nineteenth-century America' 137–138
social events 38–39
socialist feminists: anti-imperialist feminists division 63; class 46; equal rights feminist policies 16; NAC role 77; *Womens Voice* 126
Socialist Workers Party (SWP) 126
Society for the Protection of the Unborn Child (SPUC) 34
solidarity: working-class 48, 53–54
Spare Rib 8, 119, 124–126; history of suffrage movement 152
SPUC (Society for the Protection of the Unborn Child) 34
Stansell, Christine: migration enforced onto women by their husbands 140–141
starting point of WLM 15
state resource redistribution 100
stay-at-home motherhood 76; Mother-Led Union (MLU) 79–81; NAC denial of stay-at-home motherhood as a legitimate option 87
Stegner, Wallace's *Angle of Repose* 135–136; argument with feminists 144; damage to Foote 142; fictional warping 136; gender politics 141–142; lesbian theme 145; loss of ownership of Foote's life and work 136; recovery in the history of the American west 141; sexuality 137; Walsh's intervention of his warping of Foote's sexual life 143–144
Stiegler, Bernard: vulnerability of the human 158
The Subversive Stitch 19
'Succubi and Other Monsters: the women in *Angle of Repose*' 142–143
Suck 119
The Suffrage Movement 153
Sutcliffe, Peter 35
Sweetie Pie 31
SWP (Socialist Workers Party): *Womens Voice* 126–128
sympathizers: activists comparison 95

'take back the night' 3
Taylor, Helen 30
Taylor, Lisa: blanking out or removing perpetrators of patriarchy 21–22; female bodies 21; 'It was as if she had painted with the brush between her toes…' 7–8; male bodies 20–21; reproductive and sexual inequalities 18–19; unshaven hairy bodies 17–18
tertiary education: gender inequalities 96
Thatcher, Margaret: non-selective education 106
Thompson, Becky: newer histories of US WLM problems 60; white feminist participation in militant white groups 64
Thompson, Emani: Jane Alpert open letter to Weather Underground women 68
Tickner, Lisa: decolonising the female 19; vaginal motifs promoting self-knowledge 10–11
Tillem, Laura: Boston-area women's liberationists 61
Tomlinson, Natalie: threadbare historiography of WLM 27
trade unions: activism 11; Dagenham equal pay strike 48; membership 50–51; Trico equal pay strike 52
transition of non-selective co-education 106
transmission of cultural heritage 161–162; balancing 161; historical record 160; organizing artefacts 159–160; selection and emphasis 160–161
Transmissive Field, 18-Channel Snapshot 160
transnational influences 3
transportation: grammar schools 102
Travis, Trysh: feminist publishing history 116; US Women in Print (WIP) movement 117
Trico equal pay strike 51–53
Trouble & Strife: seizing of publishing power 116–117
Turbville, Vicki: formation of Bolton women's liberation group 29

UK WLM: adult education lecturers 31; all purpose local groups 36; Bradford Dykes 32; campaigns 34–37; communication 30; conferences 31; consciousness raising 30–31; cultural production 37–38; direction action 31; diversity 36; establishing 29–30; first Women's Studies MA 15; language of empowerment 30; local campaigns 37; London Women's Art History Collective 13; modes of organizing 29; municipal feminism 37; peace movement 37; personal lives and changes in lifestyles 38–39; public urban spaces 31; race 36; regional diversity 28; revolutionary feminists and heterosexual women problems 39; Silver Moon bookshop 120; sisterhood 31–32; US feminist art history approaches comparison 9–10; women only physical spaces 29–30;

INDEX

women's centres 32–34; Women in Print (WiP) movement in London 117
underground press: WLM relationship 118–119
'Underneath We're Angry' 12
unfulfilled expectations of parents: daughters carrying 98
uniforms: grammar schools 102
union membership: Night Cleaners' Campaign 50–51
University of Portsmouth conference 3
urgency: release of political prisoners 65
US recovery of foremothers 134–135; containing within domestic space 139; descendant control 136; fighting for 135; finding duplicated feelings 145; letters and representation of the life 138–139; Mary Hallock Foote 135–139; misogyny against feminists 142–143; pioneer womanhood 140–141; Smith-Rosenberg's 'The Female World of Love and Ritual: relations between women in nineteenth-century America' 137–138; valid form 145–146; western history 139
US WLM: anti-imperialist feminists 61; Black Panther Party-hosted Revolutionary People's Constitutional Convention 62; Black Panthers 2; Boston-area women's liberationists 61–62; British feminist art history approaches comparison 9–10; Feminist Art Program at California Institute of the Arts 10; Feminist Bookstore Network 120; Harvard University occupation 62–63; Jane Alpert open letter to Weather Underground women 67–68; motherhood activists 75; NOW 2; organizing whites against racism 64; race 60–61; racism, sexism, and imperialism connection 69–70; violence relationship to resistance 65; Weather Underground response to Jane Alpert's letter 69; white anti-feminists links with militant white groups 64; Women in Print (WIP) movement 117; Women's School 66–67; Women's School conflicts with Women's Center 67

vaginal imagery: symbolizing intrinsic essence of womanhood 10
Valk, Anne: national debate over politics of women's liberation 67; RPCC direct interaction among white women's liberationists, gay liberationists, and Panther men and women 62; white feminists organizing against racism 64
Vickers, Jill: welfare rights activist mothers 76
Vietnam War: Harvard University war research 63
violence: against women campaigns 36; relationship to resistance 65
Virago: duality of self-conception 119; Modern Classics series 152

Wages for Housework see WFH
WAI (Women Against Imperialism) 46
Walsh, Mary Ellen Williams: feminist response 144; lesbian theme in *Angle of Repose* 145; misogyny against feminists 142–143; pioneer women becoming feminist pioneers 142–143
Ward, Lyman: recovery of Foote 137
WARF (Women Against Racism and Fascism) 46
Warner, Marina: artefacts as open wounds 161
WAVAW (Women Against Violence Against Women): 'Reclaim the Night' protests 15, 35–36
waves in feminist history 2
Waysdorf, Susan: 'Resistance, Repression, Rebellion' class 66
WEA (Worker's Educational Association) 31
weak feminine touch of women artists 14
Weather Underground 67–69
welfare rights activist mothers: mainstream women's movement differences 75–76; marginalized low-income women's groups 78–85; NAC agenda 77–78; NAC denial of stay-at-home motherhood as a legitimate option 87; WFH and NAC tensions 86
Welfare Rights Coalition (WRC) 83
welfare state: adjustments 100; family wage 105; post-war generation of girls 106
West Yorkshire: revolutionary feminism 35; women's aid and sexual violence 35
WFH (Wages for Housework) 36, 83–85; alliances 85; assisting welfare rights mothers' groups 84–85; class 84; double slavery of paid employment 84; Marxist ideology 83–84; NAC tensions 86; race politics 85; state concessions 84
White, Hayden: history 150
white feminist movement: Boston-area women's liberationists 61–62; consciousness to racism 70; gender injustice focus 64; Harvard University occupation 62–63; Jane Alpert open letter to Weather Underground women 67–68; links with militant white groups 64; racism, sexism, and imperialism connection 69–70
Whitehorn, Laura: Boston-area women's liberationists 61; Harvard University occupation 62–63; organizing whites against racism 64; violence 65; Women's School 66–67
'Whose Feminism? Whose History?' 60
Wilderness Women 140
Winchester Women's Liberation Group 120
WIP (Women in Print) movement 117
WIRES (Women's Information and Referral Enquiry Service) 30
WITCH (Women's International Terrorist Coven from Hell-Norwich branch) 36
WLM (women's liberation movement) 1; 1978 national conference collapse 16; anti-nuclear

INDEX

protests at Greenham Common 15–16; consciousness-raising 16–17; divisions 16; influence on feminist art making 14–17; starting point 15
Women Against Imperialism (WAI) 46
Women Against Racism and Fascism (WARF) 46
Women Against Violence Against Women *see* WAVAW
Women and Music 152
'Women and their Families on the Overland Trail to California and Oregon, 1842–67' 140–141
Women As Furniture series 13
Women in Media Group 117–118
Women in Print (WIP) movement 117
'Womenmagic' touring exhibition 10
women only physical spaces 29–30
women's aid movement 34–35
women's centres 32–34; boy children 39; Brighton 33–34; Bristol Women's Centre 33; Cambridge Women's Center 63; funding 34; Harvard University occupation 62–63; hierarchical management structures 35; Leeds rap crisis 35; Norwich 33
Women's Images of Men exhibition 13
Women's Information and Referral Enquiry Service (WIRES) 30
Women's International Terrorist Coven from Hell-Norwich branch (WITCH) 36
women's liberation movement *see* WLM
Women's Liberation Music Archive 154–156

Women's School 66–67
Women's Social and Political Union (WSPU) 153
women's strikes: cross-class alliances between women 45
Women's Studies MA: first 15
Womens Voice 126–129; groups 37; socialist roots 127–128; the way forward' 128
Worker's Educational Association (WEA) 31
working-class identities 54–55
working-class women: Dagenham equal pay strike 47–49; establishing the movement 32; Grunwick strike 53–55; male workers comparison 47; Night Cleaners' Campaign 49–51; oppression 50; Trico equal pay strike 51–53; *Womens Voice* activism 127
Working Women's Charter 37
workplace demands: conflicts with family needs 105–106
WRC (Welfare Rights Coalition) 83
writing: consciousness raising through 98–99; power 114
written competitive exam for grammar school selection 101–102
WSPU (Women's Social and Political Union) 153

YBA Wife 36–37
Yorkshire Ripper 35
York Street Band drum, shoes, and socks 157
'You don't' know what is happening, do you, Mr Jones?' 13

Printed in Great Britain
by Amazon